WEAVING WORK
AND MOTHERHOOD

In the series

WOMEN IN THE POLITICAL ECONOMY

edited by Ronnie J. Steinberg

WEAVING WORK AND MOTHERHOOD

Anita Ilta Garey

TEMPLE UNIVERSITY PRESS
Philadelphia

Temple University Press, Philadelphia 19122
Copyright © 1999 by Anita Ilta Garey
Published 1999
Printed in the United States of America

⊗ The paper used in this publication meets the requirements of the American
National Standard for Information Sciences—Permanence of Paper for Printed
Library Materials, ANSI Z39.48–1984.

Library of Congress Cataloging-in-Publication Data

Garey, Anita Ilta, 1947–
    Weaving work and motherhood / Anita Ilta Gary.
      p.   cm. — (Women in the political economy)
    Includes bibliographical references and index.
    ISBN 1–56639–699–9 (cloth : alk. paper).
    ISBN 1–56639–700–6 (paper : alk. paper)
    1. Working mothers—United States—Case studies. 2. Mothers—Employ-
ment—United States—Case studies. 3. Hospitals—United States—Staff—Case
studies. 4. Work and family—United States—Case Studies. I. Title. II. Series.
HQ759.48.G37   1999
331.4′4′0973—dc21   98–43492

To Nicholas
and
to my sisters,
Margot and Shaaron

Contents

Acknowledgments

THERE ARE many people whose intellectual, emotional, and material support contributed to the writing of this book.

The hospital workers I interviewed must remain anonymous, but I thank them all for their willingness to invite me into their homes and offices and to give their time so generously. Their interest in and enthusiasm for the subject validated my own sense of its relevance and importance.

A National Institute for Child Health and Human Development Predoctoral Fellowship, administered through the Department of Demography at the University of California, Berkeley, and a research grant from the Department of Sociology at the University of California, Berkeley, provided financial support for the research and analysis phases of this project. A fellowship at the Bunting Institute of Radcliffe College in 1997–98 provided the material support and the intellectual space I needed to complete this manuscript.

This book began as a doctoral dissertation. My committee members—Arlie Hochschild, Nancy Chodorow, Kristin Luker, and Gene Hammel—each pointed me in directions that enriched my work, and I thank them for their intellectual contributions to this project and for their support along the way. I learned much from Arlie Hochschild's finely tuned sense of the way in which meaning is constructed, and I thank her for her continuing support. Nancy Chodorow helped me get this project off the ground, and I thank her for her enthusiastic encouragement of my intellectual interest in mothers. As graduate students, Karla Hackstaff, Arlene Stein, and I formed a dissertation group that met regularly for two years. We encouraged and critiqued each other's work, shared our setbacks and accomplishments, laughed together, and comforted each other during times of personal loss. This book benefits from that experience and from their careful readings and thoughtful comments on my work.

I thank Michael Ames for his editorial direction, his interest in the heart of this book, and his understanding about the inescapable "messiness" of the lives we seek to describe. My appreciation also to Ronnie Steinberg and the anonymous reviewers of the manuscript for their comments and suggestions.

Many people read drafts of the book at various stages and gave me extensive and insightful comments. I particularly want to thank Terry Arendell, Lynn Davidman, Karen V. Hansen, Judy Hung, and Nicholas Townsend for their attentive critical readings and for the insight of their responses. Carol Brown, Susan Ostrander, and Paula Aymer provided useful comments on several early chapters. Shelly Tenenbaum and Andrea Walsh gave me valuable advice for a talk I gave at the Bunting Institute, advice that I incorporated into the written manuscript.

In addition to reading drafts of the manuscript, friends, family, and colleagues contributed to this work in myriad ways. The interdisciplinary community of women scholars that comprise "The Bunting" provided a stimulating atmosphere in which to try out my own ideas and to discuss the ideas of others. Thanks to the many Bunting fellows who took part in the discussion of my research. I benefited from lovely talks with Barbara Goldoftas about the process of writing, most particularly from her comment that the best writing occurs at the point where the author takes a risk. Judy Hung, my Radcliffe junior research partner, not only provided essential research assistance, but also asked insightful questions that led me to clarify certain points in the manuscript. Discussions with Maxine Baca Zinn and Nazli Kibria contributed to my thinking and encouraged me in my writing. I also thank my colleagues in the Sociology Department at the University of New Hampshire, who have been genuinely supportive of my endeavors. I wish to express my deep appreciation to Jacquelyn Marie for her constant support and encouragement from the beginning of the project; to Lynn Davidman, whose advice and caring have proved crucial on more than one occasion; to Terry Arendell, for our pact to read each other's work before we send anything out; and to Karen V. Hansen, fellow sociologist, collaborator, and dear friend, who has been there for me every step of the way.

A caring and mutually supportive family has made it possible for me to keep this project in perspective. My mother, Ann Kovach Garey, conveyed to her children the dignity of productive labor in the economic sphere and the value of family life. I think she would have liked this book, and that gives me tremendous satisfaction. Thanks to my sisters, Margot and Shaaron, for their unfailing support of me in all areas; to my children, Kelley and Sasha, for the richness they have added to my life; and to Susan, Nick, and TyAnn for presenting me with the challenge and delight of new familial roles.

My gratitude to Nicholas Townsend spans many years and is greater than my words here can express. His contributions to this book, to my work in general, and to my life are immeasurable and are always given with grace and generosity. My own interweaving of work and family has been greatly facilitated by the constancy of his support and by our sharing of life's projects.

An earlier version of Chapter 5, "Motherhood on the Night Shift," was published as "Constructing Motherhood on the Night Shift: 'Working Mothers' as 'Stay-at-Home Moms'" in *Qualitative Sociology* 18, no. 4 (1995): 415–37.

WEAVING WORK AND MOTHERHOOD

1 "Working Mothers"

I GREW up in the 1950s, but my 1950s was not the one I read about, many years later, in sociology texts, where families were nuclear, fathers were the sole breadwinners, and mothers stayed out of the labor force and were called housewives. And because children assume that the world they know represents the way the world is, my 1950s family was my norm. And in my 1950s, mothers were employed.

My grandmother, my mother, my aunts, and the woman down the street all held jobs. They weren't always full-time jobs, or year-round jobs, or day jobs (although my grandmother sometimes held two jobs), and they certainly weren't "careers," but the women I saw around me were employed. Everywhere I went I saw employed women: my elementary-school teachers, the receptionist and the assistant in my dentist's office, the nurse at the clinic, the beautician who did my grandmother's hair, the grocery clerks at the A&P, the "cafeteria ladies" at school, bank tellers, the school secretary, the salesclerks at Woolworth's and at the candy store, the ticket-seller at the movie theater, the saleswomen in the clothing department of Sears, the "Avon ladies" who came to the door, and the voices of the telephone operators. I had no doubt that women, including mothers, *worked*; I would have been surprised to find that they didn't.

What I've discovered since then is that not all work counts *as work* in discussions of "working mothers." As a child, I had not yet learned that what counts as *real* work is full-time (forty hours or more), day-shift, year-round employment in a defined occupation. I had not yet learned how not to see the employment of large numbers of women, many of them mothers. This disjuncture between my experience of women and employment and what I read about the 1950s family sensitized me to the missing stories in generalizations about families, mothers, and employment.

The research on which this book is based began from questions and understandings that originated in my own experience of and exposure to mothers who were employed, and in the disjuncture between that experience and the social-science concepts used to describe women's relationship to employment and motherhood.[1]

EMPLOYED MOTHERS AS INVISIBLE WORKERS

What is the real story about employment and motherhood in the 1950s? It is true that at any one point in time, according to official national statistics, most married women were not in the formal labor force during the 1950s. But most is not all, and some groups of mothers were more likely to be involved than others. Mothers moved rapidly into the labor force over the decade. Only 12 percent of married women with children under the age of six were in the labor force in 1950, but the labor-force participation rate of married women with children between the ages of six and seventeen was just over 28 percent (U.S. Bureau of the Census 1975:134, Series D-63–74). By the end of the decade, 39 percent of married mothers with school-age children were employed, as were almost 19 percent of married mothers with children under the age of six (U.S. Bureau of the Census 1996:400, table 626). If we counted employment in the informal sector or in family-owned businesses as well as in the formal sector, the proportion of "working mothers"* would be even greater. My point, however, is not that the proportion of mothers employed in the 1950s was high, but rather that the presentation of nonemployed mothers as normative either has

---

*In writing this book, I faced the problem of how to approach the term "working mother." I discuss the problems with this term later in the chapter. I have avoided using the term when I am discussing an individual woman unless I am making a particular point, in which case I enclose the term in quotation marks. I use the phrases "employed women with children" or "employed mothers" when talking about these women as a group. I use "working mothers" when referring to this group as it is thought about in the culture. Terminology is a fascinating issue. One Harvard undergraduate said he thought my use of the phrase "employed women with children" was "anti-family."

characterized the "working mothers" of the 1950s and later as deviant or has rendered them invisible.

Often, mothers' employment is also made invisible within their own families. For instance, when I interviewed Ruth, a forty-six-year-old registered nurse, she told me that her mother was a housewife and added, "She was from the old school, she stayed home and raised her kids." In response to follow-up questions, Ruth "remembered" that her mother had been employed part time in a newspaper office when Ruth was in school. This kind of invisibility continues today. In an undergraduate course I taught on work and family intersections, students interviewed their own mothers or grandmothers about their work histories. Rosemary, a college senior, was amazed to "discover" that her mother had been employed when Rosemary was in high school. "I thought all she did was get on my case all the time," she added, clearly puzzled that her mother had had time to hold a job *and* to be such a presence in Rosemary's life. Several other students were surprised at their own discoveries, learning (or, rather, seeing) for the first time that their mothers and grandmothers had been employed while raising children.[2] This discrepancy between the fact that their mothers were employed and their experience of their mothers as stay-at-home moms intrigued me.

"WORKING MOTHERS" IN THE UNITED STATES: WHAT KIND OF WORK?

Since the 1950s, there has been a steady increase in the proportion of women in the formal labor force. The major part of this increase has been the result of married women entering the labor force, and this has been true across racial-ethnic groups (Amott and Matthaei 1996:304–6).[3] Two dramatic changes have drawn significant attention to the topic of "working mothers": the increase in the percentage who are employed of mothers with children under six years of age (U.S. Bureau of the Census 1990c) and the increase in the percentage of employed mothers not working in home-based employment (Bose 1987; Matthaei 1982:282–83). In 1995, 63.5 percent of married women with children under six and 76.2 percent of married women with only school-age children were in the labor force (U.S. Bureau of the Census 1996:400, table 626).

Although more than two-thirds (70 percent) of all married mothers with children under the age of eighteen are in the labor force, scholarly and popular attention to the topic of working mothers has been for the most part narrowly focused on the small percentage of those mothers employed in managerial or professional positions. While there are a number of excellent studies of women employed in blue-collar or pink-collar jobs, sociological studies of work and family use primarily a dual-career family model that focuses on elite and restrictive careers, despite the fact that this does not reflect the experiences of most women, particularly those of most married women with children (Benenson 1984). The general image of the "working mother" in popular magazines or in most scholarly discussions of work and family is of the professional or corporate woman, briefcase in hand. The women I saw around me when I was growing up do not fit this image.

In popular culture, advice books and magazines for employed women with children also presume that women are employed in professional or prestigious, white-collar occupations. The magazine *Working Mother*, for example, features a mother-of-the-month on the cover of almost every issue, with an accompanying feature article on the mother's "work and family" story. In the five years from 1993 through 1998, the mothers on the cover have held the following occupations: actor, astronaut, attorney, broadcast journalist, college administrator, concert violinist, corporate executive, engineer, entrepreneur, fitness expert, opera director, photographer, professor, and radio producer. Waitresses, salesclerks, secretaries, and nurses are still the invisible working mothers.

While inroads have been made by women, including women with children, into male-dominated, professional occupations, most employed women are concentrated in particular categories of work. In 1990, more women were employed as secretaries than as any other single occupation (Reskin and Padavic 1994:53). Fifty-two percent of employed women in 1995 were in nonsupervisory positions in sales, service, and secretarial occupations (U.S. Bureau of the Census 1996:405–7, table 637). Of all employed women in 1995, for example, only 0.3 percent were physicians, 0.4 percent were lawyers, and 0.7 percent were college and university professors (U.S. Bureau of the Census 1996:405, table 637).[4] There is a perception that mothers are employed in managerial and professional positions in far larger numbers than is the case, because the majority of employed mothers are missing from cultural images and social analyses of working mothers. In the 1990s, as in the 1950s, critical disjunctures still exist between the experiences of employed women with children and the representations of working mothers in both popular culture and scholarly literature.

THE ORIENTATION MODEL OF WORK AND FAMILY

Historically, women with children have always been involved in productive labor (Folbre 1991; Jones 1987; Kessler-Harris 1981). For most women, that productive labor took place in their households, and for some women that labor also took place in the households of others. We also know that, with industrialization, most productive labor moved out of households, and many women joined the formal, paid labor force (Kessler-Harris 1982; Matthaei 1982). We know that certain groups of mothers have consistently had higher rates of labor-force participation than the native-born, White population of mothers (Amott and Matthaei 1996; Harley 1990), and we know that the relatively low labor-force participation of White women during the 1950s was an aberration in the trend of women's labor-force participation (Bergmann 1986:19–24; Coontz 1992:155–63). Despite all that we know about changes in the labor-force participation of women in general and of mothers in particular, most discussions of women's employment are embedded in an ahistorical and homogenizing model that rests on concepts of "choice" and "orientation."

Although there is great variation by race-ethnicity and class in the work experiences of women in the United States, most discussions of women, work, and family are embedded in a conceptual frame that I have termed the orientation model of work and family.* For women in the United States, employment and family have been portrayed dichotomously—and women are described as being either "work oriented" or "family oriented." These concepts are not similarly linked for men. To be a "family man" not only includes, but necessitates, providing economically for one's family (Bernard 1981; Coltrane 1996:4; Townsend 1992), and while some men may be referred to as workaholics, this term is reserved for those perceived to be extreme in the time they give to their employment. For men, employment and family are not portrayed as inevitably detracting from one another. For women, work and family are represented as oppositional arenas that have a zero-sum relationship. In this representation, the more a woman is said to be oriented to her work (employment), the less she is seen as oriented to her family. Regardless of the experience of work and family for individual women or within particular groups of women, *the dominant cultural portrayal of work and family for women in the United States classifies women as either work oriented or family oriented.*

People's everyday reactions to mothers who are employed reflect this representation, as demonstrated by research conducted by Claire Etaugh and Gina Study. Etaugh and Study asked 192 people to rate personality and performance attributes of hypothetical mothers who differed only in terms of whether the woman was married or divorced, had either a one-year-old or an eleven-year-old child, and was either employed or nonemployed. The findings revealed that mothers described as employed "were seen as simultaneously less dedicated to their families and more dedicated to their careers, as well as more selfish and less sensitive to the needs of others" (Etaugh and Study 1989:67). The inability to conceptualize *for women* the integration of a commitment to work

---

*Patricia Hill Collins argues that, "in contrast to the cult of true womanhood where work is defined as being in opposition to and incompatible with motherhood, work for Black women has been an important and valued dimension of Afrocentric definitions of Black motherhood" (Collins 1987:5). However, the dominant culture in the United States continues to define employment and motherhood as incompatible. So while that combination may be valued within the African-American community, it is likely to be defined as a problem from outside that community. I am talking here about the conceptual frameworks that shape the images we see in popular culture and about the frameworks used in scholarship and policy-making.

and a commitment to family means that employed women with children are seen as less than fully committed mothers. This has not been true for perceptions about fathers. For men, employment is perceived as an integral part of what fathers do, *as fathers*, to support their children. Thus parenthood and employment are gendered institutions; that is, the systems of social relations embedded in these social institutions are organized differently for men and women and perpetuate gender differences.

The orientation model of work and family, which has framed most sociological analyses of work and family, fits into a larger ideological framework of separate spheres. The ideology of separate spheres divides the social world into two mutually exclusive areas: the public realm of economic and civic life and the private realm of domestic life. This ideology relegates women to the domestic sphere and men to the public arena (Welter 1973). It is not surprising that this ideology emerged in England and the United States in the wake of the industrial revolution, when production moved out of households and into factories. With respect to family life, this meant that men, as fathers, were expected to go outside the home to work in the public world, while women, as mothers, were expected to stay home and be in charge of the domestic world of home and children (Parsons and Bales 1955; Rothman 1978; Skolnick 1991:30–33). Phrases like "breadwinner father" and "stay-at-home mom" epitomize the ideology of separate spheres. But when mothers are employed, the model cannot accommodate them very well; thus employed mothers are described in terms of divided relationships to arenas that are seen as separate and oppositional.

In the same way, conceptualizing women's involvement with employment and family in terms of an orientation obscures the integration and connectedness of that involvement.[5] For example, women who postpone having children until they complete their education, or are established in their occupation, or have saved a certain amount of money are acting in ways connected to *both* family and employment considerations, but they would be categorized as work oriented in an orientation model. Women who work non-day shifts or part-time schedules are also attempting to mesh work and family, but anyone using the orientation model would categorize these women as family oriented. The orientation model of work and family is primarily a behaviorist model that categorizes observable behavior, including what people say, without considering the meaning and context of the behavior to the actors.

Even feminist sociologists who write eloquently about the need and capacity of women to combine motherhood and employment use descriptive frameworks that are embedded in an orientation model. Kathleen Gerson's book, *Hard Choices* (1985), provides one such example. Although she makes the case for the individual's capacity to integrate work and family (200), she nevertheless categorizes the women she interviewed on the basis of orientations. Gerson describes these women as either "work-committed women," "domestically oriented women," or "reluctant mothers." Although the latter category refers to the women "who chose to combine committed work with parenthood" (158), they are described in terms of their disinclination to integrate children into lives already oriented to the workplace. Their decisions to have children, Gerson notes, were based on the fear that not having children would ultimately be worse than having them. Although Gerson's point is that women can and do change orientations, my point is that the concept of orientation obscures the integration and connectedness of employment and motherhood in women's lives.

Similarly, in her book on working women, Mary Ann Mason, a professor of law and social welfare, categorizes women workers as either "women who live to work" or "women who work to live" (Mason 1988). And in a two-stage survey about the employment and family plans of women college students (Granrose and Kaplan 1996), the researchers grouped women into two sets of oppositional categories: Women whose decisions were consistent with their original plans were labeled either Careerists or Homemakers; women whose decisions did not correspond to their original plans were called either Breadwinners or Nesters. In each set, women were typed as oriented toward either employment or family—there was no integrative set.

The move from an analysis of structural incompatibilities between employment and motherhood to a typology of women with orientations to either work or family is a problem common to studies of women and employment. It is one thing to say that the workplace is organized in ways that conflict with the way family life is socially organized and another thing to say that individual women are thus oriented toward one or the other of these social structures.

It is possible, of course, to find women who are completely immersed in their children to the exclusion of any other interests and who therefore fit the description of "family oriented." And it is possible to find women who are exclusively focused on their work lives. The problem is that the orientation model implicitly assumes a bimodal frequency distribution of mothers into these two categories. If what we have is really a normal distribution, with the categories "work oriented" and "family oriented" at the tails of the distribution, then the area of greatest concentration, in the middle, is also the area that has been most neglected in scholarly work: employed women with children who are interweaving work and family in their lives.[6]

Analyses that are cast in terms of an orientation model are firmly connected to the formulation of research questions. Gerson's research question, for example, was how women "choose between work and family commitments" (Gerson 1985:2). "Choosing between" implies that *choosing both* is not an option. At present, we lack a model, framework, metaphor, or language that adequately describes women's lives as *both* workers *and* mothers.[7] We need a way of understanding what it means to choose both, and we need a way of thinking about women's employment that doesn't presume a zero-sum relationship between women's commitments to employment and to their families.

"Working Mothers": Making Sense of Oppositional Images

The way in which work and family are conceptualized in the dominant culture* in the United States in the late twentieth century helps explain the puzzle of why people often did not know that their mothers were employed or, if they knew, why they still thought of them as stay-at-home moms. Embedded in the

---

*I am using the term "dominant culture" to convey the idea of hegemony (Gramsci 1971), which includes concepts of both "culture" and "ideology" and which encompasses both the expression of particular meanings and the embeddedness of those meanings in institutions (Ortner 1990).

concepts "work oriented" and "family oriented" are cultural norms about what it means to be a good worker and a good mother. In spite of their oppositional relationship, these concepts are brought together in the term "working mother."

In this book I ask, What does it mean to be a working mother, given that work and family are portrayed as conflicting with each other? How do employed women with children think about their lives and about the ways in which work and motherhood fit into those lives? What does it mean to be a worker with children—and a mother who works?

Basically, a working mother is an employed woman who is also responsible for and in a parental relationship with one or more children. But clearly more is contained in the term "working mother" than this simple definition. We don't, for example, have an equivalent term, "working father," for men—even though most men are employed and most men have or will have children. "Working mother" is a conceptual category meant to encompass the relationship for women between being employed and being a parent, but since that relationship is presented as oppositional, it is a conceptual category that often creates more confusion than clarity.

When I interviewed Danielle, a thirty-six-year-old, Euro-American, full-time clerical worker and the mother of a five-year-old child, I told her that I was interested in what being a working mother meant to women who were employed and who were mothers.[8] Danielle's response illustrates the confusion that can occur in the attempt to get at the meaning of "working mother":

> I don't think that means anything. Not to me. I have a real problem with that phrase, because it implies that women who are at home don't work; it also—men who are parents are never called working fathers [exasperated laugh]. And I guess, from that, men who are parents work and a lot of women who are parents work and that's just, that's what *is*. And it's just this nice phrase that can be attached to one group of those parents—but anyway, I'm trying to think if I would describe myself as a working mother. I don't think I would! I think I'd have to take a few sentences to describe myself. I mean that's just too easy a phrase . . . and it doesn't have a lot of meaning.

This employed mother finds that the term "working mother" doesn't fit her experience; it is a gendered and asymmetrical conceptual category. She wonders what it says about her relationship to work if men are not called working fathers and what it says about the work of mothering if the term "mothers" is qualified by "working" when mothers are employed. She does not, however, find available alternative terms or concepts that simultaneously capture her identity as a mother and an employed person; as she says, "I think I'd have to take a few sentences to describe myself."

Why does Danielle have so much trouble using the term "working mother" or finding terms that would articulate her identity as both a worker and a mother? I suggest that the difficulty stems from the fact that the term "working mother" juxtaposes two words with antithetical cultural images: worker/mother; provider/homemaker; public/private. The problem Danielle faces is twofold. First, the term "working mother" does not adequately convey her experience, and second, the terms that would describe her experience do not yet exist in our daily shared vocabulary. This problem is an example of what Dorothy Smith (1987) describes as a disjuncture or schism between the way in which women experience the world and the concepts constructed by "experts" to explain that world.[9]

Concepts are intended to direct or focus attention, but concepts can also work to redirect attention and desensitize perception (Blumer 1969:168; Hughes 1971:339; Smith 1987:61–64). The very construction of the term "working mother" points our attention in particular directions: "mother" is a noun, and "working" modifies "mother." We do not say "mothering worker," which conjures up an image of a nurturant employee; nor do we say "mother worker," which sounds more like a job category for nannies. Clearly, when one goes from being a "working woman" to being a "working mother," it is "mother" that, linguistically, stands for the essential self. It is the mother who works, not the worker who has children. It is the mother who must fit into the workplace, not the workplace that must adjust to the needs of workers with children. When workers do adjust their work to their family responsibilities, their actions are interpreted as the actions of their selves *as mothers*, not of their selves *as workers*. It is "mother" that is an identity, "working" that is an activity; it is "mother" that is *being*, "working" that is *doing*.

On the one hand, when we conceptualize mothers as being rather than doing, the work of mothering is hidden. I mean not only the work of maintaining children, although that is certainly a part of the work mothers do, but also all of the ways of acting in relation to one's children that constitute not only the expected norm, but also the actual practice of a great many people.[10] On the other hand, by directing our attention to working as *an activity*, we divert our attention away from what it means to women, including mothers, to *be* workers. Everett Hughes (1971) notes that "a man's work is one of the more important parts of his social identity, of his self, indeed of his fate, in the one life he has to live" (339). Whether Hughes meant men or humankind, it has been shown that work is also an important part of the social identity or being of women, including mothers (Bennett and Alexander 1987; Ferree 1976; Komarovsky 1967 [1962]). Therefore, instead of the orientation model of work and family, we need a framework that makes sense of both the experiences of employed women with children and the experience of *being* an employed woman with children.

WEAVING: AN ALTERNATIVE FRAMEWORK

More than twenty years ago, Jessie Bernard (1975) stated that much of the research on women's roles as workers and as mothers suffered from what she referred to as "the Pickwick fallacy": "When Mr. Pickwick had to write a paper on Chinese metaphysics, he read everything in the *Britannica* on China and everything on metaphysics. He was then well prepared to write his paper on Chinese metaphysics. A growing research literature tells us about women in the labor force; another tells us about women in the family. Just as we need policies that help women themselves integrate their two roles, we need an integrated research approach that will help us see the lives of women as unitary wholes" (242). The research on which this book is based represents precisely such an attempt. This study focuses on working mothers simultaneously as mothers and as workers. By focusing on working mothers *as mothers* and not simply as women who have responsibility for child care, I ask what it means to be a mother and how mothers enact these meanings in the structure of their daily lives and in their presentations of self. By focusing on mothers *as workers* and not simply as women who have jobs, I ask what it means to be employed and how women with children negotiate the meaning of work in their lives. Thus this is also a study of meaning and of the ways in which women negotiate strategies of being that are meant to reconcile their identities as mothers and as workers.

The literature on women in the labor force has added greatly to our understanding of women and work,[11] but there has been little research that attempts to answer Bernard's call for an integrated vision of the lives of women who are mothers and workers "as unitary wholes." While sometimes mentioning the impact of women's family roles, the general literature on women and employment has seldom concentrated on women workers' family relationships. Those studies that do focus on this (see, for example, Hertz 1986; Hochschild and Machung 1989; Rosen 1987; Zavella 1987) have directed attention to the negotiation of spousal relations and housework rather than to the work of mothering or the meanings of being a "working mother." In general, motherhood has not been a constitutive part of most studies on women and work.

Similarly, the burgeoning literature on the institution, experience, meaning, and social reproduction of motherhood has not focused on mothers as mothers in the labor force.[12] Martha McMahon's discussion of the evolution of the research for her book *Engendering Motherhood* (1995) provides an example of the way in which women's identities as mothers and as workers are not examined together. McMahon explains that she originally planned to study the meanings of both motherhood and employment in women's lives but ended up focusing solely on motherhood (4). While her book is an insightful analysis of "identity transformations through motherhood," it leaves unaddressed the problem of unification that Bernard set for us.

Most of the existing research on the way in which employed women with children mediate work and family has focused on the household division of labor, relations between spouses, effects of mother's employment on children, and measures of role strain or role conflict.[13] In these studies, the problem has been conceptualized as one of conflict, and the meaning of motherhood has been reduced to role-specific tasks, such as the provision of child care. While it is absolutely necessary to examine the conflicts that employed women with children face as workers and as mothers, this should not be the only way of analyzing women's relationship to employment and motherhood. An excellent ethnographic study that nevertheless incorporates this view of motherhood and mothering is *Sunbelt Working Mothers* (Lamphere et al. 1993). The authors write: "At home, mediating the contradiction between their roles as mothers, wives, and workers involves *replacing their reproductive labor*. First and foremost this means finding someone to care for their children while they are at work" (20, emphasis added). The practicalities of providing child care are a central issue for employed women with children, but I found that when women talked about child care they also revealed deeply rooted concerns about their identities as mothers and expressed how much they valued their identities as workers.

I suggest that we use the metaphor of weaving as a way to look at the lives of employed women with children. Weaving is both a process (an activity—to weave something) and a product (an object—a weaving, something constituted from available materials), and I use the image in both senses. As a process, weaving is a conscious, creative act. It requires not only vision and planning, but also the ability to improvise when materials are scarce, to vary color and texture in response to available resources, to change direction in design, and to splice new yarn. As a product, a weaving reveals both grand patterns and minor designs; it reveals the connections between pattern changes and how what has come before is linked to what follows; and it reveals the richness or thinness of the materials used.

The metaphor of weaving illuminates the meaning that the women I interviewed gave to their life stories by capturing the interconnectedness of work and family within women's lives.[14] In her book *Composing a Life*, Mary Catherine Bateson (1989) compares the ways in which people design and fashion their lives to throwing a pot or building a house. Bateson suggests, too, that a life story is a composition in which the musical note, the brush stroke, or the written word is not simply a step toward a finished product but also an elemental part of the score, the painting, or the manuscript. I use a modified "composite" approach in my research on employed women with children. I do not look at every aspect of their lives, but I focus on two major areas: their lives as workers and their lives as mothers. This leaves out large areas that comprise a person's life: sexuality, religion, politics, community, marriage, and friendships. But as a central metaphor, weaving incorporates Bateson's sense of "composing a life" and runs counter to a model in which work and family, for women, are seen as inherently competing claims. The women I interviewed are each trying to weave a life pattern in which employment and motherhood are integral parts of the fabric.

METHOD

Because I wanted to talk to women whose employment resembled the employment of the majority of women in this country, I located my study in the health service employment sector and interviewed women hospital workers. In 1995, the health service industry employed 14.8 percent of all employed women (U.S. Bureau of the Census 1996:410, table 641). This segment of the labor force includes the occupations held by the women I interviewed: registered nurses, licensed practical nurses, nurses' aides, secretaries, typists, clerks, and janitorial service workers. The group of women I interviewed is not intended to be representative of all employed women with children, but occupations within the hospital are typical of the kinds of female-dominated occupations that account for most women's employment in the United States.

Because hospitals operate twenty-four hours a day, seven days a week, they are work sites with a wide variety of work schedules: shift work, a range of part-time possibilities, full-time work, and weekend as well as weekday schedules. As I illustrate in this book, these scheduling options provide some mothers with the means to be the kind of "working mothers" they aim to be, while

at other times or for other mothers a hospital's scheduling requirements constrain their abilities to fulfill those aims. The hospital setting takes us closer than many other work sites could to
the kinds of employment and the range of work schedules experienced by the majority of employed women.

I interviewed thirty-seven women hospital workers who had
children. Most of the interviews were conducted between 1991
and 1992, and interviewees were selected primarily from two
medical-surgical wards of a large private hospital in California.[15]
I designed this study from an ethnographic perspective, beginning with a group that existed as a group in a particular place at
a particular time.[16] While the people I interviewed shared a work
setting, they occupied different positions within that setting. Of
the thirty-seven mothers I interviewed, twenty were nurses, two
were nurses' aides, three were nursing directors, five were clerical workers, four were janitorial workers, two were administrators, and one was a union official who had been a hospital ward
clerk for twenty-four years.[17] A diversity of qualifications and
resources exists within, as well as between, each of these occupational areas.[18] Two-thirds (twenty-five) of these women had
full-time positions, and one-third (twelve) held part-time
positions. Twenty-two of them worked a day shift, and the
remaining fifteen worked evenings (five), nights (seven), or a
combination of shifts (three). Most of those in part-time positions worked the day shift.

The women ranged in age from twenty-seven to sixty years;
four were in their twenties, twelve were in their thirties, fifteen
were in their forties, five were in their fifties, and one was sixty.
Twenty-four of the mothers were married at the time of the interview, six were divorced, two were separated from their husbands, and five were single and had never been married. One of the
divorced women and one of the single women were living with
partners, which meant that twenty-six of the mothers were living
with a spouse or partner and eleven were single parents. The number of children born to each woman ranged from one to six. More
than half of the women (nineteen) had two children; eight women
had one child, and four of these indicated that they planned to
have at least one more. At the time of the interviews, eighteen of

the mothers had a child under the age of six years; twelve mothers had a youngest child between the ages of six and eighteen, and in seven cases the youngest child was over eighteen years old.[19]

The group of women I interviewed is racially and ethnically diverse, but ethnicity and race are by no means straightforward categories (Montagu 1963 [1945]; Montagu 1964; Waters 1990). I asked people how they identified their race-ethnicity,* and I categorized the women on the basis of their answers. When I am referring to individual women, I follow Amott and Matthaei's (1996) use of terms that denote racial-ethnic group origins, such as African American or Euro-American. When I am talking about a social category, I have used terms such as Black, White, or Latino. In grouping my interviewees into categories, I placed women who answered the race/ethnicity question with "White," "Caucasian," or terms such as "German" or "Swedish" in the social category "White." I have included two Jewish women in this category, although when referring to them individually, I refer to them as Jewish American.[20] I have used the terms Mexican American and Chicana interchangeably. Two of the women identified themselves as Mexican American, and one identified herself as Chicana. The Filipinas I interviewed were all immigrants, but some had immigrated with their families of origin when they were children and had attended school in the United States, while others had immigrated as young adults.[21] Many Filipinas qualified for immigration because they had training and skills that the U.S. government classified as needed; a nursing degree was one such qualification and accounts for the relatively high proportion of Filipinas working in California hospitals. Filipinas have "eight times their labor force share of nursing jobs" (Amott and Matthaei 1991:246).

*I am following Maxine Baca Zinn's (1991) use of the term "racial-ethnic" to point to ways that groups of people are "labeled as races in the context of certain historical, social, and material conditions. Black, Latino, and Asian American are racial groups that are formed, defined, and given meaning by a variety of social forces in the wider society, most notably distinctive forms of labor exploitation. Each group is also bound together by ethnicity, that is, common ancestry and emergent cultural characteristics that are often used for coping with racial oppression. The concept racial-ethnic underscores the social construction of race and ethnicity for people of color in the United States" (130 n. 1).

I interviewed sixteen Black women, twelve White women, five Filipina immigrant women, three Mexican-American women, and one Chinese-American woman. I identify the race-ethnicity of each woman I interviewed in my discussion of individual women, but race-ethnicity is not treated as an a priori category of comparison. This was also my approach to differences in resources, occupation, age, and marital status.

Research based on interviews with a group that is so demographically diverse raises problems for many sociologists, who argue firstly that there are too many variables for the size of the group, thus making comparison and analysis impossible, and secondly that the experiences of people belonging to different racial and ethnic categories are so different that studies need to be limited to one group or to the comparison of specific groups. My response to the first problem is that this study is not a comparison of categories; rather, it is a study of an actual group of workers in a particular place at a particular time—and the diversity of the group is represented in the interviews. My response to the second problem is that the question of difference is *a question* and should not be used as a way of eliminating people from the group being studied (for example, the group "women hospital workers" or the group "working mothers") because they don't share some other characteristics (such as ethnicity or age).[22] Another problem with limiting the group studied in order to control for difference is that findings of difference are built into the research design (Fausto-Sterling 1992).

My study of employed mothers on two wards of a hospital represents that group in its diversity. The approach I am using has been referred to by Barrie Thorne (1993) as "starting with the whole." Thorne writes, "To move our research wagons out of the dualistic rut, we can, first of all, try to *start with a sense of the whole rather than with an assumption of gender as separation and difference.* If we begin by assuming different cultures, separate spheres, or contrastive differences, we will also end with a sharp sense of dichotomy rather than attending to multiple differences and sources of commonality" (108, emphasis in original). Thorne is addressing research on gender, but her argument is relevant for any divisions based on assumed differences. We must not presume that the social processes being studied will differ along predetermined lines such as class, race, or age— although those findings may emerge from the research. *

In-depth, open-ended interviewing allows me to study the meanings people give to their actions.[23] It is also a way of hearing, and making heard, the voice of the person interviewed, in this case the voices of employed women with children.[24] In contrast to research that examines women's experience of employment, career, or vocation in terms of the existence and effects of structural incompatibilities between work and family responsibilities, my focus on the experiences of employed women with children is aimed at understanding what it means to be *a worker with children* and *a mother at work*.[25] To examine the lived experience of employed mothers and to focus on the meanings that experience has for them is not to place the researcher's analysis of that experience in the hands of her interviewees. The experiences of employed women with children constituted the beginning of the research, and those experiences pointed me in particular directions, often ones that otherwise might not have been evident.[26] The sociologist, however, is the one who attempts to make sense of it all by illuminating connections between individual experience and social relations and thus deepening our understanding of the social world.

The women I interviewed all gave generously of their time, thoughts, and feelings about being workers and mothers. In the chapters that follow, I have tried to do justice to their stories, to fairly represent their voices, and to bring a sociological imagination to my analysis.

---

*Of course there are differences between the women I interviewed, and ethnicity, race, and class are important variables. There have been, however, serious consequences, sometimes explicit and sometimes implied, of restricting samples on the basis of ethnicity, race, or class. When samples are restricted to the White middle class, the consequence has been the positing of that group as the norm. In addition, the race and class specificity of the sample is rendered invisible. Studies of White, middle-class women, for instance, are often titled and referred to as studies of "women." Studies that are restricted to non-middle-class or non-White groups have the consequence of foregrounding the criteria of selection. Studies of working-class or African-American mothers, for example, tend to become framed as studies of class or race rather then studies of motherhood.

2   Strategies of Being

"I KNOW exactly how I'm going to do it. I'm going to get a very good job in the public health sector, work for two years, and make myself indispensable to my boss. Then I'm going to have two children by the time I'm twenty-seven, take six months off with each child, and return to work while one of my family members does child care for me. My boss will have to take me back because I'll be so indispensable." When asked which family member would care for her children, this twenty-one-year-old, female college senior replied: "Well, my mother says she won't do it, so I guess it will have to be one of my sisters."

The year was 1991, and I was teaching a sociology seminar on the intersection of work and family. The faces of the young women in the room were solemn; they had been reading several sociological articles on the difficulties of combining career and family, and no one was reassured by her fellow students' plans for integrating work and motherhood. Another student said quietly, "I don't know. My boyfriend and I are both going to go to law school. He's going to get a job in a big corporate law firm, and I'm going to work until we have children. Then I'll quit until the children are older. But I don't know—my parents have put a lot into my education, and all that work to become a lawyer, and then . . ."

These college women are not unusual. In 1985, Anne Machung interviewed graduating seniors at the University of California about their career and family expectations (Machung 1989). Not surprisingly, she found significant differences in how men and women talked and thought about their futures. Comparing her findings with several large-scale surveys, she concluded that "the majority of [college] senior women across the country hope to be able to stop working for extended amounts of time when they have small children" (48). Their responses reveal underlying assumptions about family income and breadwinning, parenting, and the structure of the workplace.[1]

20

The first student's concisely expressed long-range plan may sound unrealistic in view of current structural realities, but it nonetheless expresses a strategy for reconciling what she foresees as the salient issues in her plans to combine career and motherhood. Her plans for employment and family are intertwined. She has selected a field, the public health sector, and intends to get "a very good job," by which she most likely means a job that is not only interesting and fulfilling in its own right, but that also provides a salary high enough to help support a family and benefits that enable an employee to take the desired amount of maternity leave. She plans to work for two years before she has children, a timetable that she thinks will enable her both to establish herself at work and to begin establishing her family at what she feels is an age-appropriate time. She wants to take time away from her job for a maternity leave that is longer than legally mandated and to return to her job full time while her children are in the care of an unspecified family member. The second student plans to work in the field of law until she has children, after which her husband will support the family on his income alone. Her long range plan, however, is to return to her legal career when the children are "older."

Both students, the future public health worker and the future attorney, are constructing, albeit at an embryonic stage, their identities as "working mothers." Both students hold a definition of motherhood in which women (and not men) are primarily responsible for children and in which children (and not other involvements) are women's primary responsibility. It is *in conjunction with* this definition of motherhood that their definitions of themselves in terms of their labor-force participation or occupational identities are formed. Although the future public health worker did not mention a husband in her statement, she had previously indicated to the class that she plans to marry and to be part of a heterosexual, dual-career couple. Nowhere, however, do her stated plans mention paternal involvement in child care or the intersection of her husband's career with family life. The future attorney mentions her future husband in terms of their parallel education plans and their not-so-parallel occupational trajectories: "He's going to get a job in a big corporate law firm, and

I'm going to work until we have children." The mention of her future husband's career path, however, serves the same function as the public health worker's plan to make herself "indispensable" to her boss—each provides the material basis on which the woman can implement her work/family strategy. The future attorney is able to quit work until her children are older only if her husband can make enough money to support the family, therefore he needs a well-paying job in "a big corporate law firm." The future public health worker is able to take the maternity leave she wants only if her boss is willing to hold her job for her; therefore she must become "indispensable" at work.

Both the future public health worker and the future attorney assume, probably correctly, that the addition of children and the maintaining of family is something that they, as mothers, will have to reconcile with their participation in the labor force. While each woman addresses what might be termed a child-care issue, their strategies are not only aimed at how their children will be cared for, but are also about their identities as mothers and their definitions of motherhood.[2] Neither talks about sharing child care with her husband.[3] The future attorney plans to pursue a strategy of sequencing—that is, dropping out of the labor force to raise her children and returning to work when they are older. She will be the person who cares for her children while they are young. The future public health worker plans to use a female family member to care for her children. If it can't be me, she implies, it will have to be someone who has a familial and cultural relationship to my children—someone who is like me.

While these students are worried about how they will reconcile their labor force participation and occupational identities with their identities as mothers, they are not thinking about either in isolation. Their work lives and their family lives are already inextricably linked in their plans and hopes for the future. They may be vague or unrealistic, but they are negotiating a future in which their choices about employment and about motherhood are interconnected, and their task is to try to make them support rather than undermine each other.

The hospital workers I interviewed already had children and jobs; they were not vague or unrealistic about what was entailed in being both workers and mothers. But they faced the same tasks of reconciling the points of structural conflict between the two and constructing identities as workers and as mothers. To weave life patterns that incorporate both employment and motherhood, they employ what I call "strategies of being."

STRATEGIES OF BEING

A strategy is a plan of action—a way of doing things to achieve a particular goal. When the goal is the construction of identity, the strategies to achieve this are what I call strategies of being. By this I mean a way of thinking about and representing oneself that attempts to reconcile actions with a sense of self. Strategies of being include not only external representations to others, but are also ways of representing ourselves *to ourselves*. I indicate to myself what kind of person I am through both my actions and the meanings I give to those actions.

I base the concept of strategies of being on the insights of symbolic interactionist theories of the self (Blumer 1969; Goffman 1959; Hewitt 1997; Hochschild 1979; Mead 1962 [1934]). In his theory of self and society, George Herbert Mead (1962 [1934]) argues that human beings are reflexive—that is, that a person has the ability to look at and reflect on his or her own behavior, feelings, or planned actions (an ability Mead calls "reflexivity"). This reflection on our own actions means that we can look at ourselves from the outside, taking the perspective of another person, and therefore that we have a sense of how we appear to others (a process Mead calls "taking the role of the other"). Mead further argues that not only are we able to reflect on our actions from the perspective of another person, but also that we learn to reflect on our actions from the perspective of the group (which Mead calls "the generalized other"). The ability to reflect in this way about what we have done or are planning to do enables us to shape or alter our actions so that we act in ways that are intended to represent particular definitions of self. People are therefore indicating, through their actions, their definitions of self—and their definitions of self are, in turn, used to guide their actions.

Definitions of self are not, however, constructed in isolation. Strategies of being are influenced by social norms and forged in interactions with others. For example, when I interviewed Gretchen, she told me that she reads to her eight-year-old son at bedtime. Gretchen reads to her son because she likes the activity of reading to him and believes that he benefits from being read to. Yet she is also aware that reading to her child is an action by which she indicates her self as mother—and as a *good mother* who is acting appropriately. She did not, however, invent the expectation that mothers should read to their children at night; it is conveyed to her through interactions with family members, other mothers, teachers, the school system, child-rearing books, and the media. When she reads to her son, she does so in private, but she knows that others would approve of her reading to him, and she approves of herself for doing so. In the United States at this historical moment, the norms of the dominant culture suggest that good mothers read to their children at night.[4] Reading to children at bedtime has become an indicator of good parenting, with particular connection to good mothering, and mothers point to this activity to indicate themselves as good mothers.

People do not, however, simply accept social norms or respond to them in unthinking, determinative ways. People adapt, interpret, reject, or negotiate social norms (Blumer 1969). Gretchen, for example, told me that she works three evenings a week and said, "The nights I go to work [my son] doesn't get a story, *but the nights I'm here, he sure does.*" Gretchen's husband was home with the children on the nights that she worked, but she never mentioned the fact that her husband could have read to her son on those nights, or whether he did, or why he didn't. This is consistent with my point that she is referring to the action of reading to her son as an indication of herself as mother. She isn't trying to tell me about her son's experience as a child who has books read to him at bedtime; she is telling me that her son has a *mother* who reads to him at bedtime. She is telling me that she is the kind of mother who reads to her child. In emphasizing that she reads to her son on the nights she is home, she is also countering the implication that, by being employed, she is not fulfilling social definitions of good motherhood. Gretchen points to the activity of reading to her child to indicate herself as a good mother, but if she didn't read to him, she would most likely have emphasized different actions as indications of herself as mother. For example, other mothers talked about how they made it possible for their children to participate in the soccer league or the Girl Scouts, or how they organized their children's birthday parties.

The meaning of "working mother" for each individual woman has to take into account cultural meanings of being a (good) mother and of being a (good) worker. Employed women with children construct identities as working mothers in interaction with other individuals (such as coworkers or family members), collectivities (such as workplace definitions, as manifested in company rules and benefits, or legal definitions, as indicated by legally mandated employee benefits), and with cultural images (such as depictions of employed mothers in the media or advice to working mothers in self-help books). Arlie Hochschild (1988) notes that popular advice books "recommend to the reader a 'social self'" and "tell the reader what tacit social rules sustain this self" (2). Advice books aimed at employed women with children present a social self deemed appropriate for the working mother. Strategies of being are attempts to connect our actions with the social selves we are trying to indicate. Strategies of being thus both direct and interpret action.

What kind of strategies of being do employed women with children use to indicate themselves? How do they reconcile definitions of self as mother and as worker when the dominant orientation model of work and family defines these as oppositional? And how do they indicate themselves, to themselves and others, as both mothers who work and workers who mother? The chapters that follow will explore these questions in the context of the lives of the women I interviewed. In the remainder of this chapter, I present themes and concepts related to strategies of "being a mother" and "being a worker" that emerged from my analysis of the interviews. I analyze "being a mother" and "being a worker" separately, for they are not the same thing. But neither are they oppositional in the lives of women. They are intertwined, as I illustrate in Chapters 3 through 7, which explore the interweaving of women hospital workers' identities as mothers and workers.

DOING MOTHERHOOD

People's actions are described by themselves and others in terms of social understandings about appropriate behavior. Appropriate behavior at any particular time is defined in terms of both the situation (how one should behave at the theater, in the grocery store, at work) and the position one occupies (as actors or audience members in the theater, as a produce manager or shopper in the grocery store). People in particular social positions and situations thus confront role expectations, which they negotiate in various ways. It is misleading, however, to talk about individuals as occupying roles, as if roles were precast molds into which people fit. John Hewitt (1997) suggests that the concept of role should be thought of "as a perspective from which conduct is constructed. . . . A role is thus a place to stand as one participates in social acts" (59).

Looked at in this way, we can talk about how women construct their conduct as mothers in relation to a set of expectations associated with the social position of mother. There are strong cultural expectations for how someone who occupies the social position of "mother" is supposed to feel and behave. These expectations will vary over time and between cultures, but people know what the dominant cultural expectations are for the society in which they live, whether they adhere to them or not.

Women confront these cultural norms from varying social locations and with varying access to resources; and they respond to these norms by adopting, modifying, reinterpreting, or rejecting them—but, in any case, they have no trouble identifying these norms and locating themselves in relation to these expectations. People are "doing motherhood" in the same way that West and Zimmerman (1987) argue that people are "doing gender": "We argue that gender is not a set of traits, nor a variable, nor a role, but the product of social doings of some sort. . . . We claim that gender itself is constituted through interaction. . . . [Gender is] exhibited or portrayed through interaction, and thus seen as 'natural,' while it is being produced as a socially organized achievement" (129).[5]

Women with children "do motherhood" by managing their conduct in interaction with dominant-culture conceptions of mother-appropriate activities, and it is *as mothers* that their actions are assessed. Certain activities, for example, are seen not only as appropriate for mothers but also as less appropriate for other family members and as clearly inappropriate for nonfamily child-care providers, regardless of their sex category. Consulting with a child's pediatrician is an example of an activity that mothers are expected to engage in. While it is becoming more common for fathers to take their children to the doctor, it is deemed unusual and less acceptable if mothers do not perform this activity. Someone else can occasionally "fill in" for mother if she is not available, but a mother who handed over the responsibility for meeting with her child's pediatrician to her child-care provider would warrant comment as not living up to normative conceptions of motherhood.

The concept "doing motherhood" also refers to the way in which the performance of certain activities tangibly creates the person performing those actions as "mother." In her study of families and food, Marjorie DeVault (1991) uses the concept of "family work" in a similar way, not only to indicate work that is done within the family group, but also to indicate work that "actually constitutes a social group as 'family' from day to day" (30). Similarly, "doing motherhood" does not refer simply to activities done by women with children—rather, it also refers to the phenomenon by which women with children are constituted as mothers in the performance of certain activities. For example, mothers are doing motherhood when they meet with their children's teachers—that is, they are performing a mother-appropriate activity, and *in the doing* are creating and constituting themselves as mothers through their interactions with the teachers, the schools, and their children.

Symbols of Being a Mother

It can be difficult to see the symbolic nature of mothers' actions for two reasons: because of our taken-for-granted assumptions about what should be done for children and about who should do it, and because the symbolic is intertwined with the instrumental and practical. An example from my own childhood illustrates that cultural norms change as to who should do what for children and helps to illuminate how the taken-for-granted can blind us to the symbolic aspects of actions that we assume are solely instrumental. When I was in primary school, we all got our polio inoculations at school. On the appointed day, we would wait until our class was called and then stand in single file as we inched forward toward the nurse with the needle. Most of us were frightened, and all of us were relieved when it was over. But I would venture to say that none of us felt that our mothers had abandoned us to face this experience alone. The teachers, nurses, and other mothers certainly did not construct the situation that way. Indeed, a mother might have been criticized as neglectful if she did not allow her child to be inoculated with the other children. Years later, when my own children were in primary school, it was still expected that they would have the proper inoculations, but the responsibility belonged to the parents, not to the school; and parents, usually mothers, were and still are expected to be there with their children to reassure and comfort them through the experience. Which one of these arrangements is better is a matter for empirical study—and it may be that it doesn't matter, or that the first arrangement is better for some children (who are reassured by their peers and by the standardization of the experience) while the second arrangement is better for other children. In neither case is the presence of the mother necessary for the inoculation to take place or be effective. Each arrangement, however, incorporates different cultural expectations for mothers. When I accompanied my children to the physician's office for their inoculations, I was demonstrating that I was living up to those expectations, just as my mother was being a good mother by sending me to school when I received my inoculations. The symbolic function of my action is in addition to any other functions it may serve. It represents—to my child, to myself, to the physician, to my neighbor, and to anyone I tell about this activity—that I am being a good mother.

The symbolic nature of mothers' actions is difficult to see because the symbolic is often thought to be something that stands separately, something unnecessary and added on. The star at the top of a Christmas tree, for example, is symbolic—it has shared meaning for large numbers of people and represents something more than itself—but it is not necessary to have a star for any in-strumental reason, such as keeping the tree upright. But symbols are not simply "added on"; most symbols are embedded in mate-rial things or in actions. Clothing, for example, is symbolic in many ways but is not unnecessary—clothes keep us warm and protected as well. The fur coat and the leather jacket are both outer garments that have a practical purpose, but each also serves a symbolic as well as an instrumental function. Similarly, when mothers tell me about their actions, they are presenting them as symbolic of something greater than the particular activity they are relating, even if the particular activity is useful and important in and of itself. For mothers, accompanying their children on school field trips has a symbolic function, even though there may be in-strumental reasons that a mother would want to go along. Moth-ers who volunteer to go on field trips told me that they do this mainly so that they can keep an attentive, protective eye on their children. But in going on the field trip, a mother is also indicating to herself and others that she is *the kind of mother* who acts to keep her child safe, or *the kind of mother* who is involved in her child's education, or *the kind of mother* who is not too busy to do her part to support school activities. Symbols are thus tools in constructing strategies of being. The women I interviewed told me about their actions as a way of indicating themselves as mothers. To explain who they are, they talk about what they do.

Maternal Visibility

In a cultural context in which employment and motherhood are treated as detracting from one another, employed women with children need to represent their identities as mothers in a very visible way. In a cultural context in which mothers who are not employed are referred to as "full-time mothers," mothers who are employed understandably feel the need to assert their status as mothers in a number of contexts, particularly contexts that di-rectly involve their children. They also want to be perceived this way by others. Their attempts to make their actions, as expres-sions of their identities as mothers, known to others is what I call "maternal visibility." Maternal visibility is an emphasized indi-cation of self as mother. It can be accomplished in a variety of

ways—by the public performance of certain activities, such as being "the field-trip mom," or by verbally expressing the things one
does for one's child.

Sylvia Jacobs, a forty-five-year-old, Jewish-American registered
nurse, emphasized her maternal visibility by telling me how she
makes sure that her eight-year-old son looks "cared for" when he
goes to school:

> By working the schedule that I do, I'm home [in the morning] to take
> [my son] to school. A lot of times he's all ready when I get here, but I
> can see that his teeth are brushed, his homework is all together, and
> he's going to school prepared. I see a lot of children walking to school,
> they look—they look awful, like they've had no care at all.

Sylvia's husband gets her son ready in the morning and, as Sylvia
says, many times her son is all ready to go to school by the time
she gets home. What Sylvia is expressing, however, is maternal
visibility. First, she verbally expressed to me that, as mother, she
makes sure that her son is ready and appropriately dressed. Second, she expresses her maternal visibility through her son because he goes out into the world looking like a cared-for child, in
contrast to the children Sylvia refers to who look "like they've
had no care at all."

Maternal visibility is one response to the potential criticism
that Sylvia's employment prevents her from properly caring for
her child. This type of criticism is not imaginary. Jane Bradley, a
thirty-one-year-old, Euro-American registered nurse, conveyed to
me the response given to mothers who are not "visible." Jane is
married and has two children, a five-year-old daughter and an
eighteen-month-old son. She worked a full-time, day-shift schedule until the birth of her second child and then began working
two days a week. Because of her husband's income and her own
class background, Jane is in a higher socioeconomic bracket than
most of the other nurses I interviewed, and, on her new schedule,
she often finds herself in the company of mothers who are not
employed. Jane reported,

> There's this faction that is very righteous, you know. "We are nurtur-
> ing our young, we are taking care of our young. And not only that but
> we're taking care of your children too, because you're at work." . . . and
> things that are said that I hear at the park from the at-home moms. . . .

[like] "[That mother] wasn't around, so I had to, you know, either pick [her children] up or take them here." . . . They see it as not only doing tasks and activities, structuring—which they end up doing organizationally a lot of that stuff because they're at home and have the time [laughs], um, but . . . they feel like they're really raising those other people's children. Which, which is, you know, ridiculous, to a certain extent. I mean sure they're doing this or that, but they're not *raising* their children, they're not—

Jane went on to say,

Well, it's not always easy to be at home, and we're doing all these other things to kind of maintain—particularly now in the public school system where they really need, you know, the PTA . . . they really like to have a parent monitor in each class, and it's usually all the moms and people who stay at home. They're able to do it. So you hear a lot of discussion—particularly the group of women I know, because they're like the president, vice president, treasurer, all of the PTA, the local PTA. . . . So they do take it seriously, and they do put in a lot of time and effort, but um, they're also very quick to judge those that don't, for *whatever* reasons they don't.

Ensuring one's maternal visibility is a response to an ever-present, scrutinizing gaze—a gaze with an eye on the performance of mothers *as mothers*.

Mothers aim for maternal visibility in a variety of ways, but three general themes emerged from mothers' conversations about their activities. In the words of the women I interviewed, these themes are "being there," "family time," and "doing things." Each theme is linked to a different arena of action. "Being there" represents the mother's own relationship to the child; "family time" represents the integration of children into family life; and "doing things" represents linking children to the larger, public world. Mothers use maternal visibility to indicate to others that they are performing appropriately in these arenas. Of course, differences in resources lead to differences in the strategies used to actualize or represent these mother-appropriate activities, and these differences will be illustrated in the chapters that detail the lives of the women I interviewed. Yet the general themes of "being there," "family time" and "doing things" emerged as salient in one way or another for all the women I interviewed.

Being There

Idiomatically, the phrase "being there" carries meanings of affection, engagement, availability, concern, and emotional support, in addition to denoting physical presence. Indeed, it is even possible to be there for someone without physical presence, as indicated by the expressions "I know she's there for me" or "I want to be there for him," which indicate potential emotional support. In my interviews, women often began by talking about physical presence, but the meaning would then change into being there emotionally for one's children. They made a point of stressing to me that they were "*there* for their children," "*there* during the day," or "*there* when needed." The word "there" does a lot of work, alternatively or simultaneously meaning "with my children," "attentive to my children," "at home for my children," "supervising my children," "accessible to my children," and "emotionally available to my children." Mothers used the concept of being there to convey that they were fulfilling cultural mandates about motherhood by being in the mother-appropriate places, physically and emotionally, at the mother-appropriate times.[6]

Sylvia Jacobs, who works full time on the night shift, stated: "I'm a full-time mother and I also have a simultaneous full-time job." When I asked her what she meant by "full-time mother," she replied:

> I'm a full-time mother. My mother died when I was [a child]. I had no role model, and there was nobody there for me. And I know how devastating that was for me. . . . So I need to be here.

Like Sylvia, many mothers act on the concept of being there by arranging their employment schedules, child-care arrangements, and personal lives in ways that enable them to maximize some aspect of "being there."[7] Roberta Edwards, a thirty-four-year-old African-American woman, has a four-year-old daughter and works full time in the hospital's accounting department. She explained to me that, at this point in her life, being a good mother meant not dating or being open to relationships with men. Her reply to my question echoed Sylvia's: a good mother is "being able to put my life on hold, to *be there* for [my daughter] as she's growing up."

Although the emotional aspects of being there are the ones most often mentioned, the task-related aspects are also frequently included: seeing that children are washed, brushed, fed, and supervised and making sure that children are going to school and doing well once there. Marcia Collins, a forty-two-year-old, African-American woman, has three school-age children and works as a housekeeper at the hospital. When I asked what she thought constituted a good mother, Marcia responded,

> A good mother really, for me? Okay, basically being there for your kids, having dinner on the table, [making] breakfast, sending them off to school, being there when they come in from school, help them with their homework. Love—give them love. And provide for them. [pause] Hope the best for them. . . . And actually I think a mother should be around.

When mothers talk about being there, they move from physical presence to emotional presence. Lisa Harris, a thirty-three-year-old, Euro-American woman with two preschool children, works three days a week as a registered nurse on the day shift. In response to my question about what being a good mother meant to her, Lisa replied:

> I think it's real important to be here for [my children]. I mean there are times I don't want to be here with my daughter [laughs] . . . but I think it's important that [my daughter] knows she can come to me and that I'm here for her . . . and that she *thinks* that I can take care of her [laughs]—whether I can or not is not the point [laughs].

Lisa included both physical presence and emotional presence in her definition of being a good mother. Her response further illuminates what mothers are trying to convey with the concept of being there: Lisa may not always be there *with* her children, but she must always be there *for* her children, and what is important is that her children see her this way. For mothers, being there means being the rock of stability, the shoulder of comfort, the fount of wisdom, and the source of caring. As Lisa says, whether she can always provide what her daughter needs is not the point—being there means being there in the child's eyes. It is therefore not surprising that this indication of being a mother figures so prominently in mothers' strategies of being.

Family Time

Many of the women I interviewed used the term "family time" to denote time that was separate from outside activities for everyone in the family. Sometimes family time was associated with special occasions such as Christmas or birthdays, but most of the women I interviewed identified "dinnertime" as a routine and ritualized family time. The evening meal, unlike breakfast or lunch, has become an icon of American family life. Television advertisements show busy family members grabbing a breakfast snack and running out the door or comparing individual cereal choices. Lunch is depicted as occurring at the office, in the school or workplace cafeteria, or out of a lunchbox, or as being skipped altogether. But images of families gathered together for the evening meal are ubiquitous in American culture, and the importance of dinner as a family time came up repeatedly in the interviews. For example, Joyce Anderson, a fifty-three-year-old, Euro-American registered nurse, explained to me,

> Dinnertime has always been a family hour. It might take two hours to have dinner, because everybody has to have their say about everything they did, got, or breathed during the day. So it's something we've evolved, as much time as possible to be together. And dinner is pretty much a very good time for us.

Sharing and interacting through talking together at dinnertime was mentioned frequently by the women I interviewed. The evening meal is central in contemporary Westernized families (Blum-Kulka 1997); in the United States, 82 percent of families report eating dinner together.[8] In doing the research for her book *Feeding the Family,* DeVault (1991) found that "the concept 'meal' [is] an organizer of family life" (38) and that talking together during meals is something that people planned, orchestrated, and worked at (49).

Dinnertime is not only an occasion to sit down to break bread together *as a family;* it is a time to reproduce the family, and everyone's position in it, through activity and interaction. Lisa Harris's husband works a rotating evening shift and is home for dinner only two or three nights a week. Lisa structures dinnertime differently on the nights her husband is home. She explains:

> [My daughter] sets the table and "we're having dinner together," and she sets the table and we all turn off the TV and usually turn on the stereo.

When her husband is working, dinnertime for Lisa and her three-year-old daughter takes a different form.

> When [my husband is] working, I don't eat dinner. I mean I might have a salad or something, but if I'm not hungry I don't eat dinner with [my daughter]. So then I sit there with her, you know. She sometimes watches a cartoon, stuff like that. So it's different when Daddy's not home than when Daddy is home. When Daddy and Mommy are both home it's very structured—family time.

Lisa has just described an example of what Susan Contratto (1987) calls attention to in her article, "Father Presence in Women's Psychological Development." Contratto notes that, in middle-class families with both parents present, children are shown in a variety of ways that fathers are "special" people. Indicators such as the way fathers are greeted when they return from work and the way fathers' needs (for sleep, for quiet, for particular foods) are given special priority convey the message that fathers are powerful people with a special, privileged position in the family. When Lisa's husband is home for dinner, dinnertime becomes special. Lisa's daughter can see that, for her father, the table gets set in a certain way, Mommy eats dinner too, and other activities stop. This difference between dinnertime when Lisa's husband is home and dinnertime when he isn't reproduces the position of mothers in relation to fathers, as well as reproducing a particular idea of family life. The importance of dinnertime for many mothers is that family meal times symbolize an idealized version of family in which a woman is at home and able to prepare and present an evening meal to her family.

The women I interviewed did not necessarily do all the cooking in their families or prepare and sit down to family dinners on a regular basis. Irregular schedules, shift work, marital status, and age of children all affected the structure of the evening meal. However, the theme of dinnertime was mentioned frequently by the women I interviewed. Dinnertime and other occasions marked as family time were invoked as symbols of good mothering in their strategies of being.

Doing Things

In Talcott Parsons's now classic formulation, children are socialized first into a family system and later into the wider social system outside the family. According to Parsons, it is mothers who socialize children into the family, and fathers, by virtue of their occupational ties to the public world, who socialize children into the wider social system (Parsons and Bales 1955). Although Parsons has been criticized for his limited empirical scope, his normative implications, and the static nature of his model (Morgan 1975:39–48; Slater 1964), his theory of the family and socialization remains extremely influential in sociological and psychological studies of the family.

The concept that it is fathers who socialize children into the wider social system sensitizes perception, focusing attention on occupation as the link between the family and the wider social system and locating occupation with the father. However, this linking of paternal occupational role with the socialization of children into the public sphere also desensitizes perception and directs our attention away from the work that mothers do, *as mothers*, to link their children with the public world.[9]

Linking children with the public world occurs long before children are socialized into the occupational world; it begins for most children with entry into preschool and kindergarten and with participation in organized extracurricular activities—what mothers refer to as "doing things." It is primarily mothers who implement and maintain these linkages. The activities of linking children with the public world are, for the most part, public activities occurring in nonfamilial situations. While they may be performed for the good of one's child and in order to meet cultural expectations for mothers, they are also built into the organization of this society's institutions and into the ways these institutions incorporate and socially place children. Dorothy Smith (1987) has analyzed how the work of mothering is connected to the organization of the classroom and the school:

> Along with work involved in "developing the child," there is work involved in scheduling the comings and goings of different family members in relation to their external commitments. The providing of household services facilitating the child's working schedule, supervis-

ing homework, providing cultural activities such as visits to muse-ums, movies, and the like, taking care of emotional stresses arising in the schooling process, covering for a child so that minor delinquencies such as being late or missing school do not appear as defects on her or his record, helping with the school library, baking a cake for the bake sale, driving the car when the team plays another school, and so forth—all these along with the routine and basic housework (feeding, clothing, health care, etc.) contribute to the child's capacity to func-tion normally at school. (169)

Smith points out that the dependence of the school on the work of mothers is tied to a conceptualization of mothers that provides the school with a way of analyzing and connecting children's problems at school with their family situations. It also gives a mother "a pro-cedure for analyzing her own work practices as a mother in terms of how their defects produce the child's problems in the school set-ting" (168). An example of this is provided by Marcia Collins, the hospital housekeeper whose definition of a good mother included helping her children with their homework. When Marcia told me that her eleven-year-old son's grades had declined, she added:

And it's basically because of me. My working schedule, and, you know, I'm not around, especially with his homework and stuff, and he's not the type of child who's going to sit there [alone] and do it.

Although Marcia's two other children were doing well in school, she connects her son's school problems to her irregular schedule at the hospital and blames herself for his poor grades. It is possi-ble that Marcia's son's grades would be better if she were home to supervise his homework, but it is also possible that his poor grades are related to some other factor or that his grades would not improve even if Marcia were able to make her son do his homework. But Marcia assumes that the responsibility for her son's grades is hers, and she would find that most school and so-cial service professionals would agree with her.

Teachers, school administrators, social workers, child develop-ment specialists, and psychologists all share a professional discourse in which the relationship between mothering and school-ing is embedded. Single mothers, "working mothers," and working-class mothers are viewed as being less able to provide these needed connections, solely *because* they are unmarried, employed, or not middle class. Invisible in this conceptualization is the way in which schools and other institutions construct good home-school relations around a model of mothering in which mothers are not employed. Examples abound, but here is one from my own experience. In 1989, the Parent-Teacher Association at my son's high school sent out a letter that lamented the declining numbers of participating parents and asked if perhaps it was time to change their meeting times from day to evening. Given that, in 1988, 72.5 percent of married women with school-age children were in the labor force, the answer seemed obvious (U.S. Bureau of the Census 1990b:385). Furthermore, since about 97 percent of married men between the ages of twenty-five and forty-four were in the labor force (U. S. Bureau of the Census 1990b:384), holding PTA meetings in the daytime also effectively excluded the vast majority of fathers from participating. PTA participation is thus organized so that it is gendered and becomes part of the work mothers are expected to do, and it is further organized so that only certain kinds of mothers can participate. Some parent-teacher associations do meet in the evenings, but schools as a whole are organized around the assumption that mothers are at home during the day. The scarcity of after-school child care programs and the lack of collective solutions to the problem of transporting children to after-school activities are examples of this.

The employed mothers I interviewed were familiar with the professional discourse that connects children's problems in school with their family situations, and they emphasized the ways they acted to link their children with the school and the public world in general. Maintaining these links were also ways of maintaining maternal visibility. Three areas of activity emerged from my interviews as symbolic of linking work: helping with homework, volunteering at one's children's school, and facilitating participation in extracurricular activities.

HOMEWORK.   Helping children with their homework was mentioned repeatedly by the mothers I interviewed. Children's academic success in school is not simply a sign of their abilities, but is seen as indicating their overall well being and as reflecting the stability and well being of their home life. As Marcia Collins pointed out, children's grades reflect back on mothers. Success in school is also tied to future well being, such as the potential for college and for well-paying, satisfying work. "Being there for my children" is concretized in "helping my children with their home-work," a symbol of being a good mother that is both practiced and invoked as a strategy of being by the women I interviewed.

SCHOOL VOLUNTEERING. Volunteering in their children's schools was another frequently mentioned activity. When women told me about volunteering in their children's schools they usually made a two-part statement in which the description of the vol-unteer work was accompanied by the explanation that they took a vacation day, arranged for flex-time, used a day off, or worked non-day shifts in order to volunteer. Being able to participate in their children's schools was one of the major reasons that volun-tary part-time and full-time, night-shift workers gave for their choice of schedule and their need for flexible scheduling.

Being a field-trip chaperone, assisting in the school library, working as a classroom aide, and participating in fundraisers are offered as proof that a mother's job does not interfere with her work as a mother. Being available to volunteer is a characteristic associated with nonemployed, at-home mothers, and the ability of employed mothers to volunteer enables them to invoke strate-gies of being a mother that are similar to those of at-home moth-ers. In the eyes of the teachers and other parents, volunteering in the school normalizes the deviant position of working mothers in relation to the school.

CHILDREN'S EXTRACURRICULAR ACTIVITIES. Children are required to go to school, but organized extracurricular activities are op-tional. Some children get to participate in many activities; other children participate in few or none at all. Extracurricular activities are often costly. Organized sports such as baseball, basketball, gymnastics, swimming, and soccer; clubs such as 4-H, Campfire Girls, and Cub Scouts; and lessons in swimming, piano, and bal-let are just some of the extracurricular activities available to chil-dren. Enabling children to participate in these activities not only requires the money for dues, fees, uniforms, and equipment, but also requires providing transportation to and from these activities.

Yolanda Lincoln, a twenty-eight-year-old, African-American ward secretary, is married and has two children, ages four and six years. Her mother had not been employed until Yolanda was in elementary school, at which point she started working part time. Yolanda contrasted her mother's work/family pattern to her own and concluded,

> My mom staying home had its advantages because she spent time with us, schooling-wise and things like that. But on the other hand, with one income—my father—there wasn't a lot of money. We weren't poor, but things were limited. Whereas I have my daughter, she's in ballet, she's been in ballet for two and a half years. She takes piano lessons and things like that that I missed, that I couldn't take because my mother always said, "I'm not working, and it's just your dad [working], so we can't afford that," and things like that. So that aspect, I really missed in life. So we're trying to make sure that our children have a chance to do any of those extracurricular activities that they want to get involved in.

While helping with homework represents a commitment to the present and future well-being of their children, and volunteering in their children's schools represents the normalization of employed mothers in relation to the organization of the school, enabling children's participation in extracurricular activities represents an endowment to children. While Yolanda emphasized that her employment provided her with the ability to pay for dance and music lessons for her daughter, night-shift and part-time hospital workers stressed the point that their schedules gave them the flexibility they needed to enable their children to participate in extracurricular activities and that their employment was therefore not depriving their children of enriching experiences and important links to the public world.

Homework, volunteer work, and children's extracurricular activities are ways in which mothers link their children to the public world—and are symbolic arenas in their strategies of being mothers. In all three, what is important is not just what a mother does, but how she is seen by her children, her children's teachers, her spouse or partner, and other parents. Even if a mother only reads a story three times a week, or only has family dinners two nights a week, or only volunteers once a year, it is important that she be seen and that she sees herself as the kind of mother who does these things and values these actions.

When women implement strategies of being in their presentations of self as mothers, they maximize their visibility as mothers. For employed women with children, however, maternal visibility is practiced in a context in which they are also paid workers, one in which their identities as mothers are only part of the story.

Being a Worker: Conflicting Vocabularies of Motive

When I was fifteen years old, I was eligible to apply for a work permit, and I did. I then landed a part-time, after-school job as a clerk in the hardware section of the local Woolworth's store. Delighted with this accomplishment, I was unprepared for my mother's distress at learning about my new job. My mother had been counting on me to watch my eight-year-old sister after school until she got home from work at 6:00 in the evening. I remember having a great mix of feelings: resentment at my mother's assumption that I would take care of my sister, guilt about wanting to work at the store rather than help out at home, disappointment at the response to my success at landing a job, and fear that I would have to let go of my new status as a worker. It was my first confrontation as a worker with structural problems at the intersection of work and family. For my mother, it was probably only one in a long history of confrontations with such structural conflicts. We managed to work out a solution, the details of which I no longer remember. I kept the job.*

*Employment is not, of course, the only activity that qualifies as work. Feminist scholars have written extensively about how analyzing *as work* many of the activities performed by women which are not conventionally seen as work illuminates the invisibility of women's labor and the gendered nature of institutions (Fishman 1983; Daniels 1987; DeVault 1991; di Leonardo 1987; Hochschild 1983). In this book, for instance, I talk about the "work of mothering." (For an interesting discussion of some of the difficulties of expanding the definition of work in this way, see Mirchandani 1998). However, there is a lack of terms for making distinctions between the work we do in our jobs and the work we do in other areas of our lives. Using "employment" to refer to work that is done as part of one's job might address the problem, but using "employee" rather than "worker" does not connote the same meanings as "being a worker."

The job was not particularly interesting or challenging, even when after a month on the job I was "promoted" to the cashier's office, where I was responsible for layaway payments, returns, and cashing out when the store closed. Nor, at the minimum wage of seventy-five cents an hour, did my paycheck amount to very much. But both the promotion and the fact that I was earning money gave me feelings of accomplishment and recognition, and having that job was much more important than the nature of the work or the amount of my pay. Having a job meant being a worker.

How we each feel about being a worker is not the same thing as how we each might feel about work in general or our jobs in particular. Barbara Garson interviewed people who held mundane and alienating jobs and noted the following:

> In the 1970s I spent several years learning how people cope with routine and monotonous work. I expected to find resentment, and I found it. I expected to find boredom, and I found it. I expected to find sabotage, and I found it in clever forms that I could never have imagined. But the most dramatic thing I found was quite the opposite of noncooperation. *People passionately want to work.* (1994:ix)

Our identities as workers are shaped by our individual and social group's historical relationships to work and by the social meanings and values associated with employment. In my interviews with employed women with children, I asked them about not only the details of their jobs, but also how they felt about being employed. What did it mean to them to be workers? I found that these women talked about being employed in highly positive terms. They may have disliked certain aspects of their jobs, and many would prefer to work fewer hours, but they maintained that being employed yielded a number of noneconomic rewards and was important to their concept of self. One woman told me:

> I'm just the kind of person who likes to work . . . in order to take care of myself and not depend on other people taking care of me, [is] very important.

Another said:

> I like to work. . . . I think it's what people do for the most part. . . . I mean I'm really glad that I have a job that challenges me mentally, and I feel like one of the reasons I got this job is because I'm smart and

that's a great ego boost for me. But working itself is what's important, I think. The fact that I'm earning what I need that supports me and it always has supported me and supports [my daughter]. And if I didn't have child support I could figure out some way that I could still take care of her. And I know that I can until I'm 65 or whenever.

And a ward secretary explained:

Actually, I enjoy working because it's something that involves myself, something that I'm doing or I feel that I'm benefitting or helping someone do, or just getting through a day [on the ward] that's been stressful and to help everybody there that day, it's rewarding to me. That's why I really like the job a lot and like to work. Although there are days that I say, you know—sometimes I say, "Gosh, I wish I didn't have to work," but I really don't mean that. If I could drop a few days—I think three days a week is enough.

Self-sufficiency, accomplishment, fulfillment, satisfaction, and the dignity associated with being a provider for one's children are the terms used by the women I interviewed to describe being a worker.

Numerous other studies have also found that, in addition to the economic reward of a paycheck, working-class mothers talk about and value getting these kinds of noneconomic rewards from their jobs. Even in interviews she conducted in 1959, Mirra Komarovsky (1967 [1962]) found that "[a]part from money, the working wives mentioned other rewards of working: the enjoyment of social life on the job, the pleasures of workmanship, the bracing effect of having to get dressed up in the morning, some relief from constant association with young children, and 'having something interesting to tell my husband'" (59). Referring to the positive feelings and pride in her work expressed by a twenty-seven-year-old cafeteria worker, Komarovsky notes, "A job apparently need not be a highly skilled one to yield the worker some satisfaction from its effective execution" (68–69). Subsequent studies report similar findings (Ferree 1976; Glenn 1980; Hochschild and Machung 1989; Rollins 1985; Segura 1994; Walker 1990; Zavella 1987). A study of women seeking jobs through the unemployment office found that "employment is important to women both as a source of income to support themselves and their families and as a defining factor in their self conceptions, [but] attitudes and social patterns persist that deny the legitimacy of women's labor and that ignore the importance these jobs have come to occupy in the lives of many working women" (Ratcliff and Bogdan 1988:54).

Although employment provides workers with both economic and noneconomic rewards, discussions about working mothers dichotomously categorize women as either those who have to work for economic reasons or those who choose to work for reasons of personal fulfillment. The relative weights given to motives of economic need or personal fulfillment are associated with types of jobs, social class, and marital status. Working-class employed mothers, for example, are described as needing to work to support their families, and it is assumed that they would choose to be at-home mothers if their husbands earned a family wage. Therefore, even though they are employed, they are considered to be "family oriented." On the other hand, middle-class employed mothers, particularly if they are married and employed in the professions or management, are assumed to be working primarily for the noneconomic rewards of prestige, occupational status, and achievement in their field, and are often accused of putting these values ahead of their families. These are the women who are labeled "work-oriented." Again, the orientation model of work and family divides women into women who have to work and women who want to work, as if these things are separable for most people. In a critique of the "dual-career model," Myra Marx Ferree (1987) notes that the model "tends to polarize our perceptions of women into those who receive psychological as well as economic rewards at work and those who are assumed to get little of either and so might as well stay home" (292).

The problem for employed women with children in an orientation-model culture is that talking about their noneconomic reasons for working undermines their presentations of self as mother. A 1997 *New York Times* feature article reported that women are encouraged to explain to their children that they must work to pay the bills and to buy things for the family and are advised to downplay any noneconomic rewards they derive from their work to avoid appearing selfish (Abelson 1997).[10] The women I interviewed faced the task of reconciling their positive feelings about being workers with cultural expectations about what it means to be a good mother.

The problem these women face is captured by C. Wright Mills's concept of "vocabularies of motive." Mills (1940) describes "vocabularies of motive" as words that are socially acceptable for explaining one's actions in a particular situation. Used in this way, "motives" are not the reasons we do certain things; they are the terms in which we explain what we do. Mills notes that "along with rules and norms of action for various situations, we learn the vocabularies of motives appropriate to them" (909). The terms we use to explain our behavior are thus linked to the situations in which we find ourselves.

Employment and motherhood, relegated to separate spheres and conceptualized dichotomously, have different vocabularies of motive, which make it difficult to talk simultaneously about one's behavior as a worker and a mother. This is an example of what Mills refers to as "motivational conflicts" that are created by "competing or discrepant situational patterns and their respective vocabularies of motive" (912). Three major approaches to reconciling these motivational conflicts emerged from the interviews: distancing from the concept of "career," distributing motives across time, and incorporating "breadwinning" into the definition of motherhood. Employed women with children may use one or any combination of these approaches.

Distancing from the Concept of "Career"

Many of the women I interviewed stressed the point that while their employment was important, it was not a "career." Iris, a forty-two-year-old hospital secretary, told me:

> I like to work, but I don't particularly want a professional career. . . . I personally feel like I wouldn't be able to handle the pressures of trying to rise on the executive ladder or something and being with my family. I still value being with my children more than anything else. And I feel like I don't want to be in the office till midnight writing a report when my children are home alone. . . . But I'm home by 6:00 or 6:30 so there's not a great span of time when they're by themselves. And I don't want it to be any greater span of time, because I do believe that they need their parents to be there. . . . I work for a salary. I get a little bit of money for myself and I help pay the bills, but I don't want to be an executive something making tons of money and my children are home alone.

Iris lacks a college education or the credentials that would make a "professional career" a realistic option for her, but she talks as if she chose her job as a secretary in preference to a career as an "executive something." Her rejection of career is presented as something she does in order to spend more time with her family, even though Iris works five days a week, leaving her house at 7:00 A.M. and returning by 6:30 P.M. Notice that Iris invokes the concept of "being there" ("being with my family," "being with my children," "they need their parents to be there") in her strategy of being a mother. She is actually away from her home and her children for almost twelve hours a day, Monday through Friday, but, by invoking and then distancing herself from the concept of career, she presents strategies of being in which she constructs herself as a worker who is providing for her family and as a mother who is home with her children *more than she would be if she had a career.* Sociologists Janet Hunt and Larry Hunt (1982) argue that "what is becoming incompatible with family life is not women's participation in the labor force, or the principle of sex equality, but *careers*" (503). Whether or not careers are, in practice, incompatible with family life, they are conceptualized to be in opposition. This conceptualization allows Iris to emphasize her commitment to family by pointing to the fact that her employment is not a career.

Sylvia Jacobs told me that being employed gave her the satisfactions of not being dependent on anyone and of being of service to others, but she also distanced herself from the concept of career:

> I've never looked on it [nursing] as a career. I never loved it. It was never my burning desire.

When I asked Sylvia what a "career" would be, she responded,

> A career would be to be working at what you saw as your life's goal, to achieve career steps and to be going on in your education and getting degrees and moving up the corporate ladder, and moving maybe from the bedside into management. Maybe getting out of the hospital setting and going into another area. That to me is a career.

Sylvia has touched on several aspects of career: the idea that careers are composed of incremental, ascending steps toward an ultimate goal, which may simply be to get to the ultimate step; the idea that careers involve growth and increasing expertise; the idea that career advancement is represented in the hierarchical and supervisory position represented by "management"; and the notion that careers are the manifestations of "burning desires."

The idea that work, while meaningful and important, is only one part of a person's life permeates the ways the women I interviewed constructed "being a worker." Lillian Santana, a forty-two-year-old, Mexican-American registered nurse, told me that work gave her a sense of accomplishment and fulfillment, but she distanced herself from the concept of career. Lillian had worked at the hospital one or two days a week until her marriage ended, but she increased her hours after her divorce. Her need for extra hours led her to accept increasing responsibilities and duties, and she found that she was becoming more interested and involved at work. I asked her if she saw her career differently now, but she rejected the term "career."

> I am having a hard time with that. I know I see [my job] in the sense of a career in the sense [that] I need financial stability, financial security. . . . I see it in that sense, and I'm no longer willing just to come in [to the hospital] and have no say in things. Now I come in to work—even though I'm [part time], I'm still very involved. And I do the charge nurse positions. I'm more involved. I've always been very outspoken at meetings; I'm probably even more so when we have staff meetings. Do I see it as a career? I don't want to see it as the main thing in my life.
>
> It's funny, I want to have that as a part of my life, and certainly it needs to be there, but I don't think what women do nowadays either, the other extreme, total career—and I don't want to be judgmental—and having children, I'm wondering if it's too much. I want to have—I guess I still want to have a little bit of both worlds. I want to be here for my kids. I want to have a career in the sense—maybe I'm using the wrong word—I want to have the job, I get enjoyment from it, I get satisfaction from it, I get challenged. But I—it's just as important, if not maybe more important to be able to balance the other parts of me. . . . I think it has to be kind of balanced overall. And so, I want my job, I want to go ahead in it . . . but it has to be a part of my life, not the—so in a career sense, no.

While her words express a rejection of "career," Lillian's plans and actions reveal an increasing interest in her profession and her future professional life. She is planning to go back to school to earn a B.A. (she has a two-year nursing degree) and is thinking about going on to earn a master's degree in a nursing specialty. She is planning to move out of bedside nursing and has been investigating other occupational positions within the hospital. She has started accepting charge nurse responsibility and has found that she is good at it and likes it, and she has become more involved and more verbal in her unit. Her strategy of being a worker, however, is used to interpret her actions in ways that are compatible with her strategy of being a mother. The concept of career connotes an anti-familism and an all-consuming aspect from which Lillian distances herself.

Sometimes the distancing is a matter of degree. Jane Bradley, the thirty-one-year-old registered nurse with two preschool-age children, is planning to go to law school and become a lawyer, but she wants to continue to work part time in the field of law, as she has done in the field of nursing.

> I have no—No—intention of working for a large partnership or ever becoming a partner or to go down that avenue whatsoever. And so the more I talk, people say "Well, actually you could [practice law part time]." I know a couple of ladies that work for the D.A.'s office that split positions. . . . I could wait a few more years. A lot of people are waiting and changing careers when they're older.

Jane uses the term "career," but restricts its meaning *for her* to the concept of "profession" and rules out for herself what she perceives as the all-encompassing aspects of career. She further distances herself from the concept of career by placing her actions regarding a change in profession to some future time when her children are older.

In 1970, Philip Slater criticized the alienation and anomie of contemporary society in his book, *The Pursuit of Loneliness*. Slater (1976 [1970]) noted that the rejection of "career" by many women is the product of a "formulation that makes them lose either way": "The problem once again is that 'career' is in itself a male concept—designed by and for males in our society. When we say 'career,' it suggests a demanding, rigorous, preordained life pattern to whose goals everything else is ruthlessly subordinated—everything pleasurable, human, emotional, bodily, frivolous. . . . So when a man asks a woman if she wants a career, it's intimidating. He's saying, are you willing to suppress half of your being as I am, neglect your family as I do, exploit personal relationships as I do, and renounce all personal spontaneity as I do?" (78). Slater concludes that it is no wonder that women say they don't want careers and that a career "seems like a pernicious activity for *any* human being to engage in and should be shunned by both men *and* women" (78). It is distressing that almost thirty years later, in the wake of the women's movement and the increase of women in professional positions, these notions of career are still part of the discussion. What women do want, continues Slater, "is meaningful and stimulating activity, excitement, challenge, social satisfactions—all the things that middle-class men and women get from their jobs whether they're defined as 'careers' or not" (78). The women I interviewed talk about their work in the terms Slater identifies. They talk about jobs as providing satisfaction and a sense of accomplishment and as contributing to one's ability to be a good mother.

Large numbers of employed women with children do think of their work in terms of career, including some of the women I interviewed. These women use alternative methods of reconciling the motivational conflicts that arise from an orientation model of work and family.

Distributing Motives over Time

Another way in which the women I interviewed dealt with the problem of conflicting vocabularies of motive was to distribute these motives over time. To avoid the orientation model's moment-to-moment competition between the values associated with motherhood and the values associated with paid work, they separated each vocabulary of motive in time. In this way, both vocabularies were salient, but not at once. As in distancing oneself from the concept of career, distributing motives over time refers to the discourse one uses to reconcile conflicting vocabularies of motive and does not necessarily coincide with what one actually does.

Sometimes the distribution of motives was over the span of a day, other times over a lifetime. Most of the nurses, for example, explained that when they came home to their families, they "left work at work," and that when they stepped onto the hospital ward, they didn't bring family issues with them. They thus reported separating in time and, in this case, in space the motives associated with their strategies of being nurses on the job from the motives associated with their strategies of being mothers. It didn't always work out this way, as their accounts will indicate, but their discourse about employment and motherhood was a way of negotiating conflicting vocabularies of motive as well as a design for action.

Vocabularies of motive were also distributed over lifetimes, and women would talk about "after I had children," or "when the children are older," or "when the children start school" as markers of when their actions and interests might shift. Discussions of changes in their own work lives are thus connected to culturally appropriate transitions for children—starting school, entering adolescence—and to the changes in children's needs that are culturally associated with those transitions. Lisa Harris, for example, used a discourse of distributing motives over time when she explained her future plans:

> But now, to be honest with you, my main goal is just my family, and that really does take priority. *I love nursing*—I love the giving and taking and—I mean, I just really enjoy it and I love learning about it and all that, but at the same time—it's second—or third or fourth sometimes. I mean, when I'm there I give a hundred percent. . . . I will go back and get my bachelor's, I know. When the kids are in school, I will. . . . I'd like to get into administration later, if I could make a change in it—and if I had a lot more time. Managers, I mean—Whew, they work long, long hours. . . . But you really have to be dedicated to it and put a lot of time into it for it to run right. So my kids will have to be really very busy doing other things, and not need me.

In an orientation-model perspective, this discourse would be interpreted as one in which an individual changed over time (for example, from family oriented to work oriented). But rather than changing their orientations, I found that when women distributed motives over time, they were finding a way to express the combination of employment and motherhood in their lives by presenting their lives holistically, over the life course. They thus avoided the problem of conflicting vocabularies of motive, while presenting themselves as both/and rather than either/or.

Mothers as Good Providers

Distancing from the concept of career and distributing motives over time are ways of negotiating the conflict between employment and motherhood produced by an orientation model of work and family for women, but they do not directly challenge that model.[11] Men have been "good fathers" by being good workers and thus providing for their families. Employed women with children can similarly be "good mothers" by providing for their children and by serving as role models of accomplishment and self-sufficiency. In this way, employment can be conceived of as an aspect of being a mother. It does not replace other parts of being a mother, but it no longer conflicts with them.

This more inclusive definition of motherhood has often been associated with immigrant women and with African-American women (Aymer 1997; Collins 1987; Dill 1980; Segura 1994). Patricia Hill Collins (1987) writes that "African-American women have long integrated economic self-reliance with mothering. In contrast to the cult of true womanhood, in which work is defined as being in opposition to and incompatible with motherhood, work for Black women has been an important and valued dimension of Afrocentric definitions of Black motherhood" (124). Denise Segura (1994) found that immigrant women from Mexico held a conception of motherhood that incorporated their employment and economic roles, while women of Mexican descent who were raised in the United States felt more ambivalence and guilt about combining employment and motherhood. And Paula Aymer (1997) describes how migrant women domestic workers from the Caribbean include in their definition of motherhood their economic support of the children they have left with relatives in the Caribbean.

In my interviews, it was not only or always the immigrant women or the African-American women who talked about being providers and economic role models as part of their definitions of motherhood, although they were more likely to do so. Sylvia Jacobs, for example, talked about how being employed was part of a model she wanted to convey to her children:

> What feels best is that, professionally, I'm able to go out in the world and do something that I was trained to do, do it well, detach myself from it, come home, and be Mother. I'm enormously proud of myself

that I'm able to do that. . . . It's something that I can do until I drop in my tracks. . . . I'm not dependent on someone else to take care of me. And I can teach my children that they don't have to be dependent on anyone else to take care of them.

And Lisa Harris explained,

I want [my daughter] to believe—'cause she asks why I have to work—[that] to have the nice things that we have, I have to work. And you know I had a career because I think it's important for me mentally to not just be a mommy. I mean, my knowledge, I hope I pass it off to my kids, and I guess it makes me feel more whole.

An understanding of how employment was incorporated into conceptions of motherhood did not often emerge in neat sound-bites—after all, the mothers I interviewed were constrained by the culturally pervasive language of the orientation model. Redefining motherhood to include paid work is an approach to reconciling conflicting vocabularies of motive that is still in process for many of the women I interviewed. That they were defining "being mothers" to include "being workers" emerged from the life stories women told—now this way of talking about their jobs and families, now that way—and will be clearer in the chapters that explore these women's lives in their complexity.

RESOURCE CONSTELLATIONS

Our actions are inextricably linked to our sense of self and are part of our strategies of being. Karl Marx (1963 [1869]) advised us that people "make their own history, but they do not make it just as they please; they do not make it under circumstances chosen by themselves, but under circumstances directly encountered, given and transmitted from the past" (15). Our definition of self guides our actions, but it guides them within the constraints of the possible actions available to us—and our choice of actions is expanded or limited by our access to resources. "Resources" refers not only to individual-level assets, but also to the economic, social, and political structures that produce, maintain, and reproduce those resources (Garey and Hansen 1998). Employed women with children aren't simply picking a course of action as if they were choosing different flavors of ice cream. Resources limit or expand the courses of action that may be selected. Working part time, for example, may not be viable if the mother or another family member does not make enough to support her family. The meaning and impact of part-time work depends on the social location of the worker. Part-time work can be involuntary or voluntary, achieved through superior bargaining power or accepted as a dead-end position held open for those who have no other options; a product of scaling back at work to be home more or a way of getting out of the house and into the public world.

Employed women with children base their actions and weave their life strategies from the materials available to them. These materials, or resources, include, but are not limited to the following:

Income: What does her paycheck cover? Is there another income in the family? Does the family's income enable a parent to work fewer hours, or does it require that a parent work more hours or more than one job?

Wealth and class background: In times of need, does she have access to additional resources, such as income from the sale of stocks or loans from parents or other kin, or is there nowhere to turn? Can she obtain credit based on family members who will cosign? Are other family members likely to need her material help? In making decisions and assessing risk, can she count on future income from an inheritance to cushion the years ahead, or will she only have what she can accumulate in her earning years? What cultural capital does she bring to social interactions, such as job interviews and conversations with teachers?

Education: What degrees, qualifications, or training does she have? What are her prospects for education and training in the future? What are the job possibilities for those with this amount of education or type of training?

Occupational field: Are the skills she possesses in demand or a glut on the market? Is her trade or occupation unionized? Do jobs in this field carry employee benefits?

Job security and seniority: Is this a temporary or a permanent job? What job protections, if any, exist?

Marital or relationship status and security: Is there a spouse or partner who assumes part of the financial responsibility? The care-taking responsibility? The housework and family maintenance responsibility? Or is there a spouse or partner who drains financial and caretaking resources? Is the relationship likely to continue?

Support from other family members: Where do other family members live, such as the mother's parents or siblings? Do they provide child care, shared living space, emotional support, or financial support? Are financial or caretaking resources needed by other family members, such as aging parents?

Racial-ethnic privilege: Does she benefit from White privilege in jobs, housing, and daily interactions, or does she face discrimination based on race-ethnicity in jobs, housing, and daily interactions?[12]

Public social support programs: Is there support for child care programs? Does the local school provide after-school care for children? Is a mother's job legally protected if she takes a leave from work to care for a family member?

Neighborhood context: Is the neighborhood safe? How far is her children's school from her house?

Transportation options: Does she own or have access to a dependable car? Is there reliable and convenient public transportation?

Family size and ages of children: Are older children able to help care for younger children? What are the child care costs for the number of children in the family? Are children close enough in age to be cared for together, or do they need different child care arrangements requiring separate schedules and commutes? Are her adolescent children acting responsibly, in which case they can help out at home, or are they engaging in risky behaviors, in which case they require added supervision?

Physical health: Is she a high-energy person with lots of stamina? Is she someone who needs more than eight hours of sleep to function well? Does she have chronic health problems, or is she in relatively good health? Do any of her children have special health needs, demanding intensive time and attention as well as adding to the family's medical costs? Are her children prone to colds and flu, requiring her to use up her sick leave?

These and other resources affect the course of action one can pursue. It is, however, misleading to think of any one particular resource as the determining factor in the paths these women chose, although a particular resource or its absence may be a limiting factor. In general, people are embedded in a constellation of resources. In one case, the income a woman's husband earns, the number and age of her children, and her own job opportunities form one particular constellation of resources. In another case, the lack of child support from an ex-husband, the option of living with her parents rent-free, and the potential for a good job after completing her education form a different constellation of resources. Resource constellations change over time and, with them, the options that are available.

The chapters that follow present the women I interviewed in the context of their resource constellations. Within these constellations, the women I interviewed use the materials at their disposal to weave courses of action and strategies of being. The following chapters are organized around four broad employment strategies: part-time work; full-time, night-shift work; full-time, day-shift work; and sequencing. I have organized the chapters in this manner because it best enables me to describe the ways in which these courses of action in the workplace are linked to both resource constellations and strategies of being.

3 "Calling the Shots": Voluntary Part-Time Workers

FOR WOMEN, part-time work is often portrayed as an ideal solution to the problem of combining employment and parenthood. But for many women who might desire part-time work, it is not an option, because either it does not meet their economic needs or it is not offered in their places of employment. Yet other women may not risk cutting back on their hours in organizations where salary increases, promotions, and interesting assignments are often reserved for full-time employees. For a myriad of reasons, the solution of part-time employment is not used by the majority of employed women with children. Nevertheless, for some women, part-time employment addresses many of their needs.

Thirty-two percent of employed women with children under six years of age worked part time in 1995 (Jacobs 1997:103).[1] Twenty-five percent of employed women with school-age children (six to seventeen years) but no children under six were employed part time in 1995 (Jacobs 1997:103). But these figures can be misleading if we think of part-time employment as "half time" (twenty hours a week) or even "three-quarters time" (thirty hours a week). The U.S. Bureau of Labor Statistics defines part-time employment as less than thirty-five hours a week. Everyone working up to 85 percent of forty hours a week is thus counted as a part-time worker in BLS statistics. Even with this broad definition of part time, the United States has a smaller proportion of part-time workers than do other industrialized countries, most of which define part time more narrowly than the United States does (Duffy and Pupo 1992; Rosenfeld and Birkelund 1995).[2] One likely reason for the smaller percentage of part-time employees in the United States is that most people's medical benefits are tied to their employment. Richard Belous (1989) points out that "many nations that have high part-time employment levels have developed an advanced social safety net that can compensate for many of the costs borne by part-timers. For example, the lack of employer-paid medical benefits may not be a real problem for a worker who lives in a country with a national health system" (52).[3]

People employed between thirty and thirty-four hours a week comprise 30 percent of those employed part time (U.S. Bureau of the Census 1997, table 635) and have been referred to as "intense part-time" workers (Holden 1990). Labor force scholars have argued that studies of part-time employment should distinguish between intense part-time workers and those who work fewer than twenty-five hours per week, since part-time workers are concentrated in these two categories and studies have found that intense part-time workers in professional and technical occupational categories are more similar to full-time workers than to other part-time workers (Holden 1990:161–62). At Sierra Hospital,* where the women I interviewed worked, the cutoff between part-time and full-time for registered nurses is thirty-two hours. Full-time staff nurses work an average of four eight-hour shifts (thirty-two hours a week) or three twelve-hour shifts (thirty-six hours a week), and because they are required to work every other weekend, their hours each week alternate between being more and less than that. In this chapter, I focus on hospital workers who are voluntarily employed less than thirty hours a week and who consider themselves and are considered by the hospital to be part-time employees.[4]

Part-time workers who have actively chosen to work a part-time schedule are referred to as voluntary part-time workers. It is the voluntary part-time workers we usually think of when we consider part-time work as a solution to some of the problems of combining employment and motherhood. Theoretically, part-time work is a way for both women and men to combine employment and parenting, but my discussion is limited to women, since the focus of this research is on mothers and the task of combining the work of parenting and employment is faced primarily by women. For the most part, men rely on their wives

---

*Sierra Hospital is a fictitious name for the hospital where my interviewees worked. The name of the hospital and the names of the hospital employees have been changed for reasons of confidentiality.

to reconcile any work/family conflicts they may have as fathers. As a solution for most mothers, part-time work is based upon marriages in which the husband is the primary earner. In addition, part-time work reinforces family arrangements in which fathers are seen as the breadwinners and mothers are expected to be the parents at home (Duffy and Pupo 1992:77; Smith 1983).

In this chapter, I discuss the strategies of being that are used by employed women with children who are voluntary part-time workers. These women tell a story that brings the definition of their actions in line with particular norms of motherhood, family, and employment.

Part-Time Nurses at Sierra Hospital

The choice of part-time work as a solution to combining employment and parenting is an option available only to those who can afford to earn less than full-time wages and, in most cases, also to forgo employee benefits. Of the women I interviewed, it was the registered nurses with part-time schedules who voluntarily used part-time employment as a strategy for dealing with the structural difficulties of combining employment and parenthood. As a group, the registered nurses who were employed part time had more control over their time, both at home and at the hospital, than did other nurses or other part-time hospital workers. They referred to this control as "flexibility," and they actively used this flexibility in their strategies of being mothers and workers.

There are a number of different part-time schedules available to registered nurses at Sierra Hospital. All part-time nurses are required to work every other weekend, and many nurses have a "permanent on-call" position, in which they are obligated and guaranteed to work only every other weekend. They may ask to be scheduled for additional days during the week, but they have no obligation to work extra days. These positions do not include employee benefits. In addition to permanent on-call positions, the hospital also has what it terms "two-fifths" and "three-fifths" positions. These also require working every other weekend and one or two days, respectively, during the week. As in the permanent on-call positions, additional days may be scheduled but are neither required nor guaranteed. Two-fifths positions do not include employee benefits; three-fifths positions, which do include benefits, are rare. Another part-time possibility for registered nurses is a "seven-tenths" position, in which two people work seven days each over a two-week pay period. Each works three days one week and four days the next, including every other weekend. The two people with seven-tenths positions are thus sharing more than a single full-time position and are, between them, covering every day of the week.

Which positions are available at any one time is a product of a variety of circumstances; some are historical, and some are based on the policies and preferences of the hospital administration, the nursing director of the unit, the union contract, or one's coworkers. For example, although an "intermittent" position (one weekend day a month) has been phased out by the hospital, I interviewed a woman in that position who had been grandmothered in. She would, however, lose the position if she were to transfer to another ward. Similarly, I was told by one nurse that three-fifths positions with benefits had been phased out, but another nurse told me that she had recently pushed for and obtained a three-fifths position with benefits. A seven-tenths job share position is only available in some units and only if two people can be found to share the position. When one seven-tenths time nurse decided to take a full-time position in another unit, her job-share partner faced either finding another person with whom to share the position or having to change her own position to full time or on call.

Of the thirty-seven mothers I interviewed, nine had voluntary part-time schedules at the hospital. Only one nurse had a seven-tenths schedule and regularly worked twenty-eight hours a week, the others were working at the hospital between sixteen and twenty-four hours a week on average. The following profiles of part-time nurses give a sense of the similarities and differences in this group.

Lillian Santana

Lillian Santana is a forty-two-year-old, Mexican-American registered nurse and the mother of two children, ages thirteen and sixteen. Her story provides an example of the way that a voluntary part-time position is enmeshed in comprehensive life strategies in which marriage and a spouse's income and benefits are part of the package. As is often the case, it is when such plans fail that we most clearly see their original terms and the assumptions on which they were grounded. Lillian had worked in a permanent on-call position for seven years, working at the hospital one or two day shifts a week and every other weekend (averaging sixteen hours a week) and fitting her own work schedule around her husband's schedule and her family's needs. After twenty years of marriage, Lillian's husband left her and initiated a divorce. The separation occurred a year before my interview with Lillian, and although she was still working on call, she had increased her hours to about thirty-two a week and was preparing to move into a full-time, permanent staff position that would provide a guaranteed number of hours and benefits. Lillian explained to me how her change in marital status has affected her employment needs.

> Basically we were covered by his benefits . . . as of now, I still am. But that's all going to change. We're in the process of all the legal stuff now, so [work is] going to change because I'm going to have to have my own benefits. I didn't want the divorce, after twenty years it was just sprung on me . . . but now I have to make myself independent and make the detachment from the relationship, and for me that means not only emotionally but financially. . . . So therefore [I have] to have a position I can rely on as being a permanent position at the hospital.

Lillian had been using part-time skilled work as insurance in case her marriage ended, and this bet-hedging mechanism had been the original impetus for obtaining her nursing degree. Eleven years earlier, with two children under the age of five, she and her husband had separated. The separation lasted only two months, but Lillian was left with an unshakable drive to obtain a nursing degree so that she could support herself and her children if she was ever in the same situation again. Lillian still spoke with a sense of urgency when she recounted those days:

> As soon as he got back, I started pushing for school. It took me a *long* time. I had no degree at all. . . . and because I had the kids, I think it took me a good five or six years to get through a three-year program . . . but my aim was always there and I kept pushing and just taking a class, maybe two, every semester. . . . It took me forever, but I did it that way.

Lillian's part-time strategy worked while she was married, and it provided her with access to full-time employment when her marital status changed. But as a strategy, it is bound together with other strategies and available resources. Lillian's story is important to keep in mind when thinking about both the costs and the advantages of part-time employment.

Jane Bradley

Jane Bradley is a thirty-one-year-old, Euro-American registered nurse who is married and has two children under the age of five. Jane was employed full time until her second child was born, after which she moved to a permanent on-call position. In her current position, she works at the hospital every other weekend, and she usually schedules an additional workday during the week, thus averaging two-fifths time on a regular basis. Jane says that her schedule gives her a lot of flexibility:

> When I was working full time—the weekends—you just simply don't get extra weekends off, which is hard with a family. To have four days a month with your husband, it's hard. But this way I have a lot more flexibility in that now I usually work my weekends, except we do quite a bit of traveling with my husband's work, so unless we're going somewhere, I usually work my [scheduled] weekends,[5] and then I usually work one evening shift. I work day shift on the weekends, and then I work one evening shift simply for child care purposes. That way I don't have to schlep the kids off somewhere early in the morning. I leave at 2:30, and he picks them up at 6:00. We have a neighbor down the road that watches them.

In many ways, Jane fits the media stereotype of the mother who chooses part-time employment. Her husband has a high-level, corporate management position, they live in a custom-built house in an exclusive section of the city, and Jane says that she doesn't need to work for economic reasons.

Marianna Miller

Marianna Miller is a twenty-seven-year-old, Filipina registered nurse who has worked at Sierra Hospital for three years. Marianna's son, who is just over a year old, clearly takes most of her attention when she is with him. He was in the room with us during the interview, and our conversation was punctuated with his sounds and first words and with his mother's, and sometimes my own, responses to him.

Marianna worked full time until the birth of her son and now works a three-fifths schedule on the evening shift. She is married, plans to have three or four children, likes big families, and assumes that, for economic reasons, she will not be able to reduce her hours to less than three-fifths time. They are renting the three-bedroom tract home in which they live, but she and her husband are saving to buy a home in the area, something they want to do before they have their next child.

After telling me that she would like to stay home with her children until the youngest was nine years old, Marianna quickly revised her statement and said:

> No, actually I would stay home during the weekdays and keep up with my nursing skills by working every other weekend. And being on call. Not during the week, though. 'Cause my husband would be home during the weekend. . . . And I know some moms, some nurses . . . some have worked full time and then completely dropped to every other weekend after the baby's born. . . . Because [pause] I really don't want to lose touch [with nursing] or anything. Because I went to school for a nursing degree and . . . I would feel like I was throwing it away, not keeping in touch for nine years.[6]

If Marianna could pick her ideal situation, she would not quit work, but she would be employed fewer hours. Here Marianna illustrates what I call the seven-second revision. When mothers who are employed tell me that they would like to stay home full time, I count silently to ten. Almost without exception, they revise their statement before I am finished counting to tell me that they would like to work fewer hours, but they would want to stay employed. This happens not only in formal interviews, but also in my informal conversations with mothers who are dental assistants, bank tellers, and salesclerks.

Lisa Harris

Lisa Harris, a thirty-three-year-old, Euro-American registered nurse, is married and has two children under the age of four. I interviewed Lisa in the living room of her home on a Friday, which she referred to as her domestic day. Her daughter and husband were away doing errands and the baby was awake and in his walker. The tract home they are buying in a new suburban housing division has a lived-in, relaxed feel. Lisa is a pleasant woman who smiles often. Although she mentioned occasionally getting burned out and referred to being short-tempered with the children when she is tired, she expressed contentment with her husband, her children, her home, her work schedule, and her job.

Lisa worked full time until her children were born. She now has a two-fifths day-shift position in which she is committed to work two days a week, but she is eligible to work more if she wants; she usually works three days a week. Lisa's husband, Bruce, works full time on the evening shift at another hospital. They have one day off in common each week and two weekends off in common each month. Although they use nonfamily daycare on a part-time basis, both Lisa's and Bruce's mothers do child care during the late afternoon and weekend times that their shifts overlap.

RESOURCES AND STRATEGIES

Lillian, Marianna, and Lisa use part-time employment as part of their work/family strategies. Their ability to work part time is based on the resources they can mobilize: child care (a combination of paternal, familial, and paid nonfamily child care); family support (cooperation in scheduling, help in bridging overlapping schedules); employment status (seniority, skills, security of position); and income (guarantee of hours, spousal income, benefits). Their desire to work part time is based on strategies of being that incorporate norms and identities about being a mother and about being a worker.

Education, Employment Status, and Income
Women with degrees in nursing, whether associate's (A.S.) or bachelor's (B.S. or B.S.N.) degrees, have educational qualifications that are in demand and that can command relatively good wages for women and some flexibility of schedule. A nursing shortage that began in the mid-1980s motivated hospital administrations to offer a variety of scheduling options to nurses and to increase

their pay scale.[7] In addition, because the hospital must have nurses on duty around the clock, seven days a week, it is willing to make part-time positions available and often offers part-time work as one way of covering weekends.

Another reason that hospitals have offered part-time schedules to nurses is that hospitals themselves need flexibility. The number of nurses needed in each unit at Sierra Hospital fluctuates according to the number of patients in the hospital, a number referred to as the patient census. When the hospital has many patients, the part-time nurses who work on call can be offered extra days; when the patient census is low, on-call nurses can be canceled.

Marianna had pushed the hospital administration to grant her a three-fifths position with benefits. Without her supervisor's support, her choice would have been between full time or an on-call position without benefits. In response to my question about whether many other people had a three-fifths position with benefits, Marianna replied:

> I don't know anyone at work that has the same kind of position I do . . . . initially, the kind of shift I wanted was called seven-tenths: three days one week, four days the next in the pay period. So it's a total [of] seven days. And our nursing supervisor said okay at first, but then, a couple weeks later she realized that . . . this is a job-share job, and it does stipulate it in the contract, it's a job share. So she couldn't grant it to me unless I found someone else. And everyone at work were pretty much stabilized and they were comfortable in the position they were in, and they've been there for years doing the same shift.

The support Marianna got from her supervisor was crucial to getting a schedule that met her needs. Here we see the power that middle management supervisors hold in relation to an employee's negotiation of institutional structure. Another nurse I interviewed told me that she wanted a three-fifths position, but that she had been told by her supervisor that those positions were no longer available. Individual strategies are facilitated, restrained, and shaped by institutional arrangements—and the flexibility of those arrangements is often controlled by an employee's immediate supervisor. Referring to her supervisor's support, Marianna said,

> She understood. I don't know if it's because she is a woman, or—I don't know what the reaction would have been if the supervisor had been a

man. But she was good about letting me jump down to seven days and then, finally, after she figured out I couldn't work [the seven-tenths position], I said, "Well, is it alright if I drop down to six days [in a two-week pay period]?" And she said it's okay.

Although she would prefer to work less than three-fifths time, Marianna did not want to take the economic risk of having less than a three-fifths position with benefits. Her success in her struggle against having to work more than three-fifths can be attributed to the demand for her qualifications as a nurse and to the support of her supervisor, but not everyone has these resources. For example, Shirley Roberts, an African-American nurses' aide at Sierra Hospital, had previously worked at another hospital, where she had asked to reduce her hours when her twelve-year-old son was hit by a car and would be in a body cast for several months. When her supervisor refused to let her work part time, Shirley quit.

> My son was more important to me than that job, because my husband always had a good job. . . . I'll tell you like this, you might know, there was quite [a lot of] prejudice at [Washington Hospital] in those years. They were really prejudiced a lot. And that had a lot to do with it too. But it's better now, I understand. But I think that had a lot to do with it. She should have given me part time. And I didn't know a lot about the union, like I know now. I could have taken a leave of absence.

Shirley's description of this event sums up the way her resource constellation at the time both constrained and facilitated her actions: the racial discrimination at the hospital, the racism of the supervisor, the value the hospital placed on her skills, her job qualifications, the absence of family medical leave, the activism and focus of the union, and her husband's income.[8]

Marital Status

The most striking similarities among the registered nurses I interviewed who worked part time were that they were all married and that their husbands all had college degrees and worked in professional, semi-professional, or managerial occupations. This is consistent with findings from large scale studies. In a study of women's labor force activity over a five-year period, Phyllis Moen found that those women who were continuously employed in part-time jobs were likely to have husbands in professional or managerial occupations and to have the husbands with the highest salaries (Moen 1985:129).

On-call positions work best for those who least need the income from their part-time employment. Jane Bradley and Connie Richards, both on-call nurses, are married to men who work in high-status, professional positions. Lillian Santana's ex-husband is a management consultant whose income allowed her to work in an on-call position when they were married. Marianna Miller (three-fifths time) and Lisa Harris (two-fifths time) are married to men in middle-level, semi-professional positions in the health care sector. These women are able to choose part-time work because they have the economic foundation to do so. This does not mean that their income is not needed, nor does it mean that they all fit into the same socioeconomic category, but it does mean that their husbands' jobs provide a base of income and benefits from which they can negotiate a schedule that is less than full time. The fact that there is another earner in the family, the fact that they do not see themselves as the primary earner in the family, and the fact that the primary earner earns enough and has adequate benefits gives nurses who work part time the ability to keep for themselves and their families some of the time the hospital would otherwise claim in exchange for a "family wage" or for benefit coverage.

Child Care and Family Support

Many women who are employed part time choose schedules that enable them to leave their children in the care of a family member while they are at work. Often, part-time nurses scheduled their hours at the hospital to coincide with some or all of their husbands' or partners' nonwork hours. This pattern corresponds with findings from large-scale studies that have found that child care by fathers is more common in families where mothers are employed part time than in families where mothers are employed full time (Presser 1988:140; Presser and Cox 1997).

Lisa and her husband, like about half of dual-earner couples with young children (Presser 1988:137–38) use shift work as a way of reconciling child care needs. Lisa told me:

We decided when we had kids that one or the other of us was going to work the opposite shift. Which is good, but it's not real good either, I mean we don't have a lot of time together. . . . But it's also very good. I mean we work well together.

Lisa is describing a family strategy.[9] She and her husband have a plan that they feel is good for them as a family unit, but which is not necessarily good for them as a couple. They sacrifice time together, but they reduce the time in which their children are in nonfamily child care. Lisa and Bruce have scheduled their workdays so that they both work the same two weekends a month, thereby giving them the remaining weekends to spend together as a family—"family time." They try to stagger their weekday workdays so that they do not often work on the same days.

A summary of their weekly schedule illustrates the ways Lisa and Bruce work to maximize the time they each have with their children and to minimize the time their children are with non-family members. Lisa works a day shift, leaving the house at 5:30 in the morning to get to the hospital for her 7:00 A.M. shift; Bruce works an evening shift, leaving the house at 2:00 P.M. to begin work at the hospital at 3:30 and returning home at around 12:30 in the morning. Until their first child was a year old, Lisa and Bruce only used child care by family members. On the days Lisa worked during that first year, Bruce cared for the baby until he had to leave for the hospital at 2:00 P.M., at which point Bruce's mother cared for the baby until Lisa returned around 4:00 in the afternoon. On the days Bruce worked and Lisa didn't, Lisa took care of the baby. Lisa and Bruce now use a combination of shared parental child care, child care by both grandmothers, and paid, licensed, in-home child care. On the two weekdays that Lisa works, her three-year-old daughter is cared for in an in-home, licensed child-care facility with four other children. With Lisa out of the house by 5:30 A.M., Bruce gets up with the children, gives them breakfast, and takes the three-year-old to child care. He then cares for their seven-month-old baby until Lisa returns in the afternoon. Once every other week, on a regular basis, Bruce and Lisa work a weekday in common. On these days, Bruce takes the children to his mother's house on the way to work at 2:00 P.M., and Lisa picks them up there at 4:00 P.M. on her way home. On the weekends they both work, Bruce takes the children to Lisa's mother's house on his way to work, and Lisa stops there after work, has dinner with her mother, and then returns home with the children in the evening. To cover the other days that she and Bruce might work in common, Lisa has arranged part-time child care for the baby with the same licensed child care provider who cares for their three-year-old, but that was not easy to do. Lisa told me that it was difficult to get anyone to take two part-timers in the same place, but that "they're very flexible when you talk money." Lisa and Bruce pay for two days a week for the baby, even though when Lisa is canceled at work, she keeps the baby home with her. I asked her what happens if she runs into child care problems; she laughed and said, "Then I call my mother-in-law."

Marianna and her husband, Brent, also work shifts; Brent works a day shift and Marianna works evenings (3:00 P.M. to 11:30 P.M.). Marianna emphasized that her evening schedule means that her son is only with the neighbor who does child care for them for about three hours on the weekdays that she works at the hospital. On those days, Marianna's husband picks up their son from the neighbor when he gets home from work at about 6:00 P.M., gives the baby dinner, and puts him to bed; Marianna returns home around midnight. On the Saturday and Sunday evenings that Marianna works, Brent does all the child care. In their case, outside child care is something to be used only for the time that neither parent is home.

While their children are under school age, Lisa and Marianna can effectively use shift work to maximize the time a parent is home with the children and to minimize the need for outside child care. Once their children reach school age, new timetables and needs will be added to their already complex schedules. This strategy fits a common pattern. Employed women with pre-school-age children are more likely to work a non-day or irregular schedule than are employed women with school-age children or women without children (Presser and Cox 1997:26). Marianna tells me that she is already worrying about what will happen in four years, when her son enters school:

> I [will] have to find some arrangement so that someone can pick him up [from school] and take him to the sitter for the time being. So all those thoughts have come across my mind. . . . If he got off school at

2:30, I really wouldn't be able to pick him up, and I doubt if the school would let us pick him up early. Have you ever heard of picking up early? I don't think so. They're pretty structured. . . . So that [evening] shift, it really wouldn't work out, because there's not enough time for me to get to work on time, and then in the day shift, it doesn't end until 3:30, and I wouldn't get home the earliest until 4:00 anyway, because the traffic going back this way in the afternoon is pretty busy. I don't know what to do yet! [Laughs.]

Marianna's poignant question, "Have you ever heard of picking up early?" indicated to me that she had been worrying over this, trying to figure out how she might arrange schedules so that when her son goes to school in four years, her schedule will again be compatible with her strategies of being a mother and a worker.

Several of the women I spoke with mentioned that having their husbands care for their children while they were at work was also a way of forging ties between fathers and children that was more difficult to achieve when mothers were home.[10] Marianna explained it this way:

It's just perfect, because then he gets to spend time with the baby, *alone*. Some strange things happen when we're home together sometimes. [For example] he gets to do all the yard work, male things, you know, he's home with me and we're taking the baby together, but he ends up doing a lot of male work, you know. Physically, the lawn, something in the garage, the car, and then I end up sitting with the baby. And so, not really a togetherness. But so, the time that he doesn't work, and [I do], he gets to spend time with the baby and really get to know him.

Marianna's explanation of what usually happened when she and her husband were home together points to the gendered nature of domestic work and parenting and to the way gendered relations are maintained and reproduced in daily action. Having her husband do the evening child care when she wasn't home, however, provided a situation in which her husband had to take primary care responsibility for his child.

Making a similar point, Jane enjoyed telling me the story of her husband's first weekend day alone with the children after their second child was born:

After I went back to work, just one Saturday . . . after [the baby] was born so there were the two [children], and I came home and the house was a mess and he goes [mimicking breathlessness], "I'm sorry—I'm really sorry—I couldn't clean up—but I—it was just—I was really kept busy with these kids!" [Laughs.] I go, "Really?" You know, like, what insight! So I think that they do [get] a lot more insight of all these little things you do to maintain a house that otherwise don't get done.

Jane told me that she thinks the time her husband has spent caring for the children while she is at work has made him more concerned and more realistic about issues concerning the children, such as safety and schooling. Like Marianna, she too feels that her husband is fortunate to have this time with the children.

> I think he realizes too that he has a bond that other dads don't necessarily have, and there's not all this resentment of staying and being with the kids. And also those evenings that I go to work . . . he has to pick them up, and make dinner, and put them to bed, and—those are kind of their evenings too.

In cases such as these, the resources that enable mothers to work part time are also enabling fathers to have regular times at home when they are primarily responsible for their children. Voluntary part-time workers limit the amount of nonfamilial child care they need and maximize the amount of time mothers and fathers spend with their children. At the same time, the strategy of voluntary part-time employment allows mothers to implement a construction of motherhood in which it is *mothers* who are home with their children most of the time.

BEING A MOTHER

Lillian, Marianna, and Lisa each use part-time employment as part of their strategies of being mothers. For them, nonfamily child care is a direct threat to their definitions of self as mother.[11] Lillian was not employed during her children's preschool years and didn't use child care, Lisa used child care only by family members during her first child's first year, and Marianna uses nonfamily child care only for the overlap period after her husband leaves for work and before she gets home. Their strategies of being a mother not only include keeping nonfamily child care to a minimum, but also include indicating to others that their children are not in child care for very long. Although Marianna has to leave for the hospital at 2:00 P.M. and her husband doesn't pick the baby up until 6:00 P.M. (a four-hour period), Marianna said:

> The babysitter is probably with him for about only three hours a day. And about three days a week.

It doesn't matter that Marianna isn't exact about the number of hours her child is in child care, but what her statement reveals is that she wants to indicate herself—to me, to others, and to herself—as a mother whose child is in nonfamily care for only a very short time. Marianna told me that her friends who are now pregnant and are planning to go back to work after the birth of their babies are all "scared" about the issue of child care. Marianna then explained:

> With your first child—or with any child, probably, but especially the first—you're very passionate about everything. Everything that happens to them. Everything that could happen. And most of my friends who are pregnant or have had babies do want to stay home. I think this theory of "career woman" [laughs]—I think that's going away for the first year. You know, "Let me stay home with my child and nurture him."

Marianna doesn't say that women should give up their careers or jobs or that being a mother is the only thing she and her friends want to do, but she does think that there are *particular points and durations of time* when the work of mothering eclipses career and employment. Hers is a life course perspective.

Lisa's feelings about being a mother are similar. Although she told me about her future plans to complete her B.A. degree and her interest in going into nursing administration, she was quick to add:

> But now, to be honest with you, my main goal is just my family, and that really does take priority. *I love nursing* . . . but at the same time, it's second—or third or fourth sometimes.

Lisa and Marianna like their profession and have plans for their future career development, but they take care to emphasize their identification with being a mother and its primary place in their lives. When I asked Lisa what it means to be a good mother, she replied:

> To make sure that they're comfortable and secure. I want my kids to be very secure and know that they're loved and feel safe . . . I mean I think it's real important to be here for them.

Lillian, Lisa, and Marianna can use their marital status, family income, and educational resources to more easily reconcile their actions with *being* a mother. Being a nurse, however, is also important, and the voluntary part-time workers are careful to indicate themselves as mothers who are also workers.

BEING A WORKER

The voluntary part-time registered nurses all told me that they wanted to take time to be with their children while they were young, but that they "didn't want to not work at all," and they felt fortunate to be able to be employed part time. Jane related what she felt was a telling story about a friend of hers, a nonemployed mother of three children:

> The other day . . . I said something like, "Well, I'm glad I'm going to go [to] work today, I'm feeling a little bored this week." And [my friend] looked at me, and she always seemed so upbeat and she just had her third baby and is going around doing all this stuff with the kids, and she said, "Usually I'm so bored, I could die." *And just like a flash her whole face changed for a second,* and then it came back and she got all the kids in the car and said, *said cheerily,* "See you later!" and drove off. And I just thought "Oh!" I had no idea she felt that way. Later, we talked more about it—she said, "I would just love to have something I could go to a couple days a week."

Two strategies of being are presented in Jane's story. First, Jane is telling me about her friend's strategy of being a mother—a presentation of self as mother in which she is completely and happily immersed in her children. Jane presents this strategy of being as inauthentic because it is not how her friend really feels, as Jane discovers when her friend's mask slips (*"And just like a flash her whole face changed for a second"*). The second strategy of being is Jane's own, presented by implication as a contrast to her friend's. Jane is presenting herself as a mother who can be authentic with and about her children because she can admit that being with children all day every day is boring and because she has arranged her own life in a way that she feels incorporates both her children's needs and her own.

Employment is not something that inherently creates problems for women who are mothers. All the part-time nurses I spoke to echoed the sentiment that employment gave them a break from home and children. Marianna put it this way:

> I like being able to get away—being, not being a mother for ten hours and not having to worry. I think that's when it works out well, when I think, "I'm glad I do work." Because sometimes I'm home all day and I have not even taken a shower or washed my face . . . my husband comes home and I look exactly the same as he saw me when he left in the morning [laughs]. It's very tiring. It's more tiring to stay at home than it is to work sometimes, you know.

Jane explained,

> I also think it's real hard to stay home full—full time. I mean if I didn't have my outlet of working one day or working my weekends and seeing my friends and doing something that I feel that I'm good at, that I enjoy, I get respect for. Particularly the people I work with . . . we have a real sense of camaraderie and respect for the most part. And so I get a lot out of it, the limited time that I spend there.

Lillian Santana told me that working only a few days a week had been perfect for her. She added:

> I think that's a very healthy balancing thing, and it not only gets you out there, [but it also] gives you a sense of accomplishment and a sense of fulfillment, because I don't think you can get everything from your children—or your husband.

Employment, as Lillian points out, not only provides a break from home, but it also provides a sense of self that is derived from outside one's family. All of the women hospital employees I interviewed, across occupational categories, race/ethnicity, and shift and regardless of the percentage of time they worked, mentioned the feeling of accomplishment and competence that they derived from being workers.

Marianna's ideal work schedule would be to work on call and thus to be obligated to work at the hospital only every other weekend. If she could afford to work only four days a month and to forgo employment benefits, an on-call schedule would address her concerns about child care (her husband would do it), being home with her children, and not throwing away her training and education in nursing ("I don't want to lose touch . . . I would feel like I was throwing it away, not keeping in touch for nine years"). But Marianna's reasons for staying in the labor force are not only to keep from losing out on income and human capital investment; Marianna also identifies as a worker and a nurse. She compared working with staying home all day: "It's more tiring to stay at home than it is to actually work sometimes, you know." After several days of being at home all day, Marianna looked forward to her time at the hospital. It may seem paradoxical that Marianna had previously told me that the hardest thing about being employed was wanting to be home more, "especially on those first days [when] I have to go back to work after being off all week. It's hard to go back on the first day." But both statements are true for Marianna; her identity as a mother makes it difficult for her to leave her son when she goes to work, but her identity as a worker and nurse makes her hours at work a break from the constancy of motherhood. Rather than seeing these two identities as oppositional, however, we need to understand that neither concept of self exists in isolation. Marianna is *both* mother *and* worker, but the vocabulary of motive attached to each identity makes it difficult for Marianna to articulate her identities as worker and mother simultaneously. When Marianna says that the idea of being a "career woman . . . goes away for the first year," she is reconciling the conflicting vocabularies of motive attached to motherhood and to employment by distinguishing between career and employment. Because she puts a time frame around the recession of one's identity as a "career woman," she is distancing herself from the concept of career only for specific points in the life course, and she is reconciling conflicting vocabularies of motive by distributing motives over time.

Lisa also rejects a static, snapshot view in her construction of self as a working mother. Lisa wanted to be a nurse ever since she was a child, and she had to struggle to achieve her goal. Lisa's parents could not afford to help support her while she obtained a nursing degree, so Lisa deferred her dream and went to work as a medical assistant after she graduated from high school. Fortunately, a physician for whom she was working helped Lisa get a three-year full scholarship to a hospital nursing program, and by the time Lisa was twenty-three, she had her nursing degree. Lisa talked about bringing her whole being to her work:

It's important to me to take all of my knowledge, practical knowledge as well as learned knowledge, and be able to use it every day to the fullest, and to be able to give a hundred percent and, you know, to pre- pare [people] to get better and go home, or to prepare people to die, or to do whatever the task of that day is. It's important to me to give a hundred percent while I'm there and be able to leave it there so that when I come back the next time I can be good at it still.

To Lisa, her part-time schedule does not represent a turning away from career or a lesser commitment to her work. It is, as it was for most of the voluntary part-time nurses I interviewed, a way of hon- oring both her identity as a mother and her identity as a worker.

Although the part-time nurses I interviewed express a strong work identity, management often views part-time workers as less committed than full-time workers, and those who work part time can often feel excluded and marginalized in the workplace[12] (Barker 1993; Bennett and Alexander 1987; Smith 1983). Jane Bradley told me that when she was working full time she was very "connected" at work—she knew many of the physicians, volunteered for hospital-wide committees, and organized social events in her ward. She thinks that the level of social interaction she had when she worked full time has helped her stay connected to people now that she is working part time, and that this is one of the reasons that people at work keep her informed. But Jane also makes an effort to stay connected, even when she is not at the hospital.

There was a problem that came up two weeks ago. You know, this weekend I worked again . . . everybody at work is talking to me about it again, and it's like now I know I won't be there to talk to the people I want to talk to about it, so I'm going to have to try . . . calling on the phone to [get] them this week.

Jane's actions belie the idea that part-time employees are not as committed to the workplace as full-time employees. A study that compared the work commitment of mothers who were full-time and part-time hospital nurses found no evidence to support the hypothesis that mothers who were part-time nurses were less committed to work or more traditional in their attitudes than mothers who were full-time nurses (Bennett and Alexander 1987). My interviews with part-time nurses are consistent with this finding. The number of hours they are employed each week is not a measurement of their attachment to the profession, the workplace, or their identities as workers.

WEAVING WORK AND FAMILY

In my interviews with voluntary part-time nurses, the theme of "needs" emerged: income needs, child-care needs, husbands' needs, children's needs, and the hospital's needs (in terms of available positions and current policies). These themes are all connected. Income needs, after a certain point, are subjective, and the amount of income that a couple says they need can be either a determinant or a rationalization of the number of hours they are employed. Family income needs and the kind of positions available at the hospital are major factors in choosing part-time as opposed to full-time work and in the choice of an on-call, two-fifths, three-fifths, or seven-tenths position. The type of part-time position a nurse holds affects how much flexibility she has—flexibility she uses to allocate time with her children, arrange her employment schedule and family time with her husband's work schedule, and reconcile child-care needs.

The elements that go into strategies for combining employment and motherhood are so interwoven that it is difficult to discuss them as isolated variables. Whenever we focus on one element, we inevitably include others, but the shallow focus of our lens blurs these other elements so that we miss the relationships between them. I am suggesting that we look not only at the elements from which strategies are built, but at the way in which these elements are connected and related. Marianna Miller's employment strategy, for example, takes account of myriad interwoven circumstances. Many of the elements of her strategy of part-time employment, such as the use of shift work to coordinate child care with her spouse, are common to other part-time nurses. But Marianna's situation also differs in several ways from that of the other part-time nurses I interviewed: her three-fifths permanent position requires her to work three days a week, unlike the other part-time nurses, whose schedules may allow but don't require them to work that much on a regular basis; her position receives benefits; she is renting rather than buying her home; and (4) she has just had her first child. All the other part-time nurses I interviewed were buying their homes and had two children at the time they were interviewed.

The four ways Marianna's situation differs from those of the other part-time nurses are intertwined: if she works three-fifths time, they can save to buy a house; when they buy a house, they will have their next child; if she is covered by benefits at work, having additional children is more economically feasible. All of these strands are woven together, and a change in any one affects the others. When they buy a house and have a second (or third or fourth) child, either Marianna will have to continue working three-fifths time because they need her benefits or they need the money for the mortgage payments and the cost of a larger family, or she may be able to move to an on-call position if her husband has employee family benefits, if his salary has risen enough to cover the mortgage, and if the needs of additional children convince them that she should be home more.

Some of the differences between Marianna's situation and those of the other part-time nurses may thus be artifacts of Marianna's age and life course position, and it is reasonable to assume that, in a few years, her situation may come to resemble more closely those of the other part-timers. For example, when I interviewed Jane Bradley, she was thirty-one years old, had two children, and worked part-time in an on-call position. At age twenty-seven, however, Jane had only one child and was employed four-fifths time to make the payments on a home she and her husband had just purchased. It is also possible, however, that the economic structure of Marianna's life may change, as did Lillian's, in ways that require her to increase her hours and perhaps return to full-time employment. Similarly, Marianna's plans for family size are part of the trajectory of this constellation of elements. Marianna stated that she liked big families and wanted to have four children, although she thought that three would probably be the limit. All of the other part-time nurses I talked to told me that they had no intention of having more than the two children they already had, even though several of them, Lisa Harris included, had originally planned to have three or four children. Marianna, the youngest of this group of part-time nurses and the only one with one child, may find that the norm of two children better fits with the life pattern she is weaving.

The part-time nurses I interviewed use their education and training to secure part-time employment in relatively well-paying positions. This helps to ensure that they will maintain their skills, that they will have access to full-time employment in the event of financial need (for example, divorce, widowhood, unexpected expenses, loss of husband's income), and that they will be in a position to further their careers or increase their labor-force participation at a point when they feel their children no longer need the kind of care that part-time work allows. Their husbands' incomes provide a foundation for their ability to work part time and reinforce the resulting perception of fathers as providers and mothers as caretakers. At the same time, however, the need for child care while mothers work and the preference for child care provided by parents and family members increases the amount of caretaking done by fathers while mothers are doing a share of the providing. House purchases, family size, work shift, weekly hours of employment, or job advancement are just some of the outcomes that are affected by material resources and that make up the weave of work and family in women's lives.

Lisa told me that her daughter often asks her why she has to work, and Lisa has two responses. To her daughter, she explains that she has to work so they can have the nice things they have (the house, toys, clothes, vacations). To me, she added:

> I had a career because I think it's important for me mentally to not just be a mommy. . . . I guess it makes me feel more whole. I mean I love being a mom, but at the same time just talking baby talk—it does get old. And I'm not stimulated enough with that [laughs].

Lisa presents her employment as enabling her, as a mother, to provide for her children and, as an employed woman, to engage in additional kinds of productive activity. But Lisa goes one step further, tying these identities together into a gift she gives her children.

> I hope that they're proud someday of the fact that Mom has a profession and that I went to college and that I worked hard to do it, and so did Dad, and we had other occupations first. . . . And I think that's something to be proud of.

Lisa sees the bridge between her identities as mother and as worker and employs a strategy that enables her to construct a definition of working mother in which these two identities are mutually supportive.

PART-TIME WORK AND THE STRUGGLE OVER TIME

Employed women with children are engaged in a struggle over time. The shape of that struggle varies depending on whether a mother is employed full time, is voluntarily or involuntarily employed part time, or is employed in day, evening, or night shift work. The struggle will also vary depending on the number and age of a woman's children and the resources on which she can draw. Even the nurses who are voluntary part-time workers do not have complete choice about their schedules, but they use their resources to claim varying degrees of control over the allocation of their time.

The registered nurses who were employed part time talked about the success of their strategies in terms of the degree of flexibility they could achieve. Lisa explained her position to me in the following way:

> I'm called a two-fifths person, so I'm supposedly guaranteed—my seniority plays a part—two days a week, and then I also sign up for an extra day, sometimes two, depending on their need and my need and time and all that. Rarely more than three days a week. . . . I'm prescheduled three days a week, but if I need to take another day off, I can take that day.

Lisa thus maintains control over the third day, usually working it because she needs the income, but having no obligation to do so if there are other demands on that time. Because Lisa and her husband feel that their basic family income needs can be met if Lisa works two days a week, cancellations are not seen as devastating. Lisa expresses a feeling of control over her weekly hours at the hospital:

> I don't think I could ask for a better profession and want to work three days a week and have time with my kids and make as much money as I do to be able to work part time. . . . Those are very important things, because *I can call the shots,* and if they don't need me this week, then

fine and I'll just take the time off because it's more important to be with my kids. And I'm very fortunate that I don't work at a place where I make less money and may not have that flexibility. You know, be able to call the shots that much myself.

Unlike Lisa, Marianna feels she can not afford the risk of being guaranteed less than three days of work a week. Since her seniority is much less than Lisa's, her extra days of work would be canceled more frequently than Lisa's. Marianna doesn't express the same feeling of control over her time. When I asked Marianna what was the hardest thing about being employed and being a parent, she replied:

> Wanting to stay home more. . . . that's really the struggle and then having the lack of sleep, or not enough rest. . . . It's really exhausting because parenting is really twenty-four hours a day, and then to have to go back to work where you get paid and stand there for eight and a half, really nine hours from the time you leave and get ready and then come back home, it's really about nine or nine and a half hours, and so it's very exhausting, especially if there are days when I don't get a nap. So I start from 7 [A.M.] to 12 [midnight], exhausting days . . . I don't go to sleep until about 1:00, and then to have to wake up again around 7:30 or 7:00, sometimes [my son] hollers out once in the night and that's it—I'm awake [laughs].

Time is a recurring theme in Marianna's account of what is most difficult about being a working mother: wanting more time at home, wanting less time at work, wanting more time to sleep, the twenty-four-hour-a-day time of parenting, the commute time to work, the on-your-feet time at the hospital. The struggle with and over time permeates her response, which sounds very different from Lisa's version of "calling the shots."

Flexibility is a key element in dealing with the structural incompatibilities of employment and motherhood. Over and over again, employed women with children stressed that flexibility enabled them to be mothers and to be workers in ways that reflected the integration of their identities as working mothers. And over and over again, it was the absence of flexibility that created conflict and tension. Flexibility of schedule can be of three types: flexibility of time during the work day, flexibility of work days over the week, and flexibility of work time over the year. By looking at the structure of flexibility, we can see how employed women with children use flexibility to indicate themselves as mothers and as workers.

Flexibility during the Work Day

Nurses who work in the hospital doing bedside care do not have flexibility during their time at the hospital. Lisa explained,

> It's also not very easy in nursing to say, "Gee, I'm going to take an extra hour for lunch and go see Bobby play baseball," or you know, "There's a cute little award ceremony I want to see"—you can't do that—*if you're on work, you're on work.* I do see that that is a problem as far as not feeling flexible, which is why I want to work part-time. . . . I mean it's flexible as far as I can only work part time and not full time, but I mean your time *on* is your time *on.*

However, Lisa once did leave work when her daughter cut her hand while playing. Lisa recalled:

> I had to leave in the middle of a shift, I had to drop everything and go, and, you know, it was kind of a "You really shouldn't be doing this" type of thing, and "If you have to go, go"—more regressive—whereas "Oh, no, go take care of your child" is what I more expected [from the supervisor].

Jane also recounted a time that she had to leave the hospital because of an emergency with her child:

> I remember one time [the babysitter] called and she said, "She really doesn't look good"—she'd been having like a little bit of a fever—"she's just kind of staring blank." And here I was taking care of this patient that just had open heart surgery and I just almost panicked, you know, although I realized, well, even if her fever went up and all she had was febrile seizure, you know—but when it's your own child, I was just like "I have to leave. I have to go." Luckily, I worked in a [supportive] environment. At that time our boss was the mother of two children and very very supportive, not only about children but just about anything for us—really, she was a very supportive person. And she would just say, "We can cover—I'll come out and take care of that patient. You can go." So, I mean, I was very lucky, because I can't imagine not having that—to sit there and be working. And also, these kind of patients that, you know, could die in a second, and trying to concentrate knowing that something is going on with your kid.

Jane points out that not having the flexibility to deal with problems and emergencies at home not only affects home life, but also affects performance on the job. As in the case of Marianna and her struggle to obtain a three-fifths position, a supportive supervisor is credited for making it possible to integrate family and employment responsibilities in constructive ways.

Marianna also mentioned the problem of flexibility once one was "on the job":

> There's only been one time that I know of . . . someone's father died, and *a nurse actually left the floor.* . . . I mean, it's so difficult to get out of work if you're a nurse. It's not like any other job where you can just drop everything and go. Although I would, for [my son], if something, you know, were wrong. Someone's father had died, immediately she talked to the supervisor and she let her go home. But that's the only time I know of where someone has left. Because usually, you have your patients and who is going to carry the rest of that load?

Once a nurse is working a shift, the difficulty of leaving the hospital before the shift ends makes the need for reliable, quality child care particularly important, and it further illuminates the nurses' efforts to have child care provided by family members.

Flexibility during the Week

Marianna's ward does not assign its nurses to specific weekdays, as some units in the hospital reportedly do. In other words, while Marianna must work every other weekend, the weekdays she works are not always the same day of the week. Because she now works an evening shift, during which her husband does the bulk of the child care, this irregularity does not present a child care problem and is instead seen by her as an advantage. Marianna says:

> Working only two days in the work week, I have all this time to be with [my son] while his father's not with him, and the other part of it, which is the way the hospital schedules my floor anyway, [is that] I can ask them what days I would like off so I can go do some things. If [my son] did have something for school going on in the future, then I just have that [day] off.

Flexibility is an advantage most employees would value, but for employed women with children, flexibility is what allows them to do the work of mothering when changes, snags, or opportunities occur in the work/family fabric. The ease or difficulty of accommodating unforeseen events, such as a child's illness, or irregular events, such as the school play or the soccer championship, depend largely on what these nurses all refer to as "flexibility." On-call nurses can reclaim more time from the hospital than can nurses who work two-fifths or three-fifths part-time positions. Jane, who has an on-call position, told me:

> I have flexibility, I don't have certain days I have to work. If the children are sick, I can call two hours before my shift starts and say I don't want to work. So it works out real well.

Since her divorce, Lillian Santana works at the hospital about thirty-two hours a week, but she still retains her on-call position in order to preserve the flexibility it gives her. Her children, both in their early teens, were upset about the divorce, and Lillian felt they needed a lot of time and attention from her at exactly the point when she needed to be working more hours. The need for employee benefits, however, will soon necessitate her move to a permanent, full-time position with benefits. Lillian explained:

> For me the hardest is when the kids don't feel good or they're emotional. . . . The [on-call] status I've had has been perfect for this situation because when I've seen they've been emotionally [upset] . . . I've been able to say, "No, I'm not going in." . . . What works out for me too here is, and I think that's why nursing is good, that if you take the day off . . . I'll work a P.M. shift or a night shift to make up. . . . And I've done it, because I know I have to have so many set days to have so much money. Or I'll work a weekend, which they *always* want—it never fails [laughs].

Children's behavior is often interpreted as a demand for changes in their mothers' working hours. Lisa told me:

> There are times when they need me more and if I work more I can really see it in [my daughter], and it's not okay with her that I'm not with her. And I don't feel I have the control over her. I feel like the day care people have had [the control]. "Oh, god, she's acting just like those kids," [and] I realize that's because she's *been* with those kids, you know.

Jane Bradley related a similar experience with her five-year-old daughter. Jane was employed full time until her daughter was almost three years old, at which point Jane took a part-time position. She feels that her reduced working hours have made a difference to her daughter's disposition.

My daughter was colicky, she was always kind of "fussy," "sensitive" [laughs] are different words we've used. And she's evolved and grown and done better, but part of that is my spending more time with her. And I know the old quality versus quantity—when you have certain kids I think they do okay and they do fine [with that]; other kids, like my daughter, when we would try to have our quality time, there was too much stress into it. It was never quality time because there was like this energy into the three of us, Mom, Dad, and [child] together, this is one of our few days together, we're going to have fun. We are going to do this, we're going to go to, let's say, the botanical garden, hike around and have fun. She'd be *whiny*, and I think they sense that, especially if they're a sensitive kid, they sense this energy and they react to it. So every time we'd try to have quality time, it wouldn't work out. And I have since found, since I spend a lot more time with the kids, some of my best moments and time and sharing and parenting with them are totally unplanned events.

Mothers are likely to interpret their children's negative behavior as a demand for their time, and they are sympathetic to those demands. Flexibility over the week allows nurses who are employed part time to be mothers who can "be there" to meet their family's needs when crises, irregular events, or children's additional emotional needs punctuate their normal routine.

Flexibility over the Year

Nurses who are employed part time also use the flexibility of their schedules to increase or decrease their average weekly hours of employment over a sustained period in response to needs at home. Connie Richards provides a good example of how flexibility in hours worked is used over time. Connie is a fifty-year-old, Chicana registered nurse; she is married, has two adolescent children, and works in an on-call position that only requires her to work one weekend day a month. This type of position had been phased out at Sierra Hospital, and Connie was the only nurse I interviewed who was obligated to work only one day a month. As in other part-time positions, she may be asked to work more but is under no obligation to do so; on average, she works about six to eight days a month. In order to meet the cost of her son's high-school tuition, however, Connie has recently been trying to increase her time to three days a week. During our interview, she pointed to a calendar on the wall on which the days she was scheduled to work were circled in green, with slashes through the circles on the days she was canceled, and said:

> Now I'm trying to put in three days a week. There have been months— see all those green circles [there are perhaps ten or twelve circles]—if you were to see last year, maybe there'd be three circles. But now with [my son] going to [an] even more [expensive school], I'm trying to put in a little more time.

Connie thus adjusts her weekly hours over her family's life course to meet changing needs. She also adjusts her hours over the course of the calendar year. In the summer, when her children are home from school all week, Connie works more weekends, but she says that during the school year she "can't work a lot of weekends cause that's when they're home all day and it's fun." When explaining to me that she doesn't work the week before or the week after Christmas, she said, "But then I just take off those two weeks because, you know, that's family time." Control of the ebb and flow of one's time over the course of weeks or months is as important as control over time during the week.

This type of flexibility could be made available much more widely. Which jobs are seen as lending themselves to flexible scheduling, reduced hours, or home-based work is primarily a product of how work is constructed conceptually rather than in-herent structural features of the work itself. Annemarie Gerzer (1986) reported on a department store in Munich that instituted a creative system for enabling its employees to vary their work schedules. A survey of women employees at the store found that many wanted to work less than full time and wanted more flexi-bility in scheduling. An individual work time (IWT) plan was de-vised in which each employee decided in advance how many hours a month she wanted to work on average (ranging from 60 to 173 hours a month). Employees work out the distribution of hours with their departments. At times when the needs of either the employee or the department result in lower monthly hours than the agreed-upon average, the employee's monthly salary is not affected, and she makes up the time over the course of the year. If an employee works more than her agreed-upon monthly average in any month, she gets "time credit" and can take time off in compensation. Gerzer concludes that the IWT scheme "has created something quite new in the working world: it has shown that it is possible for the obligations staff have towards their families, as well as those they have as employees, to be recognised as equally important. Family obligations which spill over into work time can be accommodated when individuals' work schedules are drawn up; and this happens not simply on an informal level, organised through personal relationships, but is built into the official structure of the company" (132).

The existence of work structures such as this one at the department store in Munich and of the job shares, nonmarginalized part-time work, and flexibly scheduled jobs that do exist point to some of the ways that people's work and family needs can be built into the organization of work. Working more hours to pay for a child's tuition or working less in order to be at home more during holidays are ways the women I talked to use the flexibility of their positions to do things for their children and to implement their strategies of being employed mothers.

The part-time nurses I interviewed are continually contesting control over time at the hospital. They all want to be employed for noneconomic as well as economic reasons. They want to work more hours when they need additional income, and they want to work fewer hours when they need time at home. When I asked Jane why she worked on call rather than quitting work altogether or working a part-time position with more hours, she replied:

> Even with our good [child-care] arrangements, there were just times where I just felt like I didn't spend enough time with my daughter, and then realizing that with the second I'm gonna spend even less time, not only with her but with the other one. . . . I mean we were able, financially, I don't really need to work. So that's kind of nice, but I knew that I didn't want to not work at all. I needed to be out a little bit. . . . I really feel that I have, as far as being a parent, nowadays, I really have kind of the best in many ways, you know. I'm very fortunate, anyway.

Nurses who are employed part time earn needed income, maintain skills and employment history, and have the flexibility to deal with unexpected or irregular events in their family members' lives. Their economic situations do not require them to be employed full time and underwrite their ability to work part time.

Their days of work and shift schedules are selected with a view to maximizing child care by fathers, and nonfamily child care is kept to a minimum. Their sense of themselves as workers is important to them, and many have plans to develop their careers more fully when their children are older. But part-time employment enables these women to see themselves and to present themselves to others as mothers who are primarily at home with their children—able to provide "family time," to "do things" with their children, and to "be there" as mothers.

4 "Putting Your Feet in the Door": Involuntary Part-Time Workers

THE SUCCESS of part-time work as a strategy for combining employment and motherhood is situational. What is a solution for voluntary part-time workers can be a problem for involuntary part-time workers. Involuntary part-time workers are people who want full-time employment but have only been able to secure part-time jobs. Not all women who work part time do so by choice—it is a work schedule sought out by some and forced upon others.

The distinction between voluntary and involuntary part-time work is crucial to any discussion of the place, meaning, and implications of part-time work. In 1995, over one-fourth (27.6 percent) of employed women were employed part time (Jacobs 1997:103). How many of these women are employed part time because they choose it, and how many of them want and need full-time employment? As a proportion of part-time work, involuntary part-time employment has been growing since the 1970s (Clark 1997; Kahne 1994:418), and many of the new part-time jobs being created are filled with involuntary part-time workers (Smith 1997:327).[1] In 1972, 16 percent of women part-time employees were involuntary part-time workers; by 1992, the year in which I conducted my interviews, that proportion had increased to 24 percent (Smith 1997:419). Part-time workers are more likely to be involuntary if they are Black or Hispanic or if they have only a high school education or less (National Center for Education Statistics 1996, Supplemental Table 33–2). Involuntary part-time workers are often the most powerless employees, forced by economic need to take jobs that don't offer enough hours and that often require working undesirable shifts.

INVOLUNTARY PART-TIME WORKERS AT SIERRA HOSPITAL

For some women, part-time employment is not the way to a more balanced and fulfilling life, but is both the result of and a contributor to being one of the working poor. The women I interviewed who were involuntary part-time workers were either janitorial workers or nurses' aides, and most of them were in a job status the hospital termed "casual—on-call." This job category operated in the following way: at Sierra Hospital, new employees in several occupational categories, such as janitorial workers, are hired for a ninety-day probationary period with no guarantee of a minimum number of hours and without benefits. They are "on call" to come to work at any time and on short notice, and their future status depends on their willingness and ability to be instantly available. After the first ninety days, these employees are either terminated, retained in the "casual" position, or reclassified to a permanent on-call position with a guaranteed number of hours. If casual employees have not averaged twenty hours of work per week, they retain their casual status. Reclassified employees are guaranteed the average number of hours that they worked during the previous ninety-day period, and will get benefits if they are reclassified over twenty hours a week.[2] As one of my interviewees remarked, a casual position is "like putting your feet in the door."

The following profiles and discussion of involuntary part-time hospital workers illustrate the way in which the resources available to them both limit their options in the labor force and enable them to participate in it. For mothers who are involuntary part-time workers, part-time work is a problem, not a solution. They not only face difficulties in providing economically for their families, but they also face difficulties in their strategies of being "working mothers."

Marcia Collins

Marcia Collins is a forty-two-year-old, African-American woman who is employed as a janitorial worker at Sierra Hospital; she is divorced and has three children, ages fifteen, eleven, and seven. I interviewed her one morning in the living room of her home in an older, residential, Black, working-class section of the city. Marcia had gotten home from working the night shift only a few hours before our appointment, her children had left for school, and the house was quiet.

Marcia had been working at Sierra Hospital for only two months; she was classified as a casual employee, was still in the initial ninety-day probationary period, and was hoping that she could work enough hours during this period to be reclassified to permanent part-time and eventually to permanent full-time. She told me that she needs to work forty hours a week and was getting to work almost that amount now, but that it varied from week to week. As a casual employee, Marcia has no guarantee of hours and no benefits; she is on call for any shift and any day. Technically, she could tell her supervisor that she is only available for certain shifts, but it is in the interest of casual employees to work as many hours as possible, not only because they need the income, but also because they want to be reclassified. For this reason, many casual employees make themselves available to work day, evening, and night shifts and usually work a combination of all three.

Her irregular schedule undermines Marcia's family life. She said that her children had not adjusted to her working different hours—sometimes she is there for dinner, sometimes she is not; sometimes she needs to sleep during the day and her children, used to having their mother available to them, knock on her bedroom door and wake her. When she works a night shift, the children sleep at her sister's house, which the fifteen-year-old does not want to do. And Marcia never knows which day or which shift she is working until she is called. When I asked Marcia how she was going to continue managing with this kind of schedule, she told me that she had decided to send her eleven-year-old son to live with his father.

> Actually, my middle child I'm going to send to [my ex-husband], after Christmas, and he's going to keep him until he gets grown, you know, until he's eighteen. Yes, he's going to stay there. Because me and [my ex-husband] talked it over, and I agree with him, it's a little too much right now with my working schedule. And I feel my oldest son I can deal

with. The [seven-year-old] baby, with my other sister, I can deal with. My middle child, that's the one I think I can let him deal with him.

Her response did not really answer the question I asked, which was about how she managed her schedule. Instead, she responded by telling me that her schedule made it difficult for her to handle and supervise the behavior of her eleven-year-old son and about her decision to handle this problem by sending her son to live with his father. Her son's problem behavior preceded the two months she had been working at the hospital, but her difficult work schedule was clearly the proverbial straw. Throughout my interview with Marcia, she connected her decisions and actions to her concern for her children (e.g., how much income she needed or what kind of child care was acceptable) and her desire to be a good mother. The decision to send her middle child to live with his father, who lived in another state, had been difficult to make and was difficult for her to talk about. I asked Marcia how she felt about seeing one of her children leave to live somewhere else.

> Right now with my working schedule, I feel that it's the best. Now this was brought up before I started to work at [Sierra Hospital], and I told him no. I said, "I want the boys to be raised together, they can come and visit you in the summertime like they always have." But now it [has] become a problem, because I'm not here as much and I just feel it would be better for [my son] now. I feel [my ex-husband] could be a better parent than I would be, put it like that. Before it was different. I was more around here. So that's the reason why I'm letting him go, you know, right now. But before, "Oh, no no no, just summer." . . . But now, I feel—and I called him—and I said "Well —" and he said "Well, okay." So, okay.

Marcia would rather work a full-time, permanent, day-shift schedule so that she could earn enough to provide for her family and be home with her children after school to make dinners, help with their homework, and supervise their nonschool time. But Marcia is an involuntary part-time worker with few marketable skills and no other source of income, and that choice isn't available to her.[3]

Sandra Wells

Sandra Wells is a thirty-six-year-old, Euro-American woman who works as a nurses' aide; she is divorced and has two children in elementary school who are both living with their father. I interviewed Sandra in her home, an apartment that appeared to be a converted garage and to consist of two rooms. There was only one window, and my eyes needed to adjust to the dim light in the apartment—it was dark and crowded and very tiny. The room I walked into served as kitchen and living-room space and contained a double bed (where Sandra sleeps). Sandra shares this apartment with a woman roommate, who occupies the one bedroom. Sandra's two children stay with her every other weekend, and her roommate's children are also there on weekends.

Sandra had been working at Sierra Hospital for eight months. She started in a casual on-call position, passed her ninety-day probationary period, and was then guaranteed sixteen hours of work a week but is often able to work as much as thirty-two hours in a week. Although she is regularly working two to four days a week, she receives no employee benefits. Sandra has achieved more secure employment than Marcia, but she still needs to worry about picking up extra days since the guaranteed two days a week are not enough to meet her economic needs. She also has a more regular schedule than Marcia's, working only the day shift and being permanently scheduled to work every other weekend. This amount of regularity makes it possible for Sandra to schedule her children's visits, but she told me that her indefinite schedule would make it difficult for her to have her children with her on a full-time basis.

Sandra's situation is not typical of the women I interviewed, but it is typical of the way that the presence or absence of resources (education, income, family support) shapes one's options and circumstances. The life story that Sandra told me was one in which a destructive marriage contributed to emotional instability and depression. Unable to financially support her children when she and her husband separated, Sandra lacked the family support used by so many other part-time workers, and she was overwhelmed by her own emotional problems. Sandra's husband received physical custody of their children. Sandra told me that she left the children with her husband so that she could get on her feet again; later she added:

> If I would have been making a better amount, well, I'd probably still be at home . . . at a job that had an adequate pay scale so that I could afford child care. I wouldn't have had the problems with adequate

child care and having to have [my ex-husband] around to help out *some* anyway. So [laughs ruefully] my life probably would have taken a whole different course. . . . Always being broke makes a big difference.

In her studies of divorce, Terry Arendell notes that, after divorce, many mothers who had, like Sandra, been living in middle-class families immediately found themselves living near or below the poverty line (Arendell 1986:37; Arendell 1995:38), and that the economic uncertainty and financial hardships mothers experience after a divorce are connected to the emotional turmoil, depression, and despair many of these women experienced. She writes that "these women who were new to poverty had no ideas about how to cope in their new situations, and they found little help in the society at large" (Arendell 1986:49).

Sandra answered my questions in a thoughtful manner, considering the questions and taking time to form a response. The lack of support came up in many of her answers—if she had had support from others during her divorce, if she had had support in the form of adequate child care, then perhaps things would have turned out better. When I was leaving, I told her about the child care centers at the Kaiser Shipyards during World War II and how women were sent home with hot meals after their shifts. "Now that's support," Sandra replied.

Wilma Robinson

Wilma Robinson is a thirty-seven-year-old, African-American woman who is employed as a janitorial worker at Sierra Hospital. I interviewed Wilma in the dining room of her home, a rented duplex in an industrialized part of the city, where we sat at the table and talked about her work and her family. Her four-year-old daughter kept running in and out, and we would often stop and respond to her; the baby woke from his nap during the last part of the interview, and we talked while bouncing him on her knee or mine. Wilma also lives with her twenty-year-old daughter, Susan, and Susan's two-year-old baby.

Wilma had been working at Sierra Hospital for two years and had moved from the casual on-call position to a permanent part-time position, which guarantees her three days of work each week and also provides employee benefits. She wants to move to a full-time permanent position, and so is willing to take any shift she is offered in order to reach a higher average number of hours worked weekly. This means that her schedule, like Marcia's and Sandra's, is irregular and uncertain. Wilma and her daughter Susan provide child care for each other, and Wilma told me that she requested night shifts when Susan was working days. Like dual-earner couples who work nonstandard hours, "many grandmothers work 'split shifts' with their daughters to provide child care, especially when the daughters are not married" (Presser and Cox 1997:26). At the time of the interview, Susan was not employed outside the house and was available to provide child care in response to Wilma's erratic work schedule. Wilma said, "It's been working out pretty good," but Susan was leaving for three weeks to visit relatives, and Wilma was concerned about child care during that period. She had made arrangements to send her four-year-old daughter to stay with the child's father for three weeks, and, while she was at work, she planned to leave her one-year-old son with a girlfriend. Wilma explained:

> It worries me when [Susan's] not here. Like I say, that means that I have to go out—and I don't want to get nobody else out of the family [to do child care]. I really don't, I don't know, I'm just leery about that. 'Cause I know ain't nobody gonna take care of them like family. See my girlfriend, she's been around for a long time, so she's family [laughs].

Wilma's employment status is more secure than Marcia's, but, like Sandra, she is still scrambling to get enough hours to make ends meet. The combination of her permanent part-time employment status and her family support system enable her to continue working an involuntary part-time job with an irregular schedule while keeping her family together.

RESOURCES AND STRATEGIES

Marcia, Sandra, and Wilma are involuntary part-time workers, and like most involuntary part-time workers in the United States, they are poor (DuRivage 1986:7). Involuntary part-time work, however, is preferable to the alternatives of unemployment or, in the case of these employees at Sierra Hospital, working more regular schedules somewhere else for far less money. Several janitorial workers and nurses' aides, for example, told me that they made twice as much at Sierra Hospital as they previously had made working in convalescent hospitals. Their ability to accept employment that provides less than the full-time work they need and that wreaks havoc on the structure of their family life is based on the resources they can mobilize.

Education, Employment Status, and Income

The involuntary part-time employees I interviewed had no more than a high school education. The skills they had to offer were learned on previous jobs and, while helping them to obtain their present positions, were not highly technical or in great demand. They were not offering their labor in a seller's market.

The hospital uses its casual on-call positions to screen employees, to save on benefits, to fill in for absent permanent employees, to reduce the number of permanent employees, and to pay wages only for the exact number of hours that need covering. As one union representative told me, employees who are on probation or who are waiting to be called for additional hours are not likely to ask for changes in their work conditions, and the hospital has no incentive to grant them if they do ask. She explained:

> You can say, "I'm only interested in days," or "Because I have a kid, I want P.M.'s [evenings] to make sure they're home from school" or whatever . . . but I think that because you're new and coming in, they say "Well, we have an on-call, that means you work all shifts. And people—you know, they want the job. . . . Now I had a person who said that she had a problem with child care and she talked to the manager [in her unit] and it was no problem, but later on I don't think she ever finished her probation; things kind of happened. . . . So they have to be very careful, so they don't complain.

Wilma Robinson, who has a permanent part-time position with benefits, has tried changing her hours. She wrote to her supervisor saying that she couldn't work nights anymore and asking to be scheduled for only day or evening shifts. The supervisor agreed, although Wilma may find that she is working less as a consequence. When I asked her how flexible the hospital was about such requests, she laughed and said that she did not think they would go for another change, unless it was a change back to the night shift, "because they need people on nights."

Marital Status

These involuntary part-time hospital workers are also similar to each other in marital status; Marcia and Sandra are divorced, and Wilma is separated from the father of her youngest daughter after a long-term, live-in relationship with him. For these women, husbands do not provide a second income or an economic base from which to work part time. While lack of education translates into lack of employment opportunities, the absence of a spouse's, partner's, or other adult's financial resources translates into a greater need to accept the terms of available employment. While the voluntary part-time registered nurses I interviewed are in a position of strength by virtue of having skills that are in demand and having husbands who provide additional income, these involuntary part-time workers are forging employment strategies from a position of relative weakness in these areas.

Child Care and Family Support

Involuntary part-time workers need to work more hours to meet their economic needs. Therefore child care is an expense they can't afford, even if they could find child care that would meet their scheduling needs. Because their hours fluctuate, they can't depend on having enough income every pay period to cover child-care expenses, nor can they plan on how much child care they will need. Not only are they often called at the last minute, but they may be canceled from days they were scheduled to work. As I mentioned earlier, one of the voluntary part-time registered nurses I interviewed paid for child care two days a week, even though she might need it for only one day during some weeks, in order to guarantee that she had the care if needed. This option was not economically feasible for the involuntary part-time workers.

Although "child care" is usually associated with caring for young children, women who work evening or night shifts want to know that someone is caring for, supervising, or protecting their children regardless of the child's age. Marcia's eldest child, at fifteen, is too old for formal child care, but Marcia takes him to her sister's house when she works the night shift because she doesn't want to leave him alone all night. Marcia told me,

> At work I don't want to worry. Even when I leave my son here [at home, during the evening shift], my oldest here, there's always something in my mind.

Her son objects to this; he wants to stay home and thinks he is old enough to take care of himself, but Marcia insists. She tells him that taking him to his aunt's house is not the same as having a babysitter, and sometimes she lets him stay at a friend's house. Marcia told me that she is not so worried about her son getting into trouble when he is on his own, but that she does worry about a fire or a break-in if her son is sleeping alone in the house. This concern with danger was echoed in an interview I conducted with another single mother who worked the night shift; she solved this problem by having one of her adult sons, who no longer lived at home, come over to her house on the nights when she worked and had to leave her twelve-year-old daughter. On nights when this was not possible, she carried her sleeping daughter to the home of a cousin who lived near the hospital. For single women with school-age children, working evening or night shifts presents particularly difficult child care dilemmas. The primary way of resolving these dilemmas is through the help of family members.

The preference for kin as child-care providers and mother substitutes is something that came up repeatedly in my interviews with employed women across racial/ethnic groups. There is a closely woven web of reasons given for this preference: the caregiver has a relationship and bond to both the mother and the child, mother and caregiver share cultural and familial rules and customs, the mother knows the caregiver, care is given on an emotional rather than an economic basis, the caregiver is someone the child relates to outside the caregiving situation, and the caregiver is someone who, in important ways, is seen as "similar" to the mother. By this last point, I do not mean that they are personally alike, but rather that there is a blurring of the boundaries between, for instance, grandmother and mother

(mother and daughter) or aunt and mother (sisters) that con-
tributes to the mother's feeling that she is leaving her children
in the care of someone who is an extension of herself. Of course,
this is not the way all mothers feel, and some women would not
want their mothers or sisters to care for their children, but for
many women, the issue of similarity is salient. The importance
of family-based similarity was expressed forcefully by a registered nurse who explained to me how she felt when her own
children were in nonfamily care and why, if her daughters returned to work after they had children, she would care for her
grandchildren rather than see them be cared for by nonfamily
members.

> You know, it was the oddest thing, and I tell people this and I feel so
> weird—I hated picking my kids up from the day-care center because
> they smelled funny to me. And it was this very visceral, primal kind of
> thing that only a woman would get into. But I didn't like my babies
> smelling like other women. And I'd smell her perfume and the only
> thought in my head was: "the day-care lady." Rather than being happy
> that she held her, I was like, "I don't like that!" So I'd want to wash it
> off them because they weren't supposed to smell like other people. . . .
> I remember [my oldest daughter] refused to eat something I cooked one
> time, and she only wanted what this woman cooked. And that just
> burnt me. Just all kinds of little things like that would happen that I
> just didn't like—did not like! And you know, if I'm their grandma and
> I'm taking care of them, chances are I'm going to be cooking what their
> mom cooks, and chances are she'll wear the same cologne I wear. . . .
> And she won't have to worry about abuse and all of that kind of stuff.
> And if she's too tired to come and get them because she and her hus-
> band need to rest—fine. I'm not going to charge her an extra hundred
> dollars [laughs].

Female kin from the mother's family of origin are thus seen as
surrogates for the mother. They do not replace her; rather, they
represent her or stand in for her.

Most of the women I interviewed preferred child care by family members to nonfamilial child care. This preference became a
necessity for the involuntary part-time workers, whose schedules
precluded the use of regular outside child care. Marcia Collins
and Wilma Robinson needed someone to be available for any shift
on any day, weekends included. Who but another family member
can be so enmeshed in one's life?

Family support is a crucial resource, and certain kinds of family support are used to offset the lack of other resources, such as income and wealth levels or opportunities to increase income and wealth (such as education or occupational status). For the women I interviewed, child care for very young children (under three years of age) by family members other than the child's father was common across occupational status and ethnicity. Sometimes the child care was for short durations, to get families over a temporary child-care crunch, but often it was for the first year or two of a child's life, when neither parents nor grandparents felt comfortable leaving the baby with a nonfamily member. Family support in relation to child care was mentioned most often in terms of its perceived necessity—"I don't know what I would have done without it"—and was given as a reason why people were not able to deal with serious troubles—"Her family all live out of state and she has no one to help her." Lack of family support in the lives of the women with whom I spoke was rare and usually had negative consequences.

Sandra Wells is an example of someone who has little family support and none of the support she needs to keep her children with her. She is an exception that proves the rule. Sandra has no family in the area, her relationship with her parents is strained, and she does not get along with any of her siblings. In a family of college graduates and professionals, Sandra is the only one who did not attend college, and she is poor. The reason Sandra did not go to college, or the reason she receives so little family support (or so little of the kind of support she said she needed) is not the point here. In any case, I have only Sandra's perspective. But her story does indicate, by that absence, the kinds of family support that affect a woman's ability to support her children when she has few skills and minimal education. What she said she needed was assistance, either financial or personal, that would provide care for her children while she worked. This had not been forthcoming, and Sandra felt that the absence of support had contributed to the conclusion that her children should live with their father. It may be that the children's father would have been awarded custody in any case, but it is noteworthy that Sandra pointed to the lack of child-care support as the reason her children do not live with her. It takes an ongoing support network to be an employed mother who is part of the working poor.

Families as Resources

There are many varieties of family support, some more visible than others. The personal family support in working-class and poor families, often involving sharing living space or helping to raise each other's children, appears different in kind than the less personal style of family support found in middle- and upper-middle-class families, which usually involves the giving or loaning of money for such things as sending children to college, buying a home, or contributing to grandchildren's private school tuition.[4]

The type of family support that Marcia and Wilma can mobilize resembles the kin support described by Carol Stack (1974) in her study of an African-American community in the Midwest. This support is personal, immediate, ongoing, and both labor and time intensive on the part of the provider. Patricia Hill Collins (1990) discusses how, among African-Americans, "othermothers" help biological mothers care for their children: "Grandmothers, sisters, aunts, or cousins act as othermothers by taking on child-care responsibilities for one another's children" (119).

In the African-American community, the reliance on othermothers does not mean that men are not involved in family and child care. Many of the women I interviewed shared child care with their husbands, and some of the ex-husbands or ex-partners of the single mothers in my study were involved with the care of their children. In some cases, it was a woman's father or brother who provided child care. Collins states that "the centrality of women in African-American extended families reflects both a continuation of West African cultural values and functional adaptations to race and gender oppression. This centrality is not characterized by the absence of husbands and fathers. Men may be physically present and/or have well-defined and culturally significant roles in the extended family and the kin unit may be woman-centered" (119). Wilma, for example, relies on her adult daughter, Susan, to provide child care for Wilma's two younger children, but when Susan is not available, Wilma turns to other members of her extended family. I called Wilma a few months after our interview to see how the child-care arrangements had worked out when Susan was out of town. Wilma told me that her brother had ended up taking both children for that period. She did not explain what had happened to the previous arrangements, but in both cases it was family and close friends who were looked to for help with child care.

Marcia explained that she managed to be on call for any shift by referring to her family support system.

> Right now, I'm dealing with it because I have help with my boys. . . . What good help I have is I send them over to my sister's house.

Marcia told me that her mother also lives close by and helps out sometimes, that one of her other sisters did the child care twenty years ago when her first child was born, and that a few years ago she would pick her sister's child up from school and keep her until her sister came home from work. Both of Marcia's parents were factory workers, and I asked her who took care of her when she was young while her parents were at work. She explained:

> Well—we all watched each other. Because, you know, with my family I had fourteen sisters and brothers. So, I was a babysitter for a while, one of my sisters was over me and she was a babysitter. So it was like, it always was like seven or eight at home, maybe the rest of them was married or something like that.

The reciprocity and interconnection between family members in matters of child care is something that Marcia grew up with and now reproduces.

I found the reliance on kin for help in caring for children to be common among the African-American hospital workers I interviewed. I did not, however, find this type of reliance on kin to be restricted to African Americans. What distinguishes the involvement of kin in caring for children among African Americans from the child care provided by kin among Euro-Americans is the history and pattern of such networks (Collins 1990:119–23). Many of the African-American women I interviewed, including the women mentioned in this chapter, had not only used "othermothers" to help them with their own children, but also had themselves been "othermothers" to siblings, nephews, nieces, or grandchildren. There was continuity and reciprocity in these arrangements. Shared child care was something they had experienced growing up, used with their own children, and provided for others. There was a tone of matter-of-factness and acceptability in their telling of these arrangements. The Euro-American hospital workers I interviewed did not share this norm, even though many of them relied on family members for child care.

BEING A MOTHER

Marcia, Sandra, and Wilma, like the other mothers I interviewed, share a general understanding of what it means to be a good mother. They differ from many of the other women I interviewed mainly in their abilities to carry out this mandate. These are differences of implementation rather than of definition. Both Marcia and Sandra explained that their inability to meet certain expectations for mothers was the reason that their ex-husbands, with the help of new wives, could be better parents than they could be at that time.

Although the support Marcia received from her family of origin helped her to care for her children while working irregular hours, it did not solve all her problems. Marcia's older two sons did not like going to their aunt's house, and Marcia's eleven-year-old son was starting to have trouble at school. Marcia felt that her middle child's problems were a product of the way her job interfered with her ability to do the things "good mothers" do, like helping with homework and "being around."

> I think a mother should be around because a lot of times when things happen to kids—that's what I'm scared of—if something happen, you can pick up on it. Now [if] something kind of happen, you know, that's going on with my kids, [I'll] be tired and you can't really pick up on it. See, I can pick up on things. If something happen to my son, like before I was working this shift, when he walked in the house and stuff like that, I would observe him. [I would notice] "That ain't right." Then I would go and ask him, I might say, "Frederick, did anything happen in school today?" Then he could tell me, 'cause there would be something that happened in school. But right now, I'm scared that I'll be too tired that I wouldn't pick up on that. You know, maybe a fight or someone gonna jump on him, or he got mad at somebody or maybe he cut school, or something like that. And if you're at home and really *there* for your kids, you can pick up on all of that stuff. Cause the first time he cut school, I knew it. [Laughs.] I could pick up from

different things when he walked in the house, he was acting funny. I said, "Something's going on, something's happened." He thought maybe I'd called and checked up or something. And I say, "Frederick, something is going on," and he say, "What you talking about! What you talking about! Somebody called you!" [Laughs heartily.] So that bothers me, you know, because I really be too tired to deal with that.[5]

"Being around" was a refrain that Marcia used both to convey that mothers should be there for their children and to convey the problems she was having with her irregular schedule. It was not just that she could not be home as often or be home at needed times that worried Marcia, but she feared that her fatigue from working all hours was affecting her ability to be there fully when she was home. She worried that her attention would waver, that she would be too tired to see a child's need or to sense when something was wrong. The control that the hospital sought over Marcia's time was interfering with her ability to care for her children and with her strategy of being a mother.

Sending children to live with their fathers, and often with their fathers' new wives, is perceived by mothers as an alternative to rather than a support for their mothering. For mothers, sending children to live with their fathers is qualitatively different than sending them to live with an aunt or a grandmother. Although Marcia often leaves her seven-year-old son at her sister's house for the entire week, Marcia does not feel that her sister is raising her son. Instead, Marcia says that her sister is "a really good help." Allowing their children to live primarily with their fathers, however, is not easy, even when mothers say that they feel it is in the best interests of the child. Being a good mother, for all the women I interviewed, meant "being there." How can a mother feel she is fulfilling this expectation when her children are not living with her? How can she indicate to others that she is still "being a mother"? Sandra, the nurses' aide whose ex-husband had custody of their children, told me:

I feel real bad that I'm doing this [leaving her children with their father]. I feel like I'm copping out as a mother. . . . There are people who have worse situations. There was a program on TV . . . about a mother who had a little girl, a seven-year-old daughter, her husband had walked out on them . . . she ended up losing her job cause her daughter was sick and she got kicked out of her apartment because she didn't have money and she ended up homeless. . . . The little girl was scared that her mom was going to leave her, and her mom says, "I'll never leave you, you're my reason for living." *And my kids are watching this movie* and I'm sitting there and I'm not part of their life. Well, that's not true, I am part of their life and at least I haven't left completely. . . . I'm doing the best I can with what I've got right now, but it seems like there's others who have done a whole lot better.

The message that Sandra is "copping out as a mother" is reinforced in the culture by stories such as the one conveyed in the television drama that Sandra recounted and by her own self-comparisons with other single mothers. Sandra told me about a nurse at the hospital who had two small children, was going through a divorce, and was having child care problems and custody disputes with her husband. Sandra saw this woman as someone who was succeeding where she had failed, because she was able to keep her children with her. Differences in resources (income, skills, education) and in the circumstances of their divorces made their situations very different, but Sandra's focus was on their respective abilities to "be there" as mothers.

Given Sandra's circumstances, she finds it difficult to claim that she is being there for her children, but her emphasis that she "hasn't left completely" is part of her strategy of being a mother, reminding me and herself that she is still there for her children—she has not abandoned them. She then highlights the connection between her plans for employment and her strategies of being a mother by telling me that she plans to continue working as a nurses' aide, to begin a nursing program to earn her degree as a registered nurse, and then to find a well-paying nursing position that will enable her to increase her share of the physical custody of her children. At a time when "working mothers" face cultural pressures to feel guilty for participating in the labor force, Sandra finds that her economic position presents her with additional and contradictory pressures. Sandra thus represents the fact that her children are living with their father as a situation that provides time for her to "get on her feet" in order to be with her children more in the future.

Marcia, Sandra, and Wilma share an understanding of the cultural expectations for being good mothers, but they have a difficult time meeting some of them. Nevertheless, rather than re-defining motherhood in ways that incorporate their situations, each employs strategies of being that reconcile her situation with her sense of self as mother.

BEING A WORKER

Involuntary part-time workers, like most adults, don't have a choice about whether to be employed or not. They have to engage in paid work to support themselves and their families. But in addition to the income, employment provides each of these women with a sense of self that embodies competence and the ability to provide for herself. Marcia told me:

> I enjoy being with my kids, but I know I have to work. Even if I was rich, I'd have to do something. . . . [work] just makes me feel . . . good about doing something. Actually at the hospital, you help other people. I feel like I'm doing something. I go in there and I talk to the patients, and I get a kick out of that.

And Sandra commented that when she was still married, she managed her home life better when she returned to work part time:

> When I got out and got to work and was doing something that I knew I was good at, and getting contact with people who appreciated what I was doing, and seemed to like me, then I came home and I looked around and I had the energy to do it [housework]. And I didn't mind doing it. It felt good doing it. And the competence that I had at work carried over into the home.

When I asked Wilma what the hardest things were about being employed and raising young children, she thought about my question for several moments and then said, "I don't know. 'Cause I really don't look at it as hard, because it's something I got to do." My question, which voluntary part-time workers answered without hesitation and at length, was not a question that resonated with Wilma's experience. But while she sees work as something she had to do, Wilma also feels positive about herself as a worker. About her work, Wilma said:

> It gives me a good feeling. . . . It gives me a sense of responsibility, and to know that I am taking care of stuff, by myself, that this is my job.

And as long as I can make it, this is what I'm gonna do. But I like it—
and I to try to show my kids—well, I always have tried to show my
kids, you have to work. Ain't nobody going to give you nothing. And
as you get older, you really gonna have to work, you know. Because
nobody gonna take care of your old butt.

All three women talk about work in positive terms. They may
complain about the conditions of work or the effects of work
(mainly fatigue), but they don't question employment itself.
There would be no point in their considering whether "to work
or not to work," since employment is an economic necessity for
these women. But being employed is also connected to concepts
of self—to ways of "being" in the world

Weaving Work and Family

Marcia Collins, Sandra Wells, and Wilma Robinson are each
weaving a work/family strategy that must incorporate an involuntary part-time employment status—a pattern not of their
choosing. They are limited by educational level and economic resources, but Marcia and Wilma are enabled by strong family resources. Support from kin networks enables them to take what
would otherwise be unworkable schedules, thereby providing for
their children and living up to a definition of motherhood that includes being a good provider. When there are problems with family support, as when Wilma's daughter leaves for three weeks or
when Marcia's sons do not want to stay with their aunt, the ability of mothers to stay employed or their ability to do the work
mothers are expected to do is called into question.

Involuntary part-time employment for mothers is connected
both to low educational and economic resources and to the ability to mobilize family support. For involuntary part-time workers, the lack of education and technical skills devalues their time.
Time is what they have to sell, and the hospital takes advantage
of their need not only by controlling their actual hours of labor,
but also by claiming access to all potential hours of labor. Casual
on-call hospital workers make themselves available to work as
many hours as possible, any hours of the day or night, in order to
get enough paid work and to work toward a more stable schedule.

Their irregular work schedules also force them to give up much of their control over time at home.

The meaning and purpose of part-time work is different for voluntary and involuntary part-time workers, but for each it represents a struggle in the workplace over the control of time. The voluntary part-time workers see part-time work as the solution to their income and family needs and as a way of furthering their identities as mothers. For them, it is the negotiation of flexible work schedules that enables them to be mothers in ways that mesh with cultural expectations about motherhood. But for other employed mothers, part-time work is not a solution to balancing employment and motherhood, but a problem that prevents them from adequately providing for their families. Involuntary part-time hospital workers face the problem of employment arrangements that are not compatible with their needs for income or their needs as mothers. In this situation, the flexibility mothers seek is in their child care arrangements. Access to flexible and kin-based child care arrangements enables them to take the jobs they need to support themselves and their children, even though that employment does not provide enough of what they need.

In the next chapter, I discuss how employed mothers use shift work to construct an image of motherhood that resembles the one that voluntary part-time workers construct.

5   Motherhood on the Night Shift

"MY GRANDMOTHER worked in a cannery for forty years, and I never knew it! She was just my grandmother. We'd go to her house and she'd bake cookies and—she was just *there*. I never knew she worked. I never knew she was a cannery worker." In the seminar in which my students interviewed their mothers and grandmothers about their work histories, they were now exchanging "discoveries." Many students were amazed to find that their mothers had been employed while their children were school-age. One student asked herself aloud: "How could I not know she worked?" How indeed?

In the aggregate, women's labor-force participation can be "invisible" in a number of ways. Feminist scholars, through their research and writing in the 1970s and 1980s, reclaimed what had been a hidden history of women's employment and economic production. Women's economic role had been omitted from most historical accounts, and feminist historians put women back in (Kessler-Harris 1982). The invisibility of mothers' labor-force participation has also resulted from the way in which survey and census data have been collected. Women engaged in agricultural labor, for example, are disproportionately undercounted in the censuses of most countries (Dixon 1982). Christine Bose found that, despite changes over time in the technical definitions of "employment," women's employment has been consistently undercounted in U.S. censuses.[1] Bose argues that although changes in the way employment is counted have corrected a great deal of the undercount of women's employment that occurred in censuses before 1940, much of women's employment in the informal or irregular economy is still not counted (for example, in-home child care, piece work, domestic service, or giving piano lessons). Her larger point is that "census definitions, enumeration, and verification methods can be molded to conform to, and thus sup-

108

port, gender- or race-related ideologies" (Bose 1987:109). In other words, employment can be counted so that certain types of employment and employment of certain types of people remain invisible.

The students who were surprised to learn that their mothers and grandmothers had been employed were pointing to a different kind of invisibility. Rather than the aggregate invisibility of histories and censuses, they had touched upon the ways an individual woman's employment can be rendered invisible. Patricia Zavella's interviews with Chicana cannery workers revealed that although these women had worked in the cannery for many years, some of their husbands would deny the fact that their wives were employed by discounting seasonal work or by describing as temporary and short term a work history that had become ongoing and long term (Zavella 1987). The refusal to recognize their wives' employment status is connected to an ideology that sees women's labor-force participation as secondary, nonessential, and a potential threat to men's identification with being the family provider (Potuchek 1997). Mothers themselves often downplay their employment, and together wives' and husbands' presentations of self perpetuate the ideology of the male breadwinner (Hochschild and Machung 1989; Potuchek 1997; Zavella 1987). For example, many women emphasize maternal visibility in relation to their children by restricting their hours of employment to the hours their children are in school or to the hours their children are asleep. This strategy can render less visible the fact of a woman's employment. It is this kind of invisibility that my students discovered when they took the time to ask their mothers and grandmothers about their labor force participation.

Night-shift work takes place when no one is looking, when the house is quiet and everyone is asleep. Mothers who choose the night shift talk about their reasons for doing so in remarkably similar terms. None of them refers to herself as a night person; all of them talk about their fatigue and their need for more sleep; and all of them describe how working the night shift allows them to be the kind of mothers they want to be. The night shift enables these women to implement a strategy of being a mother that most closely resembles nonemployed "at-home mothers."*

Mothers who work the night shift (11:00 P.M. to 7:30 A.M.) link their strategies of being a mother to which hours they are at work—or, more accurately, to which hours they are at home. They leave for work after their children are in bed for the night and usually arrive back home after their children have left for school or day care. During the night, children have been with fathers or other relatives, and it is predominantly the fathers who get the children off to school in the morning. One thing that mothers who work the night shift thus avoid is the morning rush at home. Mothers who work day shifts at the hospital, which begin at 7:30 A.M., either have to leave before their children are awake, or they have to get both themselves and their children up and out the door at a very early hour. The morning is not only rushed and tense, but the mother's work schedule and her child's needs and wants are brought into head-on collisions on a daily basis. Some of the night-shift workers reported getting home before their children left for school, and these mothers emphasized the fact that they could then make sure that their children looked "cared for" before they left for school. But they were not the ones who actually got the children ready, and they did not need to hurry their children because of their own schedules, but only in terms of the children's school schedules. Night-shift nurses tiptoe out after the children are asleep and thus avoid the conflicts of a frantic morning exit.

Night-shift workers are home at the other end of their children's school day, when their school-age children return at around 2:00 or 3:00 in the afternoon. Day-shift hospital workers, on the other hand, leave work at around 4:00 or 4:30 in the afternoon and head into rush-hour traffic for the commute home.

---

*The common phrase "at-home mothers" infers that mothers who are employed are not in their homes, when clearly employed mothers are at home some of the time and nonemployed mothers are not at home all the time. It serves the same purpose as the phrase "full-time mothers," which is to signify that employed mothers are not "fully" fulfilling their roles as mothers. I use quotation marks to indicate that I am using these phrases to refer to the cultural conceptions embedded within them, conceptions with which both employed and nonemployed mothers must contend.

They rush to pick up children at child care, or they return to waiting children and dinner preparation as soon as they walk in the door. The importance of this after-school and evening time to mothers who choose the night shift becomes evident when we compare them to workers on the evening shift. If mothers work the evening shift (3:30 to 11:00 P.M.), they are home in the mornings to get their children up and off to school, and they are there during the day to be with their preschool-age children, but they are not there in the afternoons and evenings to help with homework, have dinner with the family, or put the children to bed.

In general, mothers with school-age children do not find the evening shift conducive to their strategies of being a mother, and the mothers I talked to who worked the evening shift fell into two categories: they worked part time and had children who were not yet in school, or they worked full time and had children who were grown and out of school. Thus being at home when children returned from school was not an issue for the women in these two groups.

Mothers who work the night shift use shift work to present themselves as mothers in ways that resemble the voluntary part-time workers' strategies of being employed mothers. Although most of the full-time night shift nurses said they would prefer to work part time, they did not have the economic resources that would enable them to take part-time employment. All of the night shift nurses I interviewed worked full time. Most of them were married, but their husbands were not employed in the professions and had less education and lower positions in the occupational hierarchy than the husbands of the voluntary part-time nurses.[2] In addition to needed income, wives' full-time employment at the hospital often provided the medical insurance coverage and other benefits that the family needed.

There are direct economic reasons for nurses to choose the night shift. For example, the hospital gives a pay differential to nurses for working nights, and so nurses on the night shift earn more per hour than they would on the day shift. But my interviews reveal that financial factors are only one part of a matrix of reasons for choosing the night shift and not the sole determining factor. Several nurses reported turning down opportunities for promotion and higher pay because the promotions would have entailed increasing their hours or being responsible as a supervisor even during their hours at home. Nurses explained their choice of shift in terms of their relationship to the profession, their children's needs, their definition of successful mothering, and their husbands' schedules, as well as their family's financial needs.

Another economic benefit of the night shift is that child care costs are reduced because other family members are home at night to look after children. Night-shift nurses may not have the economic resources to work part time, but they are able to draw on family support resources for nighttime child care. The use of shift work by couples with young children is clearly a way of solving the child-care problems of availability, quality, and expense, and many dual-earner couples deal with the issue of child care by working different shifts and sharing the care of their children (Hertz and Ferguson 1996). Dual-earner couples with children under fourteen years are more likely to work non-day shifts than are dual-earner couples with children older than fourteen (Presser 1987:108). In one-third of dual-earner couples with children under six years of age, at least one parent works a non-day shift, and there is a strong correlation between non-day shifts and high rates of child care performed by family members, including fathers (Presser 1988, 1989).

But child care by family members was not primarily motivated by economic considerations. When it is the woman who works a night shift, the solution resolves more than the provision of child care. Concerns about leaving children with nonfamily child-care providers, coupled with concerns about their identities as primary caregiver mothers, were strong forces motivating these women's child-care arrangements.

When their wives are working, the husbands of the married night-shift nurses are the primary caretakers of their children. For the most part, it was fathers who got their children up and ready for school. Fathers' contributions to the care of their children remain important even when we remember that most of this care occurs between 10:00 P.M. and 8:00 in the morning. It does not occur during the hours when children are doing their homework, going to after-school or weekend activities, having their dinner, taking their baths, being read to, or getting tucked in for the night. The nighttime care of children does not occur when children have appointments with doctors and dentists, during parent-teacher conferences, during friends' birthday parties, or when the stores are open so that one can buy school supplies, clothes, Halloween costumes, sports equipment, dancing shoes, and the present for the friend who is having the birthday party. When fathers care for children while their wives are working night shifts, most of the care occurs while the children, and the fathers, are sleeping.

These men are not necessarily trying to escape parenting work. It is true that men are often resistant to sharing the second shift (Hochschild and Machung 1989), but some women are also reluctant to surrender symbolically key activities, especially those connected to their identities as mothers. In his study of dual-earner couples, Scott Coltrane notes that "the routine care of home and children are seen to provide opportunities for women to express and reaffirm their gendered relation to men and to the world" (Coltrane 1989:473). In addition, Coltrane found that fathers who perform activities normatively assigned to mothers often face negative reactions from male coworkers. Men may refuse to take on these responsibilities for the same reasons that many women are reluctant to relinquish them: because the performance of these activities is symbolically linked to constructions of gender. The night shift enables mothers of school-age children to maximize "family time"—it does not take up after-school time or evening family time, and it gives mothers the most waking time with their children. Working the night shift is the way that some women attempt to reconcile the structural conflicts and the conflicting vocabularies of motive attached to motherhood and employment.

NIGHT-SHIFT NURSES AT SIERRA HOSPITAL

Most of the hospital workers who work nights are nurses. My interviews with night-shift workers included registered nurses and nurses' aides, in addition to the involuntary part-time janitorial workers discussed in Chapter 4. At night, the physicians, physical therapists, social workers, secretaries, receptionists, administrators, and food service workers have all gone home. Several of the night-shift nurses remarked that this was one of the things they liked about working at night.

At Sierra Hospital, the night shift nurses work eight-hour shifts, which begin at 11:00 P.M. and end at 7:30 in the morning. Many of these nurses live outside the city where the hospital is located and have commutes of up to an hour each way. Most of them reported getting home between 8:30 and 9:00 in the morning. Although they are entitled to a half-hour break during the night, heavy patient loads and exceptionally busy nights often mean that these breaks are not taken in an effort to keep up or catch up with the work that needs to be done. One night shift nurse put it this way:

> Doing a midnight shift on my area, *rarely* do we get half an hour break—*rarely*. You've got to move real fast. Why should I move real fast constantly? You know, even if you take the half an hour break, I'd be so far behind.

Skipping their break also helps them to leave work on time or reduces the amount of time that they must stay after their shift ends. Before a nurse can leave her shift, she must update each patient's chart. Often nurses can not finish their charting until the next shift arrives to take over the direct patient care. Nurses reported having to extend their workdays by thirty to forty-five minutes in order to finish their charting. Although nurses are technically entitled to overtime if they work after their shift, overtime is frowned upon by a budget-conscious administration, and the message conveyed to nurses is that "good nurses" finish their charting during their shift. Therefore, nurses who don't get their charting finished before their shift ends do so on their own time rather than risk being judged inefficient.

Being a worker is important to the night-shift nurses. However, while part-time nurses were sometimes frustrated by the extra effort it took to stay connected at the workplace when they came in only a few days a week, many of the night-shift nurses preferred the way that the night shift separated them from the daily activities of the ward. One nurse noted that working the night shift was "a family-like business" and different from the day shift, when "the bosses and everybody are there." Night-shift nurses were more removed from the professional aspects of their positions than were either part-time or full-time, day-shift nurses, and they interacted far less with other health professionals such as physicians, physical therapists, and social workers. This had its disadvantages, and several nurses remarked that they were not likely to be promoted or to have opportunities for specialization while they remained on the night shift.

Of the thirty-seven mothers I interviewed, seven were currently working full time on the night shift. All but one of these women had children under the age of twelve years, and the person who didn't have young children had worked the night shift since her children, now grown, were young. In addition, many of the older nurses who were working full-time day shifts when I interviewed them had worked the night shift when their children, now teenagers or adults, were young. Mothers who no longer worked the night shift reported either that they couldn't handle the fatigue of working nights or that they had changed their shifts when their children were older or when there were changes in their circumstances, such as the availability of family child care.

While there are patterns and conclusions to be drawn, there is both overlap and diversity within the group of night shift workers. Short sketches of six of these women illustrate their commonalities and differences as well as the contexts in which each weaves a life.

Shirley Roberts

Shirley Roberts is a sixty-year-old, African-American practical nurse who has worked the night shift for twenty-six years.[3] She is married, has five adult children and eight grandchildren, and lives in a older, working-class neighborhood with well-built and well-maintained Spanish-style homes and well-tended gardens. After her youngest child was born, Shirley went to night school for a year to get her practical nursing training, and her husband stayed with the children while she was in school. Shirley noted that after being home with five children for more than twelve years, evening classes had provided a break for her: "It was an outing for me also, to get away from the house." When her youngest child was six years old and in school, Shirley started to work at the hospital.

> So my husband would be home with them at night and I would be home in the daytime. They would be in school until like 3:00, so that gave me a chance to sleep in the daytime, get up and cook dinner, then, you know, help them with their homework. And then that's what I been doing ever since.

Shirley does not live far from the hospital, and she does not have to do charting as the registered nurses do, so she is able to get home soon after her shift ends. When her children were growing up, she made sure that she got home before they left for school.

> I always got home before they went to school, and I would see that they had their breakfast—their daddy would start it sometimes—and comb their hair, make sure they're okay when they're underage and all.

Shirley told me that her husband, who is a skilled laborer with a civil service position, worked the evening shift when the children were growing up. He would come home at night just as she was leaving for work. Between work schedules and sleeping, Shirley and her husband didn't see each other very much. Shirley explained:

> But you have to be able to understand that. . . . You have to have a nice husband who understands that and helps you with the children. You can't do that alone, it's too hard. I mean mothers are doing it, but it's really hard. You need someone to help you. Fortunately, my husband was nice. . . . I didn't have no trouble with the children either.

Shirley never had to rely on nonfamily child care. She was home with the children while they were young, and when she went to work nights, her husband was with them. If the children were ill, Shirley would take vacation days or take the sick child to her mother's house. In the summer the boys would go to summer camp, and the girls would split the summers between both sets of grandparents. At Christmas, Shirley would take vacation time, which she told me was "a big family time for them." Now that her children are grown and she is near retirement, Shirley continues to prefer the night shift because, she explains, the workload is lighter than on the day shift, when patients have to be fed, bathed, and moved. At sixty, Shirley finds that the night shift continues to work for her.

Janice Ramos

Janice Ramos is a thirty-year-old, Filipina registered nurse. She immigrated to the United States with her parents when she was a teenager. Janice is married and has two children, an eight-year-old child and a fourteen-month-old baby. Her husband, also a Filipino immigrant, works as a technician. The family lives in a large, custom-built, two-storey house in a small town about a forty-five-minute drive from the city where Janice and her husband work.

Janice was very articulate, but there was a flatness in her voice, a lack of intonation and a strain that conveyed long-term fatigue. Janice is a planner: their children were planned, their house was planned, her continuing education and career goals were planned. "We plan our life situation," she told me. But Janice has had to face the unplanned and unexpected. Janice's ultimate goal is to become a nurse practitioner. That plan, however, was postponed when Janice's second child was born with health problems. The baby was in the hospital for five months and was still plagued by respiratory illnesses. This experience affected Janice's plans to continue her education and her and her husband's plans about future children (they decided not to have any more).

Doris Chavez

Doris Chavez is a thirty-four-year-old, Mexican-American registered nurse. Her parents both had eighth-grade educations, and she was the first in her family to attend college, where she earned her B.S.N. degree. She is proud of her parents, whom she described as having come from very poor families and as working hard and doing well. Doris and her husband, an electrician, have two children, ages seven years and four years.

I interviewed Doris at the hospital just after her shift ended at 7:30 in the morning. Doris's home is an hour's drive from the hospital and, although she makes this commute four days a week, she feels more sympathy for her husband, whose commute is almost twice as long. Doris and her husband could not afford to buy a house in either of the urban areas where they work, and commuting is the price they pay for buying a house in a more affordable outlying area. Doris added that where they live is "calmer" than the urban area where she works, and that she liked that for her family.

Doris had a lively manner and a quick sense of humor. While she did not hesitate to say that being a "working mother" is "hard" and that "it's not easy to do," Doris thinks of herself as fortunate. Often, after describing a problem or a difficult situation, she concluded, "But we do okay," or "But it works out."

Angela Cordova

Angela Cordova is a forty-three-year-old, Filipina registered nurse who immigrated to the United States when she was sixteen years old. Both of her parents and all four of her siblings have also immigrated. Her mother lives "mainly" with her, but "goes around" to the houses of her other children, being cared for by them and helping them to care for their own children. "In my family," Angela said, "we help one another." When she returned to work when her second child was six weeks old, it was her mother who cared for the baby: "She's the best—the mother of the mother."

Angela is married and has two school-age children, ages nine years and six years. Her husband, also a Filipino immigrant, has a college degree but has been unable to find a job commensurate with his education and now works for a package delivery company. The Cordova family lives in large, six-bedroom house in a suburb that is a forty-five minute drive from the city in which Angela and her husband work. When I arrived at her door, Angela opened it and told me that she had just woken up and that her house was not clean. I sat on the sofa while she darted around picking things up and cleaning off the dining room table, where we would sit to conduct the interview.

Angela was friendly and eager to help me with my research project. She was also very tired, and several times during the interview, when I thought she was too tired, I would start to wind it up, at which point she would launch off on another topic with renewed enthusiasm.

Julia Ginzburg

Julia Ginzburg is a forty-three-year-old, Jewish-American registered nurse. Julia's upper-middle-class parents had higher ambitions for her than nursing, but Julia worked in poorly paid social service jobs after college, became pregnant with her first child, and married a man with no education or skills. A nursing degree for Julia was seen as an answer to the problem of how to support her family while her husband obtained his GED and went to college. Julia, her husband, and her first child lived with Julia's parents, who paid for her nursing education, while she went to nursing school. After Julia began her career as a nurse, she and her husband moved into their own rented apartment and had another baby.

At the time I interviewed her, Julia had been working as a nurse for three years, and her children were nine years old and one year old. While still considering themselves a married couple, Julia and her husband have recently separated and live apart. Julia is the primary and often the only breadwinner in the family. Julia's husband takes care of the children during the nights she works at the hospital, and he is there many evenings on her days off, but the bulk of the child care and daily maintenance is left to Julia. Unlike Janice, Doris, or Angela, she is renting the house they live in, and she said of herself, "I'm old, I'm forty-three, and I've got— I've got—nothing—to fall back on."

My overriding impression of Julia was of weariness and disappointment; unlike Janice, Doris, and Angela, hers was not a story of upward mobility, future aspirations, and hope. Julia grew up in an upper-middle-class family; her mother stayed home to raise the children and support her husband's career, and a college education for Julia and her sisters was assumed. Julia's background and the idealism and optimism of the period in which she came of age promised expanding opportunities, but that sense of possibility and promise is no longer a part of Julia's perspective on life.

Patricia Anderson

Patricia Anderson is a fifty-three-year-old, African-American registered nurse. She has worked as a nurse for twenty years, is divorced, and has three adult children and a twelve-year-old daughter. Patricia and her daughter live in a two-bedroom rented apartment in a new apartment complex in a middle-class section of the city. Although most of the full-time nurses at Sierra Hospital work four shifts a week, Patricia works five shifts a week because, she told me, her daughter's dance lessons and other activities are expensive, and she needs the money.

Patricia likes being a nurse and she likes interacting with patients, but she does not like working in the hospital because of the administration, the paperwork, and the speed-up on the ward. If she got married again, which she would like to do, she said she would change her schedule from full time to part time. When I asked if she would quit working altogether if she could, she replied that she wouldn't take that risk and would stay working two days a week to keep her hand in "in case anything goes wrong."

Nationally, African-American nurses comprised only 4.2 percent of registered nurses in 1996 (Malone and Marullo 1997), and the number of African-American registered nurses at Sierra Hospital is larger than the national average but still a small minority. In an occupation in which 90 percent of the total population is White, Patricia had experienced a number of incidents that she characterized as "subtle racism." Patricia explained, for example, that whenever she was in a new situation, White people would assume she was not a nurse. Applying for her first nursing job twenty years earlier, she was told that applicants for the janitorial positions should apply at the office down the hall. After working as a nurse for a number of years, she interviewed for a different nursing position and discovered halfway through the interview that the personnel director assumed she was applying for a position as a nurses' aide. At Sierra Hospital, nurses and nurses' aides can be sent from their regular wards and loaned to another ward if needed; this is called floating. Patricia remarked that different assumptions were made when White women and Black women "floated": "If a White person floats to another floor, they assume she's an R.N. If I float, they assume I'm a nurses' aide."

Most of the African-American nurses I interviewed mentioned both institutional and personal racism in the hospital.[4] Different hospitals and different units within the same hospital had varying reputations regarding whether they were better or worse places for Black nurses to work. "Each floor has a personality," Patricia told me, "like states—Louisiana is a man's state; Illinois is a White man's state; and California is strictly for kids." Sierra Hospital was considered a better place than many of the other hospitals in the immediate area, but some wards were considered definitely better than others.

A Mother's Place: "Being" at Home

The house as a symbol of family life is a recurring theme in the stories my interviewees told. Regardless of shift or occupational category, most of the women I talked to emphasized the importance of owning their own homes in the context of their feelings and plans about children. But there was another way in which the house as symbol was particularly salient for the night-shift workers. A house, to be a home, is where a mother is.

One of the most powerful images in modern theater is the door shutting as Nora Helmer leaves her husband and children in Ibsen's *A Doll's House* (1958 [1879]:68). This image juxtaposes the physical boundary of the house with its symbolic importance in the definition of family. Houses, the spaces within which homes are made, are important symbols in the construction of meanings about family. Ibsen represents Nora's desertion of her family with the sound of a closing door, by which the audience knows that she has crossed the threshold and is outside the physical space of the house. When the woman is removed from the house, definitions of home and family are called into question and must be reconstructed to account for or to conceal the fact of their missing central element.

The emotional content of home is mirrored in cliches such as "Home is where the heart is" and "Home is the place where they have to take you in." Another well-known saying is "A woman's place is in the home," the corollary of which may be "A home is where the woman is"—especially where a mother is. Night-shift "working mothers," in common with nonemployed mothers, are able to be home during the day.

Being at home during the day is related to cultural ideas of what a mother *does* and what a mother *is*, to both *doing* and *being*. To be at home during the day is to emulate nonemployed mothers, often referred to as full-time mothers. The term "full-time mothers" incorporates the idea that to be employed lessens the fullness or completeness of one's mothering. It is in response to this perspective that the night-shift workers are constructing a "working mother" who is a "full-time mother" because she does what "full-time" (nonemployed) mothers do. Even if her husband and children are not at home, the woman *of* the house is the woman *in* the house.

Janice Ramos, Doris Chavez, and Julia Ginzburg each have one child in elementary school and a child under five years old in some form of day care. Despite differences in ethnicity, age, and seniority at the hospital, their stated reasons for working the night shift are remarkably similar.

Janice had been at Sierra Hospital for less than a year but had worked in several hospitals before that, and I asked her if she had worked the night shift in her previous positions. Janice responded:

> I was always working nights. 'Cause it's easier to work nights with my young children. I like to be home with them, even [if] I'm sleeping, I like to be, you know, around.

Doris, who had worked at Sierra Hospital for ten years, immediately mentioned both owning a house and being home during the day when I said, "Tell me about working and having children." Doris replied:

> It's hard, real hard. I want my kids to go to college; we bought a house. I want them to have a house. The things that I feel are important and so that's why I do it. And that's one of the reasons I work night shift. I feel more comfortable being at home in the daytime while they're— well, they go to day care. So my husband takes them to day care and then I get home in the morning and sleep. And I know that I'm home by the phone in case something happens to them. The school's right down the street so during school time it's nice—he walks home.

Julia, who had been at Sierra Hospital for almost three years, gave a similar response to my question about her reasons for working the night shift.

> For me, it allows—I mean, if—I'm available. There's always a parent at home. If there's anything that comes up; if the kid is sick, it's no big deal, I'm here. Like now, when—during the summer—when my son is finished with his program at noon he comes home. I'm here. He can handle himself around the house. My small one I have in child care, but the big one comes home and can go and play with friends, he can go to the library himself, but—I'm here. . . . I'm asleep! But I'm here. If something comes up, I'm available.

"I'm here," "I'm home," "I'm around," "I'm available": these are striking refrains in two ways. First, they are coupled with the statement "I'm asleep." Second, for a large part of the time when these women are home, their children are not. Notice that both Doris and Julia use the word "comfortable" to describe their reasons for wanting to be home in the daytime. But being at home during the day, even if they are asleep and their children are at school or in child care, fits with their definition of motherhood. It not only enables them to respond instrumentally to daytime child-related needs and emergencies and to be home when children return from school, but it places them in the symbolically appropriate place for mothers: in the home. A look at how each organizes her daily schedule illustrates this.

Janice gets home from the hospital at about 8:30 in the morning. Her husband, who has to be at work by 9:00 A.M., has already gotten their older child off to school, taken the baby to the neighbor who does child care for them, and left for work. Janice returns to an empty house and immediately goes to sleep. At 1:30 in the afternoon, she wakes up, gets the baby from the neighbor's house, and meets her son at the bus stop. She spends the next few hours feeding the children, playing with the baby, and helping her son with his homework. When her husband returns from work between 4:30 and 5:00 P.M., she goes back to bed and sleeps until about 9:00 P.M., at which time she gets up to leave the house at 10:00 P.M. for another night shift.

Shirley Roberts reported a similar method of getting enough sleep by going to bed as soon as she got home from work in the morning, sleeping until the children got home at 3:00 P.M., and then going back to bed after dinner and sleeping for another two or three hours. These routines are exceptions to the pattern reported by most of the other night-shift nurses, who don't go back to bed in the afternoon or evening for additional hours of sleep. Janice's intended routine gives her more sleep than the other nurses I interviewed. However, my interview with Janice indicated that things were often not routine in her household and that she averages far less sleep than claimed in her report of a typical day.

Except for her two days off each week, Janice spends about three of the thirteen-and-a-half hours she is home during the day with her children. The rest of the time the children are at school or child care, or they are home and Janice is sleeping. For Janice, working nights cannot be a way of spending more time with her children, since day-shift workers would have about as many child contact hours as Janice does. Nor does working nights give Janice more time with her husband, who takes over the care of the children as soon as he returns from work so that Janice can sleep. But, as Janice says, what working nights does do, is to allow her to "be home with them"—to "be around."

Long commutes contribute to mothers' concerns about being at home during the day, near their children's schools and child care locations. While the concern with being far from home does exist for commuters, many women cited the same reasons for working nights even when they had lived near the hospital in which they worked. Julia Ginzburg and Patricia Anderson, both of whom live within five miles of the hospital, talked about being home during the day in the same terms as did those with long commutes: they wanted to be around, to be available, to be home.

Doris Chavez lives over an hour from the hospital and usually does not get home until 9:00 in the morning. Her husband, who has a two hour commute to work, gets the children up at 5:00 A.M., leaves the house by 5:30 to drop them at the child care center, five minutes from their house, and then continues on his way to work. Their oldest child will be at the child-care center until 8:00 A.M., when he is bussed to his elementary school, which is also near their home. Unlike Janice, Doris does not immediately go to sleep when she gets home; she does some housework, thinks about dinner preparations, unwinds a bit. She said she usually sleeps between 10:00 A.M. and 3:00 P.M., but when I asked her if that meant that she usually gets five hours of sleep, she told me that she averages about four hours of sleep on the days she works. She wakes at about 3:00 P.M. to welcome her son home from school and goes to pick up her youngest child from the child-care center. Doris spends the rest of the afternoon preparing dinner, helping with homework, and caring for the children. When her husband comes home from work, they all have dinner together. Doris reported that evenings are spent playing games, reading with the children, or facilitating the oldest child's participation in sports or Cub Scouts. Doris tries to have the children in bed by 8:00 P.M., a challenge in the summer during Daylight Savings Time, so that she can take a half-hour nap on the sofa in the living room before getting ready for work. She leaves the house at 9:30 at night to drive back to the hospital for another night shift.

Doris and Janice differ in the number of hours they are home and awake while their children are home and awake. Doris reported spending about twice as much contact time with her children as Janice, but for both of them what is salient is *which hours* they are home. As Doris said, "I know that I'm home by the phone in case something happens to them." Doris told me that the "overlap" period from 5:30 A.M. until 9:00 every morning, during which neither she nor her husband are at home, is a concern to her, and adds:

> But I'm usually home by nine, and I have been called before [by the school] and they know I'm sleeping. I get that straight with the teacher [laughs] right off the bat. You know, "I work nights, I'm home."

Doris lets her children's teachers know, and she emphasized the importance that they know, that she is a mother at home during the day. The work of making her presence at home visible to her children's teachers illuminates the symbolic nature of Doris's behavior. She is gesturing to herself, to her children, and to relevant others that she is an at-home mother.

Julia Ginzburg's separation from her husband and her position as the primary earner in her family make her life very different from both Janice's and Doris's, but her schedule is similar to the others. When I interviewed Julia, she was trying to implement and maintain a healthier sleep schedule than had been the case for the previous three years. She had been sleep deprived for so long that she reported that she was beginning to have physical and emotional problems. Before she took a break and got some rest, it would often take Julia two hours to leave the hospital after her shift, because she was so tired it would take her that long to finish her charting.* On her new schedule, Julia gets home between 8:30 and 9:00 A.M., after her husband has taken the children to school and child care. She sleeps until about 3:00 P.M., when her nine-year-old son comes home from school, at which

---

*Other nurses I interviewed confirmed Julia's exhaustion and the time it took her to finish charting and leave the hospital in the morning.

time she leaves to pick the baby up from child care. In the summer, her older child gets home at noon from a summer program but takes care of himself while she sleeps.

Julia did not report as structured a family life as Doris did, but Julia is just as concerned about preserving certain symbols that represent a particular construction of motherhood, particularly one in which a mother is home during the day. Although Julia is asleep when her son returns from school, the fact that she is in the house is important to her, not only in terms of being physically present in case of an emergency, but also in symbolic terms. Julia explained:

> If I were working in the daytime, I wouldn't be comfortable with him coming home to an empty house. I don't want him to be—*I don't feel like he's a latchkey kid*. I'm here. I'm asleep! But I'm here.

Patricia Anderson expressed a similar sentiment when I asked her if it was her choice to work nights:

> I'd rather because—since I'm divorced and [my twelve-year-old daughter] is into a whole lot of different things [dance and sports activities]— to make sure that no one ever has an excuse for saying [in a singsong voice], "Well, my mommy wasn't home and I hit the streets"—just like that.

In Doris's, Julia's, and Patricia's narratives, there is an emphasis not only on the importance of being at home during the day, but also on the importance of being *seen* as mothers who are at home. Doris emphasizes that her children's teachers know that she is home during the day and available to be called; Julia stresses that her son is not a "latchkey kid"; and Patricia says that she works nights in part so that no one can say, retrospectively, that she neglected her daughter because she was away at work during the day. All three are emphasizing maternal visibility. There are two concerns being conveyed in their explanations: one is with the immediate safety of the child, and the second is with potential problems that might be said to be caused by the mother's behavior.

Being there in the afternoon to welcome children home from school and in the evening to supervise dinner, homework, baths, and bedtime is extremely important to these women. The night shift, unlike day or evening shifts, allows them to be present during both of these crucial times. Angela Cordova used a parable to explain her reasons for working the night shift:

> It's better for a mother to stay home in the evening. Because the children will be more calm. See, I grew up in the country, and I could see the chickens and the chicks, like when the sun is setting. The chicks is "cheep cheep cheep" and then the mother hen will sit down and all goes underneath.

For Angela, being at home in the evening is part of a natural order that is pan-species but sex-specific.

A woman's presence at home in the evening has a symbolic, emotional, and instrumental importance. If mothers are at home during the afternoons and evenings, they can supervise older children during those hours when children are most likely to act independently or in association with their peers.[5] The theme of supervision was particularly salient with Shirley, Angela, and Patricia, the night-shift workers with the oldest children. Angela told me with great amusement:

> I have only two [children] and I told my husband, "We have to watch them like a hawk" [laughs]—"a friendly hawk, though," I say. [Laughs.]

Shirley also mentioned the parental supervision of children as a reason for working the night shift:

> Working at night was good for my family. It kept them together. You keep your children out of trouble. . . . I don't think children should be left alone. I think that's where you find the problems. I think children should be supervised at all times.

When I asked Patricia if she ever considered changing shifts as her daughter got older, she replied:

> You know, see, every time I want to change [shifts] I see a [television] show or something about teenagers and so I think [about the] things they could do, and I know how I was. I was the goody goody two shoes *only* because my parents were exceptionally strict.

What these mothers are saying is not just that children need supervision, but that *mothers* need to be the ones who are supervising at particular times or in particular circumstances. The supervision that only mothers can do is directly linked to concepts of being—being mothers and being at home. Men (fathers) are often seen by the women I interviewed as unable to provide this all-encompassing kind of supervision and are sometimes seen as either needing supervision themselves or being incapable of adequately supervising their children. Yolanda Lincoln, an African-American ward secretary who worked full time on the day shift, remembered the problems she had when she once tried working an evening shift.

> It was hard for the kids because I didn't get to spend as much time in the evening with them. And even my husband, you know, he said today he would never work evening again while the kids are little. It's family time, and especially as a mother and with children in school, just to oversee that they are doing their homework and things like that. My husband is capable, but sometimes he can be lax, you know? Because a lot of times of time [when] I worked evenings . . . a lot of times I would come home and homework wouldn't be done and he would say, "Oh, she didn't tell me she had homework." So I knew then I could never work evenings.

Like caring for younger children, being at home to supervise older children is gendered. It is considered a mother's responsibility not only to teach young children right from wrong, but also, by her presence, to keep older children from doing wrong. Angela told me that when her nephew got into trouble and was sent to Juvenile Hall, she looked to the structure of her brother and sister-in-law's home for an explanation of "what went wrong." Angela's sister-in-law works an evening shift, from 3:30 P.M. to 11:00 P.M., and Angela blames her sister-in-law for being absent during those crucial hours. She admits that when her sister-in-law goes to work, her brother goes out to see his friends and leaves the children with Angela's mother. Angela's sister-in-law feels that her husband should stay home and help with the children, and Angela agrees. But Angela added, "And then I said to myself, 'Maybe [my brother] feels the same way, he misses [his wife] in the evening.'" Although two other adults are responsible for the children, the children's father and grandmother, Angela thinks that the key to her nephew's delinquent behavior is the absence of the mother during the evening hours, an absence that leads the husband to go out at night, leaving his children with their elderly grandmother. Angela's judgmental comments about her sister-in-law are probably glossing other unspoken family strains, but Angela's disapproval of her sister-in-law is expressed in a story about the symbols of appropriate motherhood. Earlier in our conversation, Angela had described her sister-in-law as an "ideal mother [whose] house is clean, [and who] cooks so good," and had then launched into the story about how her nephew was sent to Juvenile Hall. Angela concluded:

> [My sister-in-law] likes [to work] in the evening because she can do more work in the daytime at home. Her house *very clean*. . . . And I told [my sister-in-law], I said, "Why you don't work nights?"—"I can not function right at night," she said. But I don't know what's best. That's why the house don't get clean.

Angela was presenting a morality tale about priorities and motherhood, and she was also presenting her own strategy of being by positing what she presents as the failed strategy represented by her sister-in-law. Despite her disclaimer, Angela clearly feels that she does know what is best, and she invokes the theme of "being there" to present her own strategy of being a mother, a strategy in which she is at home during the day and early evening for her children.

"Doing Things"

When I arrived at Patricia Anderson's house at 3:00 P.M., she told me that she had not slept since she got home from work the night before; she had been trying to match the color of her daughter's dance costume so that she could dye the skirt to match the headpiece. I wondered about the balance between sleep and incremental shades of rose pink, but I was also reminded of the importance of "doing things" as part of mothers' strategies of being. There is both instrumental and symbolic importance to being available to participate in or facilitate children's school and extracurricular activities. Having the appropriate costume is a symbol in Patricia's strategy of being a "working mother." When Patricia told me why she preferred the night shift, she added:

> I get [my daughter] involved in things. So she's at karate and she's got the different dance things and so forth. So if I work nights, then she can go and I can take her. But if I work daytime, that means every other weekend she'd have to miss out because I wouldn't be here to take her

... And on P.M. shift [3:30 to 11:00 P.M.], she'd still have to miss out
cause I'd be at work.

All staff nurses, regardless of shift and weekly hours worked, are
required to work every other weekend. This makes weekend activities a problem for nurses. By working nights on the weekends,
Patricia has her weekend *days* free to spend with her daughter.

Doris also uses her night-shift schedule as a way of being involved with her children's school activities. She told me:

> If I see a field trip coming up—you could say I'm a little protective—
> not overly so—but I like to be there, if they're going to go on a bus trip
> or something, I want to be one of the ones on the bus. . . . And that is
> one of the reasons I do like working nights.

Julia told me that she used to give up sleep time in order to take
her son to after-school classes.

> I used to do all the dumb things like have him in after-school classes
> at 3:00 so that I would get about four hours —four or five hours—of
> sleep a lot of times, [and then] take him to afternoon classes. And I feel
> better about that, because we were in the public school system for the
> first time and I didn't like what was going on and he was bored so I was
> trying to get—add on—a lot of after-school classes. Now he can do
> things like ride his bike to a tennis class after.

Although Julia speaks derisively about her actions as "dumb,"
she also says that she feels better about having deprived herself
of sleep rather than depriving her son of enriching activities. Her
son is now old enough to get himself to an after-school class, but
her second child will soon require the same parental assistance if
he is to participate in afternoon classes.

The night shift thus enables mothers to participate in school-
day, after-school, or weekend day activities with their children.
Day-shift hospital workers told me that children's extracurricular
activities were a difficult issue for them and a reason that many
of them were employed part time. Given enough advance notice,
day-shift workers could sometimes arrange their schedules so that
they could attend the school play or go on a field trip; but regular
lessons or sports activities had to be arranged after work time, and
they were not able to participate regularly in their children's
weekend day activities. Nurses with part-time schedules cited the

ability to participate in and facilitate their children's activities as one of the major benefits of a part-time schedule. However, both full-time and part-time day-shift workers faced structural conflicts between their work schedules and children's activity schedules and were sensitive to the charge by nonemployed mothers that working mothers don't do their share of chauffeuring and volunteering. Whether they actually volunteer and participate or not, mothers who work the night shift know that no one can say that they did not come to the school play because they were working. Activities such as dancing lessons and sports become markers that indicate both how much one is providing for one's child and how a mother's employment is not interfering with her children's ability to participate in extracurricular activities.

DE-NORMALIZING SLEEP NORMS

The disruption of sleep patterns and the lack of sleep make it impossible for some people to work a night shift. Several nurses who no longer worked a night shift gave vivid accounts of the problems night-shift work had created for them. A forty-seven-year-old nurse remembered the time when her children were young and she had to work nights.

> You had to do a year of nights after training. I almost quit three times, but I made it. I made it through. I'm not a night person, not at all. I lose weight. I mean, I literally could not speak in the morning unless I took a nap at 5:00. So I definitely was not a night person. . . . I literally used to cry on weekends because my children could not understand why I needed to sleep during the daytime.

Arlene, a forty-year-old nurse who now works the day shift, recounted what it was like when she tried to work nights. She was twenty-five then, a single mother, and her only child was in first grade.

> I worked nights, and sometimes I would get off work late, like I did today, and I'd have to rush home, get him ready for school. My sister would give him his breakfast, but he'd really want me to get him dressed, so I'd rush home and get him dressed and take him to school. And at that time, he would get out of school at 12:00 and I'd be so sleepy. Sometimes I would oversleep, just sleep and leave him there,

and the teachers would call me and they'd be so angry that I left him, and [they would] feel like I was abusing him when it was just that I was tired, and they couldn't see that. So I decided a couple of times: "Well, I'm going to sleep in front of the school and that way [the teacher will] see me out here, and then they'll know to knock on the window and bring him out to me." But they couldn't. Even though she would see me out there, she wouldn't knock on the window. So maybe an hour would pass and then I'd finally wake up and realize that I didn't have him.

Arlene worked a night shift for five years, waiting until a day-shift slot became available in her unit. Talking about those years, she said:

It was hard. I would be confused. I would go to sleep, and of course, it's another day because you're going in at 11:00 at night and it would be another day. And then I would wake up and think it's [yet] another day, you know? And I'd have to have a clock and calendar by me to orient me to what day it is and what time it is because I'd wake up and think, "Oh, my god, I've slept a whole day away!" You know? Eventually, after it started getting close to five years, I got confused. I would pass my house and think, "Where in the world am I going?"

All of the women who were working a night shift when I interviewed them considered themselves to be sleep-deprived. They reported schedules in which they got between four and five hours of sleep on the days following a night shift. They actually got less than this, as they admitted when asked about any particular day. Asking people to tell about a typical day is revealing, not only for the substantive information it provides about their lives, but also because the report is often an indication of how things go when they go well or when they go as planned. Answers to questions about a typical day convey intentions. Therefore, after asking a woman how much sleep she typically got, I would ask, "How much sleep did you get yesterday?" The answer was usually less than the answer about a typical night's sleep and usually led the interviewee to revise downward her original estimate of how much sleep she typically got.

In general, employed women with children report inadequate sleep and frequent fatigue (Hochschild and Machung 1989; Moen 1989:47–51). But for night-shift workers, the sacrifice of sleep and sleep norms is built into the structure of their work and family lives. Their attempts to normalize family life result in a de-normalization of sleep (when one sleeps, how much one sleeps, whether one sleeps with one's spouse).

Not surprisingly, Patricia Anderson and Julia Ginzburg, both single mothers (one divorced, one separated) and both at the older end of the group, reported the most severe sleep deprivation. Patricia told me that sometimes she is "too hyper" to sleep when she first gets home from work:

> Sometimes I'm really hyper and I can't sleep. When I finally get ready to go to sleep, it's time to go to work sometimes, so I'm really bananas sometimes [when] I get to work. I'm just working on, what should I say, on nervous energy. Other times, I'm so exhausted, I'll call in sick and when I get to work I change it to a vacation day. 'Cause I don't want to use up the sick leave. Like the night before last, I just was exhausted so I just called in and said, "I got a headache." I checked and made sure there was enough people and I said, "I got a headache," and they said, "Okay," and I just—I'll go to work and I'll just sign vacation on my time card.

In answer to my question about how much sleep she averages, Patricia says:

> I average three to three-and-a-half hours. Now when I'm off, I just sleep. I can sleep until I'm rested. But I'm just hyper at night, you know.

Patricia was the nurse who had not slept the day I interviewed her because she was working on her daughter's dance costume. What became clear in our conversation was that this was not an unusual event. Patricia told me that when she gets home between 8:30 and 9:00 A.M. on Saturday mornings, she sleeps for about forty-five minutes and then gets up to take her daughter to karate and then to dance class. She told me that sometimes when she's working at the hospital, "I go to the bathroom—there's no lounge—I put my head in my lap and I sleep for five minutes sometimes." Patricia explained to me that she doesn't always get home before her twelve-year-old daughter has to leave for school, and added:

> I'm so tired, that I don't make it home [before my daughter leaves for school]. When I leave [the hospital] in the morning—I sit in that car and I sleep. Or sometimes I just drive and I get halfway home and I just have to sit in the car and I go to sleep—I can't go any further. I just, my

mind, it's like, brain is dead. You know, and the older I get, it seems like I'm having psychological problems. I'm just getting older and falling apart.

Julia Ginzburg, ten years younger than Patricia Anderson, talked about her sleep deprivation in similar terms:

> Until I took ten days off about a month ago, I was burning the candle at both ends. I mean, even before [my second child] was born, I told you I was trying to get up at 3:00 in the afternoon to take the first one to classes. And so I was functioning on a sleep deficit for probably—probably up until a month or two ago. And so I was chronically—I was getting out of work late; I wouldn't get out till 9:00 [A.M.]. And I wouldn't get to bed until 11:00 [A.M.]. I was just—I was a mess! You know, finally when, when [the baby] was five-and-a-half months old, my big one went into a tailspin. Started getting really depressed, jealous and . . . and, from about that time, I knew I had to have a break. About March I was really, God, I just had to have a break. . . . March I was about ready to have a nervous breakdown. I've never been like that but virtually ready to crack up, but I had to keep going because [my husband] wasn't going to be finished with school until [May]. . . . So finally, God, when did I finally take a break, in June? Finally I took ten days the end of June or something. Spent two days on my own and left the kids with him and the child care, you know, made everything out so it would work of course. You know. Everything was just going smoothly; I'd made all the plans, of course as we [women] do. And I just went up and visited my sister for two days without any kids and I came back and . . . I took care of a lot of things I'd been trying to get done and—just took—got sleep. Slept and slept and slept and slept and slept and slept. And since then, since I've gone back to work, I'm able to sleep better during the daytime, I'm getting out on time, I'm efficient at work, everything—all the pieces are falling into place at work finally. Sort of like I was—a basket case.

Julia said that getting sleep has become a priority for her and that she now tries to get six or seven hours on a regular basis, but my interview with her took place only a month after the ten-day break she took from work. Julia's sleep deprivation may not reach the crisis point again, but like the other night shift nurses I interviewed, she will very likely continue to be chronically sleep-deprived.

Angela Cordova told me that she averages about four hours of sleep a day. Arriving home from work about 8:30 A.M., she goes to sleep at about 10:00 in the morning. Her son's kindergarten school day ends at 11:00 in the morning. In a matter-of-fact tone, Angela explained:

I hired a lady to pick [my son] up; I just pay her a dollar, but I still have to wake up to get him in [the house] and that breaks my sleep already and I try to go back to sleep but then you cannot really go to sleep because leaving a five-year-old alone [laughs]—you don't know what he's getting into.

At 2:00 P.M., Angela leaves to pick her older child up from school. She explained that she didn't really get to sleep in the afternoon, either.

After I get them and tell them to do their homework and all those things, and then I try to get some sleep but it doesn't work anymore. So almost every night I have only four hours of sleep every day.

I could not see how Angela was getting even the four hours she claimed, and I told Angela that I did not think I would be able to function well on so little sleep. Angela replied:

You know, that's what I thought, but—I guess the sign that there is really God. Because I always, I say, "Look God, I can't do this anymore, so you have to give me the strength and the grace that I'll be able to take care of these people," and I regard my children as, they're entrusted to me, they're not mine. He just entrusted to me. And so with my patients. "Look, I'm just weak and you entrusted these people in my hands, I can't do it alone without you." That's all my daily prayer.

When I asked Angela what were the hardest parts of working and being a mother, she didn't mention lack of sleep; instead she said:

Oh, it's like you don't give your whole self as a mother, which I would like to do. I want to be a good, ideal mother, like—everything is right for my children. Like the house is clean and everything; I just want to be that way, you know.

Doris also reported getting about four hours of sleep on the days after she has worked a night shift. I asked her how it worked to get that amount of sleep and she replied,

Very rough, I'm tired a lot. My back hurts. I get a little edgy. But it works out 'cause I look towards the weekend.

Doris catches up on sleep during the weekend, when she gets about eight or nine hours a night. But four hours of sleep four days a week takes its toll:

You know, I joke around and say, "I'm only thirty-four, but I feel like I'm fifty." [Laughs.] 'Cause my body feels it. . . . I try to get about a half-hour nap—usually on the couch in front of the TV, but it works—just that little bit really helps. I can't do it if the kids are up and running around [saying], "Mommy I need this." You know, and I say, "Go ask your daddy." [Laughs.] And so they do, and he's pretty good about that.

Janice claimed that she gets four to five hours of sleep on the days after she works at the hospital. The youngest of the group at the age of thirty, she feels she can manage on this much sleep, making it up on her days off. Janice, however, has a chronically ill sixteen-month-old baby, and things are seldom routine. I asked her if the night shift is tiring, and she told me:

Sometimes it's tiring when I don't get sleep. Like when, like what happened yesterday. I got home in the morning and my husband told me [the baby] had a bad night; she was up most of the night coughing and she has her asthma attack, so first thing in the morning when I got home I called her pulmonologist at [the hospital] and he said, "Bring her over, I have to evaluate her." So meantime I didn't get any sleep at all and I had to bring her over [to the hospital], so I was there by 9:00 in the morning—nine-thirtyish. I got off work at 7:30, got home here by about 8:15 and I had to turn around and go back [to the hospital] by myself to bring [my baby] [sighs]. And we were there until, gosh, 11:00. . . . I didn't get any sleep at all until, gosh, until 4:30, till my husband came home. I was up for already twenty-four hours. But it's good I was off last night so I was able to sleep. And I'm going back to work tonight again.

Sleep has been de-normalized by night-shift nurses because on a regular basis they sleep less than they feel they need and less than most people are said to need on average. It has also been de-normalized because they sleep at times that are different from the rest of their families and because they sleep at the socially normative time for being awake. Night-shift workers have also de-normalized sleep and time in relation to their spouses or partners. Night-shift hospital workers have more family time with their children, but they have less couple time, and they don't share sleep hours with their spouses or partners on the nights they work. The night shift gives couples the least time to be alone together, either awake or sleeping.

Studies of the impact of shift work on the family life of couples reveal a similar minimizing of couple time in favor of children having more time with either or both parents (Hertz and Charlton 1989), and this may contribute to the higher divorce rate among couples in which one partner works a non-day shift (White and Keith 1990). On the other hand, low job flexibility for parents has been found to lead to problems in marital relations (Hughes and Galinsky 1994), and couples often use shift work as a family strategy for increasing their flexibility in relation to the care of their children.

Shirley Roberts emphasized that, while the night shift was good for the family as a group, it was essential to have a husband who was cooperative:

> Nights is a good shift. . . . But I find that it's good for families if you can have an understanding with your husband. But if you don't have an understanding with your husband, working nights can be a breakup.

One of the day-shift nurses who had worked nights when her children were young described her relationship with her husband during that period in the following way:

> I always looked at it as two people rowing a boat. He's alongside me— we're both rowing. I can't look at what he's doing. I just have to know that he's doing his job. I've got to know he's doing it because I don't have the time to look.

While some of the women I interviewed did express regret at not having more time with their husbands, the primary focus of their accounts was on shift work as a cooperative family strategy.

The night-shift workers I interviewed are de-normalizing sleep in order to absorb the contradictions of working away from home while trying to construct themselves as mothers who stay at home. Fatigue and lack of sleep notwithstanding, mothers who work the night shift feel that they have made the best possible choice of employment schedule given both the circumstances of their lives and their desire to emulate "at-home" mothers in their strategies of being.

BOTH "WORKING MOTHERS" AND "STAY-AT-HOME MOMS"

Mothers who work the night shift use the cloak of night to render their employment less visible. They do not deny the fact that they are employed, but they do try to implement strategies of being that highlight their maternal visibility. The night shift allows "working mothers" to appear to be "stay-at-home moms." At issue is the preservation of a family form in which the mother is available to her children during the day, both as the person who performs symbolically invested activities, such as volunteering at her child's school or taking her children to dance lessons or sports activities, *and* as the person whose very being is symbolically invested—the woman in the house, the mother at home.

Night-shift nurses implement strategies of being employed mothers in three major ways: they limit the visibility of their labor force participation to their children and in the public spheres of their children's lives; they make themselves available to involve their children in symbolically invested activities outside the home, and they position themselves in the culturally appropriate place and time: at home, during the day. All three of these strategies work to highlight their visibility as mothers.

What explains this shared concern with being seen as "at-home moms"? It is not a commonality of cultural, ethnic, or class background. Doris is the daughter of Mexican-immigrant, working-class parents who were both employed while she was growing up. Julia came from an upper-middle-class, Jewish home with a father in the professions and a homemaker mother. Patricia's parents were middle-class African Americans who both held professional positions. Shirley grew up in a working-class, African-American home in which her father was the breadwinner and her mother stayed home and was not employed until Shirley was in elementary school. Janice immigrated to the United States from the Philippines with her college-educated parents, both of whom were employed. What they all face, however, are similar dominant cultural norms about motherhood. From their different backgrounds, they each interact with prevailing definitions of motherhood—they are not creating motherhood from scratch, and they are not immune to the culture around them.

Working the night shift enables these mothers to normalize family life so it looks and feels more like the dominant cultural ideal of a traditional family: a father who goes to work in the morning and a mother who is home during the day, welcomes her children home from school, has dinner on the table for her returning husband, and tucks the children into bed at night. Judith Stacey refers to this family form as the "modern family": "an intact nuclear household unit composed of a male breadwinner, his full-time homemaker wife, and their dependent children" (Stacey 1990:5). In historical terms, Stacey is correct; the prevalence of such families was historically recent and short-lived, as well as being culturally specific. But for the women I interviewed, this family form is conceptualized as traditional. If not a common family form in their modern world, it was still an ideal by which they measured themselves, and the word "traditional" best represents the concept that these "working mothers" were trying to convey.

As a group, they have similar constellations of resources that make night-shift employment a sensible strategy for negotiating norms about motherhood in their constructions of themselves as "working mothers." Except for Shirley, they all have qualifications as registered nurses. Except for Patricia, each relies on her husband for nighttime child care. Unlike the voluntary part-time nurses, their husbands' jobs do not pay enough or provide the needed benefits that would enable them to work part time. Of course, similar resources are experienced differently by women in differing social locations and familial contexts. What it means, for example, to be the sole support of her family will be different for Julia, whose parents have economic resources she could call on in an emergency, than for Patricia, who is estranged from her parents and has grown children who still turn to her in times of need. They have traveled different paths (Cole 1986), but they talk in remarkably similar ways about how working the night shift enables them to be "working mothers" who are "stay-at-home moms."

6   Nine to Five: A Collection of Days

EMPLOYED WOMEN with children are creating work/family patterns by weaving together their constructions of motherhood, their constellations of resources, and the structure of their workplaces. Sometimes these three elements work together to form a similar pattern, as they do for the voluntary part-time workers or the night-shift workers. Among the full-time, day-shift workers, however, there was great variety in the configuration of resources, child-care situations, job categories, and work schedules. And although all of these women understood what the cultural expectations for mothers were, their responses to those expectations and their strategies of being workers and mothers varied.

Eighteen of the mothers I interviewed worked full time during the day, but many of them had worked evening or night shifts while their children were younger. Some found that they physically couldn't continue to work nights and so changed to the day shift after several years. Others had used shift work as part of a sequencing strategy, matching employment schedules to the changing needs of children over time and moving to the day shift when children moved into adolescence or adulthood. In this chapter, I focus on the full-time, day-shift workers who had children under eighteen at the time I interviewed them.[1] What kinds of work and family patterns do mothers who are employed full time during the day weave, and how do they present themselves as workers and as mothers?

SHARON BAKER: THE 300 PERCENT SOLUTION

Sharon Baker is a thirty-four-year-old, African-American registered nurse. She is married, has three children who are one, four, and seven years old, and is employed full time during the day. After telling me about her work, her future plans, her husband, and her children, Sharon concluded:

Those are the things I feel good about. All of them. It's like I want to give 100 percent to every aspect. I want to be 100 percent nurse, 100 percent community health nurse, 100 percent neighbor, community person, 100 percent wife, 100 percent mother—and that's hard. But that's what I want to do. And I feel like I do bits and pieces of it, enough to make a difference. I naturally feel like I make a difference in my kids' lives. I hope my husband enjoys marriage as much as I do [laughs]. And I like having a job, having a family and having my husband. They're all interactive. I mean it's a triangle. I keep a picture of the three kids in the car with me so when the day gets hard, I'm looking at that picture knowing why I'm working! [Laughs.] And I look at them and they all three look like my husband, so there's the interaction there. And even when I'm in school, like right now, I've gone back to school [one evening every other week] to get my public health nurse's certificate. I'll be finished with that [in a few months]. So then I can do anything I want to as far as in the community or public health or whatever. So it's like everything pools and I know that I'm going to school to fulfill what I want to do so that I'm teaching my kids that you can do— anything that you want to do, you can accomplish. And the only way to teach them is to show them. By example.

Sharon is not only active, busy, and involved in a myriad of things, but she is also aware of how each part of her life is connected to the other parts. But, as Sharon said, trying to actualize all these facets of one's self—to be 100 percent in all areas—is "hard," and she admitted that she was often exhausted. I asked her what her ideal work schedule would be, and without hesitation she replied:

Nine to three. I'd like to not have to be at work until 9:00. That would give me enough time to drop the children off and take a deep breath before I go into work, and being off at 3:00 would give me enough time in the evening with them instead of the type of thing that was going on a couple weeks ago when I run around, pick all three up, go home, cook dinner and try to listen to them in the meantime. The baby is crying 'cause he's hungry. My son: "Mommy, are you gonna help me with my spelling?" And my daughter, just because she's not being paid attention to, running in and out of the kitchen or whatever. But if I had more time in the evening with them I think that would make a *lot* of difference.

As the stories of the night-shift nurses illustrated, a primary issue for mothers who are employed is *which* hours they can be home and available to their children. And, as the stories of the voluntary part-time nurses emphasized, another key issue is flexibility in the control over time. Sharon doesn't have the schedule she thinks would be ideal, but she had moved out of hospital nursing to take a position in the hospital's visiting nurse program, and this gave her more flexibility during the day and released her from the requirement to work every other weekend.

> Well, like this week, today I wanted to only see five patients because my children have musical recitals that are coming up in June. The auditions are tomorrow. They have their lesson on Friday afternoon at 3:30, and my son has a carnival going on at school. He asked that I come to that. So Wednesday I saw nine patients to make up for today. Usually we see six [a day], but so the time worked out, because I'm seeing five and I know it's not going to take . . . it could sometimes take eight hours, but today it probably will only take seven. But I know I've made up my time on Wednesday. So there is some flexibility. [But] it's almost as if some of that is being taken away from us. Because there are more demands on us as far as how much productivity they want us to meet and things like that. . . . But there is some flexibility. If I had something that I really had to do at the end of the day, I could save all of my charting until I got home that evening. Or I could go into the office at 7:00 in the morning and start on some of my paperwork. Call my patients at 8:00, start seeing them at 8:30, and then too save my paperwork until the evening, so by noon I could be done with seeing the patients, [and then] make some calls to the physicians. I wear a beeper so if I'm [at] a doctor's appointment with my children and I get a call, generally at the doctor's office they'll let me use the phone. So it works out okay most times.

Most of the mothers who were employed full time told me that they would prefer to be employed about three days a week. Some mothers have the resources to make this preference a reality, but many do not. When I asked Sharon what the hardest things were about combining employment and mothering, she replied:

> Wanting to spend the time with my children without yelling at them sometimes because I'm tired or frustrated or something like that. I talk to myself constantly and even when I do snap at them, I come back with a smile. I have to think fast. So I just wish I didn't have to work, or work as much so that I could spend that time. Like being at my son's carnival today. Those kind of little things. He asked me this morning, and it would be nice to be able to say, "Yeah, I'll be there." Or [he says]: "How come you don't do yard duty sometimes?" To have that option—like with other things, you want options. I want those options with my kids.

Like so many of the mothers I interviewed, Sharon corrected herself when she said that she wished she did not work. The issue for these mothers is not a dichotomous one of being employed versus not being employed, nor is it an issue of being a worker *or* a mother—the issue is one of how to structure work and family life so that these two endeavors can be combined in ways that do not take such a heavy toll on mothers and their families.

At the end of the interview, I asked Sharon if there was anything she wanted to add:

> No, sounds like you hit all the points, all the major points anyway. I don't know. I was just thinking as I'm talking about everything, I don't know how it sounds when it sounds like everything is just going along. But I go crazy half of the time, and I try not to. There are some times when I have to sit down and tell myself: "It's gonna be okay. It's gonna be okay." Almost as if my brain is slipping out of my head and I'm trying to tell myself and talk to myself: "It's gonna be fine." Paying the bills is added into all that. There's just all these little things, folding the clothes, and five people in the house, there's a lot of clothes. Going grocery shopping and the weekends and the beeper. . . . It's not just the money to pay the bills, but actually physically sitting down and siphoning through and which one, juggling and—I don't know. It feels crazy sometimes. And it feels good when I've gone to bed and the clothes are folded and I've kissed the kids goodnight without yelling at them. Just those little things. All the bills are paid up to a certain point and I can actually, [although] I should be studying, and I'm going to bed and it's 11:00 P.M. And that's early for me.

Lack of sleep is not an experience reserved only for night-shift workers. With few exceptions, mothers who were employed full-time are "doing it all" by giving up sleep. Arlie Hochschild noted that the "working mothers" she spoke to "talked about sleep the way a hungry person talks about food" (Hochschild and Machung 1989:9). Sharon says that she usually gets about four hours of sleep a night.

> Seriously. Because I have to get up in the morning with the kids. And I mean there are other times when I catch up on that sleep. Where I just can't take it any more and I have to go to bed when the kids go to bed. But that time after they go to sleep, I get their clothes out for the next day, I start lunches as much as I can, do some of those things. Or fold the clothes or whatever. But when I'm not able to do those things, the next morning is harder because it takes a long time to get their

clothes out and everything else. Or my temper is a little bit shorter because the house is a mess and I don't like that. So that's when I feel like I'm losing my brain!

Sharon's daytime employment schedule is what night-shift workers refer to as a "normal" schedule. In spite of this distinction, Sharon and the night-shift workers sound very similar in the expectations they strive to meet and the sacrifices they make.

Sharon Baker is typical of most of the mothers I interviewed, regardless of shift, in her feelings about motherhood, in the way she expresses her concern for her children, in her efforts to meet the cultural expectations of mothers, in her positive feelings toward herself as a worker, and, for the full-time workers, in the stress she experiences in trying to keep it all together. But there is variation in the mothers who work a day shift, and not all full-time, day-shift hospital workers resemble Sharon Baker.

The following work/family patterns differ in ways that are connected to constructions of motherhood and of employment. These constructions of motherhood and employment are reflected in women's strategies of being mothers and their strategies of being workers.

RACHEL PIERCE: REDEFINING MOTHERHOOD

Rachel Pierce is a forty-seven-year-old, Euro-American registered nurse and the nursing director of a hospital ward. Married for twenty-two years, with two children ages eight and eleven, she worked full time as a staff nurse on the evening shift until her first child was born, at which point she cut back to a three-fifths, part-time position on the same shift. When her oldest child started first grade, Rachel enrolled in graduate school and earned a master's degree in nursing, after which she accepted an administrative position as a nursing director.

Rachel's ability to work the evening shift while her children were young and to move into a full-time administrative position was facilitated by the way in which she and her husband handled the division of labor in their family.

Well, this is how it worked. . . . When we decided to have kids, we looked at who needed to keep working and who could stop working, and I was the one who needed to continue working because he had no benefits like mine, and no options. So I continued working and he totally cut back when the baby was little, did all the primary child care. Then when that first baby was a little older—was it the first one? Gosh, I don't even know. He went into the [gardening] business, but where he could make his own hours. So he's always picked up the child-care pieces. It's wonderful. It's been wonderful. And he's still doing that, because now we're into orthodonture and piano lessons and all that stuff. So he's still the one who can do all that. . . . It turned out it was a good choice because my salary is good. And he wasn't as ambitious, you know? . . . So this has been wonderful for him, although he did give up ten years. I mean, he could never get back into a mainstream career at this point. That's behind him.

In telling me about their parenting arrangement, Rachel emphasized that it has worked well structurally and that her children have benefitted from "this real two-parent team." Buying a house in the 1970s (before the cost of housing in California skyrocketed), investing their earnings during a period of high returns, and waiting until their late thirties to have children gave Rachel and her husband the resources to take extended parental leaves when their children were born and has made it possible for one or both of them to work less than full time since then. But resources are only one part of this pattern.

A family strategy in which the father is the primary parent and the mother is the primary breadwinner rests on constructions of gender, motherhood, and work that differ from dominant cultural norms. Rachel's definition of self as mother is not expressed in terms of "being there" in the way that most other women defined being a mother, but it is expressed in terms of seeing to it that her children get what they need. She is the manager and organizer—but she does not portray herself as the main point-of-service provider. Rachel represents a small minority of women who have handed over to their husbands the primary parenting and the symbolic practices associated with motherhood. Rachel summarized their arrangement in this way:

> The kids are in terrific shape, and I can't help but think it's because they've had—well, we're two very different people, my husband and I. And we agree totally, sort of, on the course we want to take, what we want our kids to be like, and what we want to provide for them, but our styles are very, very different. And he has fun with the kids, where

I was, and am, sort of MOM. I make the dentist appointments and the doctor's appointments and make sure there's food, but I'm not as imaginative. I don't love them any less, but he would always refuse to sit around the house. I mean, the kids went every place real early on. So he's had a good time doing it, it hasn't been a real sacrifice for him because he just took them with him. And the up side is I think the kids have really benefitted on this real two-parent team. Most people get divorced, or [children] never see their parents because it's a real struggle around here to support kids. I mean, we're talking two-career families. So [our children] never experienced any kind of loss. There's never been loss of attention, loss of a parent.

But relinquishing gendered practices is not easy, and for Rachel's husband, Mark, the cost has been his own potential career and his individual earning power. Rachel presented their arrangement as wonderful for her and the children, but each time she mentioned to me how this arrangement works for Mark, she made a two-part statement, emphasizing what Mark had given up and then minimizing his loss by such comments as "he wasn't as ambitious," "it hasn't been a real sacrifice to him," or "he thought it would be fun," as if she had to rationalize his position as being "naturally" suited to him, in the same way as mothers are often described.

Rachel did not talk about mothers and fathers—she talked about parenting and parents. She described her husband as the primary parent, but not as the person who is "mothering" the children, nor did she use any of the other gendered terms usually used to describe such arrangements and relationships. When Rachel used the word "mom," it was as a contrast to the freer, more playful way that her husband parents. In practice, she and her husband have shared the parenting, using shift work and part-time work as well as outside child care. Rachel had taken a year-long maternity leave and her husband had quit his job to stay home when the first child was born, and she had worked evenings and been home during the day for most of her children's preschool years. But she did not present this as something she did as a mother, but as something that they did as a family.

And then as the [maternity leave] year went on, I was going crazy, finally, being home with the baby. The thought of actually having to spend eight to ten hours a day with a baby and without another adult just horrified me. And he thought it would be fun. So, that's it. I went back to work and it worked. And I worked evenings, so I had almost the whole day with the kid. So we were there together as a family until I had to be at work at 3:00. So it wasn't like a nine-to-five job. I missed maybe four hours of [my child's] awake time and that was it.

Rachel's children are receiving what other mothers told me they wanted for their children: lots of parent contact time, involvement in extracurricular activities, a parent to facilitate that involvement, and special family times. The difference is that Rachel doesn't feel that, as mother, she has to be the primary person to provide these things, nor does she present herself in ways that highlight her visibility as mother. If anything, the gendered role of mother has been erased from Rachel's presentation of self in favor of the gender-neutral parent, and the expectations attached to the role of mother have been denaturalized and redistributed.

No one fulfills all the expectations for mothers, and some mothers meet fewer of these expectations than others—ideology and practice are seldom isomorphic. But mothers usually employ strategies of being by which they present themselves as mothers who are fulfilling these expectations in one way or another. What is unusual in Rachel's case is not that she did not do some of the things that mothers, as mothers, are supposed to do, but that she did not define herself as someone who had to do those things.

Rachel's definition of self as worker reflected a similar modification of the expectations attached to her role as supervisor. She had worked hard for her advanced degree, clearly enjoyed her job, and was pleased to have been promoted to nursing director. But while other nursing directors told me that the job entailed an average of sixty hours a week, Rachel was clear that she was not going to devote all her time to her job.

> At the beginning of the job I was taking work home because that was the only way I could do it. And then I stopped doing that. I realized that I could take it home all the time, and I could do twice as much work here and I would just have more work to do. I put limits on—I do not take work home. I'm also fortunate that my nurses don't call me at home a lot. I have twenty-four-hour responsibility. So I've set limits with them and I've also set limits with myself. . . . I don't see my role as that of a mother [to the nurses], and I think a lot of nursing directors . . . try to do too much.

In some ways, what Rachel did was to redefine her role as supervisor just as she had redefined her role as mother.

> Well, it can't take over my life because I'd be totally useless and I'd burn out, and they would have to have someone else. There are lots of things in hospitals that I can't control, and this hospital will go on whether I'm here or not. I am not indispensable to this hospital functioning.

Rachel's position as supervisor, however, does require that she be available to the hospital at all times, and her hours at work have doubled since she went from a three-fifths staff nursing position to the full-time administrative position in which she works fifty hours a week. Despite the increase in hours, Rachel found that the day shift was more conducive to family time now that both her children were in school, and that a supervisory position allowed her to trade in the flexibility of part-time work for more control over time during the day and for the freedom from weekend shifts. In response to my question about what had changed the most since she had taken the job as nursing director, Rachel replied:

> We have much more of a routine. Weekends, we were never able to go any place on the weekends, so we have a routine where we actually go away on weekends sometimes. I am there for homework and dinner. So we've become more of a family. It isn't Dad doing it part of the time and Mom doing it part of the time. We're doing it together now that the kids are older. It worked when they were younger. So we're much more a family now. So that's changed significantly. I also have a life with my husband, where that was sort of catch-as-catch-can as well. And we knew that we couldn't function that way forever, that we would pass in the night. Our marriage is strong enough that we both said, "Well, this will be over at some point." But it was time to have it be over. I don't have as much flexibility, although being a manager, I don't punch a time clock. So I have more flexibility in this particular job than in other jobs. I can take off if there is a teacher who has to be seen or a kid who is sick. I try not to take off for the field-trip driving and stuff. But I can take off for the other things. But the downside is I really need to be here Monday through Friday.

As they did for other mothers, dinner and homework figure centrally as symbols of family time—but in Rachel's narrative, they are not necessarily linked to definitions of motherhood. Dinner, for example, is a family time, but it doesn't have to be prepared by mother. Rachel tells me that she used to cook dinner, but now that she is working days, her husband makes the evening meal.

> He's actually very sweet. I come home to a hot cup of coffee and the newspaper, and "Leave Mommy alone for a half-hour, and let me talk to her." It's very nice!

Rachel's description of coming home from the hospital was similar to the picture Mary Clark presented when I interviewed her. Mary is a thirty-three-year-old African-American ward clerk. She works days from 7:30 A.M. until 4:00 P.M., is married, and has two children, ages thirteen and one. The one year old is cared for during the day by Mary's sixty-seven-year-old grandmother. Mary reported that her husband

> drops the baby off [at my grandmother's] on his way to [work]. And on his way home, he picks her up, picks me up, and we go home. So it works out great. . . . I don't have any major issues [laughs]. I really don't. I just go to work, go home. Well, basically, when I get home from work, my child totally ignores me. It's like I'm not even there. This is the baby. The older one, she can take care of herself. I don't have to do much for her. Me and her have our little talks, you know, mother to daughter talks, that sort of thing. . . . But the baby totally ignores me. She's off to her father. She follows him all over the house. And I just sit there and relax, and get ready for dinner. But I'm just a nobody at home [laughs]. And I love it. So it's fine.

Rachel's and Mary's descriptions are dramatic contrasts to Sharon Baker's description of her own return home after an eight-hour workday when, as mother, she was in charge of picking up her three children from child care, paying attention to their immediate needs, and making dinner for her family—followed by baths, bed, stories, laundry, and lunch preparation for the following day. The "second shift," as Arlie Hochschild has so effectively shown us, is the point where women pay an enormous toll and where the skirmishes and battles of the "stalled revolution" take place (Hochschild and Machung 1989). In heterosexual couples, the participation of husbands, partners, and fathers in the work of family and home makes a tremendous difference in the ways mothers are able to weave work and family. Near the end of my interview with her, Rachel leaned forward and said, "But I think that I'm a real atypical family person. I don't think many people have had it as good as I've had it." Based on my interview data, I think she is right.

HEATHER MACLEOD: "SOMETHING IN-BETWEEN"

Heather Macleod is a forty-two-year-old, Euro-American regis-tered nurse with a high-level administrative position at the hos-pital. Heather and her husband, a professional with his own prac-tice, were in their late thirties, married for twelve years, and well established in their respective careers before they had a child. Un-like Rachel and her husband, Heather and her husband continued to work full time days after the birth of their only child four years ago. Heather took a three and a half month maternity leave. When she returned to her job, she took the baby to a child care provider who lived near the hospital. Although Heather had no doubts that she intended to return to work, she found it difficult to leave her baby with someone else.

> I really felt as though this was the end of my relationship with my daughter. I had nothing else to go on. I didn't have another child. I didn't realize—yeah, I kind of felt like I was giving up my relation-ship with her to go back to work, and someone else would be her mother on a daily basis. [The child care person] was a young woman, about my age—we had a lot in common anyway. She was very used to taking babies of busy women and helping them through that tran-sition. . . . But I was never so depressed. I don't ever remember being so depressed in my life as those few days. I don't know that I felt guilty. I really felt sad. That's not what I had anticipated. I had an-ticipated, "Oh, I want to go back and I probably shouldn't feel that way." I really remember my overriding emotion as being one of sad-ness, that this was the end of a time that had been very happy for me and it would never be this happy again. And of course now I have lots of years of real happy times with my daughter to say that that's not the case. But that really threw me for a loop. I hadn't anticipated be-ing so sad.

With the help of Jody, her child care provider, Heather was able to continue breastfeeding after she returned to work. Jody would call Heather's beeper when the baby needed feeding, and Heather would leave work and go to Jody's house to nurse the baby. Heather remembered those months fondly:

It was a hassle, dashing back and forth and dealing with pumping your breasts and that sort of thing, being caught in an elevator with wet clothing and that sort of thing. But I recall it all now as a very positive experience. It was a nice break in my day to go and sit with her.

Heather's administrative position, while requiring long hours at work, also gave her flexibility over when and how she spent those hours—flexibility that she used to continue breastfeeding. It also gave her the financial resources to find high-quality care from a person who was willing to help her combine motherhood and employment.

Within several weeks I realized that [my daughter] was going to be fine . . . it wasn't that now I was a working person and I couldn't be a mother anymore. There really was something in between. All I could see was these black and whites: I was a mom for three-and-a-half months; now I have to go back to work and I won't get to be a mom anymore. You know? . . . I was very relieved that I didn't feel that bad after a while, that things worked out pretty well.

At the time of the interviews, Rachel and Heather had similar positions and schedules, but they were employing very different practical strategies and very different strategies of being. Rachel and her husband had reversed conventional gender roles, shared most of the daily care of their children, and tried to de-gender parenting. Heather and her husband also shared parenting, but they used a child-care provider for most of their daughter's daily care while each continued to work about sixty hours a week.

James and I really credit [our child-care provider] for getting us through those toddler years. Because if I had had—either one of us, not just me—but if either one of us had had to do too much more juggling with our schedules around a day-care person who was closed or whatever, it would have been really much more stressful for us than it was.

It was the issue of work schedules that did cause problems in their attempts to share parenting. Heather, linking parental care to being at home, had problems when James too often combined the care of their four-year-old daughter with being in his office. The nature of their struggle illuminates the gendered nature of their shared parenting.

When we started in the [preschool], it was quite an eye-opening experience as to how many school days they are closed. They gave us this calendar, and I'm going, "*James,* one of us is going to have to make some changes!" [Laughs.] And the first month or two, that's a bit of a different adjustment. But again, our strategy has been to really be rigorous about calendaring each other on days we have to be there early, days we have to be there late . . . [On days the school is closed] he can bring her to his office because he has a room where she can watch a videotape. . . . And there are places there where she can lie down and sleep and do her thing. So as much as anything, if we're really stuck and neither of us can really not be at work, she usually is in James's office. . . . And we had not anticipated how long school would be closed during Christmas. I mean, we figured the Christmas holidays and a few other days. So I think the whole week between Christmas and New Year's, she was at his office every day. Now he had shorter days, he wasn't very heavily booked those days. And she's very accustomed to doing that. It doesn't seem to bother her too much. We also can get into some difficult struggles. We both travel quite a bit on our job, and what will happen to me is that I'll be away and I'll call home and talk to James and he'll say, "Oh, I had to go in and see a client." And he generally will always make accommodations for the client. And because our daughter is such a good sport, he would drag her along. And about three weeks ago, I was in Boston, and I said, "James, she doesn't have a day off when you do that." So at that juncture, that was one of about three times when I had to sit down and say, "You can't do this to her. If you had told me you were going to do that, I would have canceled my trip to Boston, I would not have gone." . . . And to him, it hadn't been a problem. He could just take her into the office. . . . And as long as she falls asleep on the couch in there, she's fine. And I'm going, "But James, I'm not sure that's really okay. I think she kind of needs to be at home."

Instead of cutting back on their hours of employment and redistributing the work of parenthood as Rachel and her husband had done, Heather and her husband were incorporating parenthood into their occupational lives.

Heather cannot step away from the norms of motherhood in the way that Rachel can, secure in the knowledge that her husband is fulfilling the expectations of "being there" and "doing things." On days when Heather wants to stay at the hospital in the evenings to catch up on her work, James is supposed to pick their daughter up from school.

He'll call me and say, "I thought I could pick her up, but I really can't. Can you come home?" And most of the time that's something I can scoop up into a briefcase and do after she goes to sleep.

Other times, rather than getting their daughter home for an early day as they had planned, her husband would take their daughter back to the office with him so that he too could catch up on some work—"and then its 8:00 P.M. before she gets dinner." Heather presents this arrangement as one that her daughter does not mind by telling me that the staff at her husband's office likes their daughter, that their daughter is accustomed to going there, and that "it doesn't seem to bother her too much." But Heather worries about the length of time her daughter is away from home, and she is bothered by the fact that her husband combines his work and parenting by caring for their daughter in his office with a video and a sofa to sleep on. Heather's daughter may indeed love being at work with her father, and watching videos at his office may be little different than watching videos at home—but Heather is "not sure that's really okay."

While Rachel Pierce noted that her new day schedule enabled them to be "much more a family now" because she and her husband were both there in the evening for homework and dinner, Heather described how she had to learn to "let go" of a certain version of dinnertime as a symbol of family life.

> I had this ethic at one point in my life, because of the way I was raised, that we all had to sit down to dinner and eat together. So that put a tremendous pressure on me, principally, because I like to cook and I do most of the cooking. . . . As soon as I got home I had to get dinner on the table because my daughter had to eat at a certain hour. And I finally realized that at that point, especially, she didn't really like to eat what we ate. We all eat in the same room. She's sort of there playing while we're eating. So I had to let go of that "we're all going to sit down at the table together" business and realize it was really okay, we were all spending the evening together anyway. Because she would be hungry, and she would get to eat [first]. James and I would have a little bit more time to just chat after she was done eating and she was playing or watching her videos or whatever she wanted to do. Then we would have a more relaxed dinner. Otherwise, we would get into these big struggles about dinner.

The symbolic practices of motherhood were not, however, completely tossed aside. Heather emphasizes her maternal visibility by immediately adding that, while they do not eat together as a family, "We have a real bedtime story routine." Similarly, as a counterpoint to the long work days she and her husband maintain, Heather emphasized that they include their daughter in all their leisure activities.

> So I think that's one advantage of having kids later in your life because you tend to do a lot of traveling. We do a fair amount of traveling now because our daughter is a good traveler. . . . We really don't do anything outside of our work hours that doesn't include her. And our friends have narrowed to other people who work like we do and have kids.

Heather's daughter is still in preschool, and the problems of accommodating themselves to children's activities, such as playing with friends after school, lessons, sports, field trips, and the class play, have yet to surface. When I asked Heather what they would do when their daughter starts elementary school, her answer indicated that this was something she had been thinking about. She explained that her home is a forty-five minute drive from the city where they both work and that they were currently using a preschool near the hospital, but that they wanted their daughter to attend the public school in the upper-middle-class neighborhood in which they lived.

> I couldn't quite conceive of this notion of leaving my child forty-five minutes away. It doesn't always take forty-five minutes, but if there is bad traffic and that sort of thing. . . . So I still haven't quite dealt with that. She will be one more year in [preschool] and then we do want her to start [school] in our neighborhood because we are within walking distance of a very good public school. So that's my next motherly hurdle is the thought of leaving her [that far away] for kindergarten if I continue to work full time. I keep sort of telling myself, "I'll cut back," and somehow—or my husband . . . he'll arrange his office hours and [so will I] so that we won't be working as hard as we do. And yet it seems every year we wind up working harder and I'm taking on more professional obligations.

Although Heather mentioned several times the possibility of cutting back her hours, she was referring to doing fewer than the sixty hours she reported or to taking more work home with her and being at the hospital less—she was not considering part-time work, or even cutting back to forty hours a week. Given this, I was surprised that she was not thinking about enrolling her daughter in a private school near their place of employment, but as Heather explained,

One of the reasons we really are committed to having her start school in our neighborhood [is] because we will build those friendships, and our neighborhood is full of little kids. And I'm really confident that there will be somebody [in case of an emergency] within walking distance. I know there are moms in our neighborhood who, if they work, they don't work full time. And we think at this point that when she does go to school there, we will likely have to hire somebody, if we're both still working at the same pace, we will hire somebody to be there in the afternoons when she comes home. And part of the reason we're working as hard as we do, that we chose the house we live in—even though we knew children were way off in the future—is we both wanted that kind of neighborhood where you could just walk to school and walk around the corner and ride your bike with your friends. And I really still am very emotionally certain that I don't want to be dragging her [to the city] as she gets any older. And I want her to feel that she can go home at the end of her school day, because she has a very long day. Today, for instance, James is in Phoenix because he's attending a meeting there, I had an 8:00 A.M. meeting obligation, so she was in school at 7:45, and I'm trying to squeeze in my teacher conference that we missed last week, to 5:00 this afternoon. So, at best, she'll get out of there by 5:30. So she has at least as long a day, if not longer, than we do.

Heather's narrative specified the elements that made up what she felt was an idyllic childhood, a childhood in which her daughter would walk to a very good public school with her neighborhood friends, a childhood in which her daughter's days away from home would be shorter because she would not have to commute to the city and back with her parents and because she could return to her own house after school. But her narrative also includes competing demands: early morning meetings, work-related travel, teacher conferences. In order to provide their daughter with the kind of childhood they want for her, Heather and her husband need to hire someone else to be at home. It may turn out that the logistics of having their child attend the neighborhood school are too difficult to maintain. Getting time together as a family is not easy even with the present arrangement.

I think our biggest challenge is trying to find a couple of hours—which is really all that it is—of time to devote to her and to each other before you go to bed and then it starts all over again. I'm sure that's what you hear from a lot of people [laughs].

Heather noted that the time she has in the car with her daughter was some of their best time together, because once she did get home she and James were busy with the second shift.

> One of the other things that I've recognized over the years is that the commute time is actually some of the best time that I spend with [my daughter], especially when she's in school because she's obviously a seasoned little commuter. She just thinks her day begins and ends in a car. And we make the car fun for her. She can eat in there. The cars look god-awful. You have this standard for cars before you ever have kids and after that it all goes downhill. But we have a pillow because she usually takes a nap, and we try to plan things that she can take in the car to play back and forth, and word games. She's a very good speller and she's just a real bright little punkin. And it's kind of like, the time before we hit home and get into dinner and stories and all the routine at home, it's almost our little respite. . . . And I absolutely never want a car phone because to me, that's the only period of time. When I hit home, I get calls from my mother. I have an aging mother in the area, [and] my husband has an aging mother, neither of whom are a terrible burden to us in any way, but it's a couple phone calls a week. And friends and whatever—social obligations. So it's almost like a different workday starts as soon as you get home, for both of us.

Letting go of some of the things they thought were important was one way of making things work.

> If dinner doesn't get made, it doesn't get made and we go out. So if I had been somebody where everything had to be absolutely perfect and orderly in both their workplace and their home place, I probably would [not] be able to do this without killing myself or killing my daughter or something.

Although Heather said that she sometimes thought about working fewer hours or that sometimes James talked about cutting back, neither saw doing so as a viable option. Heather did not think she could work less than full time in her present position, nor did she really want to do so.

> I do work a lot of extra hours. I've always seen my position as more than a forty-hour-a-week expectation. And then if I didn't do work here, I'd be taking on professional activities that put me well over that period of time. So I would say that with either my professional reading that I may take home, or work I may take home, I would judge that I probably easily work sixty hours a week. And I don't feel put upon doing that. They

are things that I like to do. I'm not saying that [I like] every single task, but basically, there's very little in my job that I don't like doing.

In an orientation model of work and family, Heather's strategies of being a "working mother" would be labelled work oriented. Heather does not distance herself from the concept of career, nor does she emphasize her visibility as a mother. She and her husband have reduced their parenting hours by hiring others to care for their child, and Heather has relinquished some of the symbolic practices of motherhood. However, the orientation model is the wrong framework to use in understanding Heather's experience, just as it is the wrong framework for understanding the experience of the other women I interviewed. First, it categorizes women in a way that is not analytically useful, and second, it erases from view the intricate interconnection of work and family in Heather's life. As a mother, Heather expends a great deal of thought, energy, and resources on providing her child with the things that she thinks will contribute to her daughter's present and future happiness and well-being.[2] As Heather discovered when she returned to work after her daughter was born, "It wasn't that now I was a working person and I couldn't be a mother anymore. *There really was something in between.*"

JACKIE PATTON: THE CENTER CANNOT HOLD

Jackie Patton is a twenty-seven-year-old, Euro-American registered nurse. She had worked as a nurse for five years, had a four-year-old child, and was eight months pregnant with her second child when I interviewed her. Although the youngest of all the women I interviewed, she was among those with the heaviest burdens. Jackie is currently separated from her husband, the father of her two children. Jackie said he could not hold a job and that, even when they lived together, he had not contributed to their economic support. Jackie had been the sole support of the family since her first child was born, and she presents herself, in contrast to her husband, as a competent and responsible person. Much of Jackie's conversation with me was about how much her son meant to her and how she was trying to handle things as a single mother.

Jackie lives in a two-bedroom apartment in a suburb an hour's drive from the hospital. The apartment was filled with brightly colored children's toys, as was the patio, on which there was a wading pool, a sandbox, a rocking horse, and a little car. She told me that her goal was to own her own house, and like most of the mothers I interviewed, she said she would prefer to work part time. She consciously linked part-time work with having a relationship in which she would not be the sole support of her family.

> Now I would love more than anything not to have to work full time. I would love to be able to work part time because nursing is really satisfying to me. I really get a lot out of it. But I would love not to have to be full time and not to be one completely, sole[ly], dependent on myself like I've been, because it's been really hard. I wish I didn't have to do that. . . . I would [go part time] in a heartbeat.

Jackie wanted her work/family pattern to resemble that of the voluntary part-time nurses. She wanted for her own children what she felt she had had growing up: a secure home life, a house rather than an apartment, parents who remained married to each other, a dependable father who provided well for the family, a mother who wasn't employed full time, a rural environment in which to play and explore. At the moment, she was not managing to provide any of these things, and the discrepancy between what Jackie envisioned and what she has been able to accomplish was huge. Paradoxically, the actions Jackie takes to weave a pattern that is closer to her ideal actually take her further from it. For example, while Jackie did not have the luxury of a part-time schedule, she did manage to work only three days a week by working twelve-hour shifts, from 7:00 A.M. to 7:00 P.M. At Sierra Hospital, registered nurses who choose to work twelve-hour day shifts work three days a week on average, including every other weekend. This "solution," however created a child care nightmare, since she could not rely on her husband in this situation.

For mothers, twelve-hour shifts offer the advantages sought by part-time workers—they are home more full days during the week, and they can present themselves as mothers who are only employed three days a week. While night-shift workers move their employment hours from day to night, twelve-hour day-shift workers distribute their full-time employment hours over fewer days. Finding child care for such an extended period, however, is a major stumbling block. And the problem of being unavailable all day every other Saturday and Sunday is another reason that this schedule is not used by more mothers. It is not surprising that the mothers I interviewed who worked twelve-hour day shifts had children who were not yet in school, nor is it surprising that family support plays an important role in their ability to maintain this schedule.

In most situations, the thirteen to fourteen consecutive hours of child care required for children whose mothers work a twelve-hour shift necessitates that some of that care be provided by family members. Family members can care for the child for the entire time, or the child can be with a nonfamily child-care provider for some portion of the time the parent is away while the family member does the remainder. Jackie remarked,

> People don't want to watch kids for twelve hours. It's too long for them. It's too expensive. Early-in-the-morning drop-off was really hard to find around here because my shift starts at 7:00 A.M. And there's just not that much available. And I was surprised for [this] area because I thought [this] area would have a lot. But it really doesn't. I've been surprised at just how hard it's been to find a program that is flexible and affordable that I really like. Because I decided to go from family care to more like day care with more structure than in a home. I found something [nearby] and she's willing to take him at 6:30 A.M. But he has to be picked up at 3:30 in the afternoon. For a while there, while my husband and I were really in a bad phase, I worked out with one of her workers, I'd pay one of her workers seven dollars an hour to stay over until I got off work at 7:30. And I did that for like a couple of months. But that just really was kind of difficult. And then weekend care is impossible to find.

Twelve-hour shifts can work out, but like so many employment schedules, it takes a support network to make things run smoothly. For example, Gloria, a thirty-three-year-old Filipina registered nurse, works twelve-hour shifts, is married, and has a four-year-old daughter. She explained to me that, when she was at work, care for their child was provided by Gloria's husband, Gloria's mother-in-law, and a preschool program. For Jackie, twelve-hour shifts would work only if her husband took responsibility for child care. This had been their agreement, but Jackie's husband had not held up his end, and his lack of dependability eventually led to their separation.

> He was going to be the caretaker of [our son] while I went to work. And that was great because I could just get up, go to work and come back. But then I'd get home and [my son] hadn't had dinner and Dad was about to pull his hair out. "I've gotta get out of here. This kid's driving me crazy!" And of course [my son] was in his terrible twos. . . . now, he's four—he can talk to you—you can reason with him. . . . So it's a lot easier to take care of him now. So of course [now] his father is willing to take him on quite a bit, like he does now. But earlier, he was tough to take care of, but those are things you put up with as a parent. And my husband has very little patience. And I have a lot. So I'd get home and [my husband would] be ready to leave, so I'd have to put [my son] to bed and I'd be tired. So that was causing a lot of conflict between us. We were fighting like crazy. I was getting to where I wasn't real comfortable with [my husband caring for my son] because when [my husband would] stay up late, it would be real hard for him to wake up in the morning. I knew there were lots of mornings where [my son] would be up by himself playing. And [my husband's] parents, too, were disturbed by that. Because they would call and phones don't wake him up. Banging on windows and doors don't wake him up. He sleeps through anything. And so it was really just a lot of conflict between us. So finally he moved out. But now he's gotten better and now he wants [our son] fifty percent of the time. And he's responsible with him. He's gotten better. He stays with his Dad half the time and me half the time. So [my son] doesn't necessarily have to go to school on a day I work.

Another nurse I interviewed referred to Jackie and her problem with child care and linked it to Jackie's lack of support from her husband, her family, and her supervisors at the hospital:

> [She is] a younger woman with a three-year-old, working twelve hours, 7:00 A.M. to 7:00 P.M., getting a divorce, and pregnant. I looked at this poor girl and I thought, "What is this gal gonna do?" She's from the East, so she has no family [here], no support system, devastated, and then she didn't get support from the job. When she needed special days off or couldn't get a babysitter at the last minute, or say her babysitter arrangements fell through, she was stuck. And it didn't seem—the manager at that time didn't seem to have sympathy for her. [She] was someone who had never had any children and really couldn't sympathize. I mean I just felt so awful for this girl, and it never worked—it never worked.

Jackie's child-care and work problems were critical, and when I asked her what she would do about child care when the baby was born, her reply indicated that she felt overwhelmed by the problem.

> Oh gosh. I haven't even thought about that. Well, see, I don't trust my husband to take care of a newborn because I know with my son I was always the one who had to get up with him every two hours. And I did everything. I bathed him and diapered him because my husband would be like, "Oh it's so gross, it's going to make me pass out!" So with a new baby I'm going to just have to find twelve-hour home care, I think. And I'm going to go with the home care because it worked real well with [my son] and just I'm going to have maternity leave about six weeks and just look [for child care]. I did find a place . . . close to where I work. And there was a place there run by an Indian lady who is really soft-spoken and sweet, and she had mostly infants there. And she had only five or six but the place was real clean. And I was thinking, "Now this might be a place to bring a baby." And she's reasonable. But I didn't say anything to her about twelve-hour care. We'll have to work out something on the weekends. Maybe the baby can go and stay with Dad on the weekends, but not stay overnight like [my son] does. Because it's just at night that I'm concerned about his dad. So during the weekdays, I only work two days during the week and then every other weekend, so it would be two twelve-hour shifts during the week or something that I might have to do this.

I asked Jackie if she had thought about hiring someone to come to her home to do child care there, but lack of a second income combined with the drain her husband had put on the family's resources made this idea unrealistic.

> I would think that having a nanny come in would be real expensive. I mean, I've been living paycheck by paycheck.

The child care Jackie needed was either unreliable (her husband), unaffordable (a nanny or au pair), or unavailable ("people don't want to watch kids for twelve hours"). Jackie told me that at one point, when she had not had anyone to watch her son while she worked weekends, she called a friend who lived an hour's drive away.

> She said "Sure, bring him over." And I'd take him over there for a couple of the weekends I worked. But it's a really long drive. And I had to wake up at 3 A.M. It was just horrible.

Jackie was hoping that things would work out with her husband, that he would be a good father to his son and eventually to the new baby. It seemed to be her desire for the conventional image of family life that prevented Jackie from returning to her own parents for the support and environment she wanted for herself and her children. With no at-hand support from her husband or her parents, Jackie was trying to emulate both the strong, provider father and the nurturant, stay-at-home mother she had grown up with. The strain was taking its toll.

> And I'll just make it. I've been praying that my husband will keep changing for the better because I really need him, because it's been really hard having to deal with all his problems and all of his craziness and everything. [My parents have] been real supportive of me, but really not like they should have, because they have their ideas of what I should be doing and they really let them be known. "Oh, Jackie, you need to move back here and let us take care of you." And they've never liked [my husband]. . . . They've always, ever since I've been married, they've been pushing for me to get out of marriage with him. So when I called them and said "I've decided to get a divorce," they were real happy about that. But they haven't been supportive in the sense that if I decide to stay out here, they'd be really mad and upset with me because they want me to come back [to Maine]. And if I stayed out here, it would be just because I want my children to be around their father and I don't know if he would be willing to move back there, even for his kids.

At this point in the interview I was struck by the fact that Jackie seemed to be saying that she was willing to work a difficult schedule, live paycheck to paycheck, worry about how to find the child care she needed for the baby due in a month, and live in a part of the world she didn't particularly like, in order for her son to have frequent contact with his father. I asked Jackie, "Are you saying that if it weren't for the fact that the children's father was here, you probably would move?"

> Yeah, just because I prefer living in Maine. . . . I'm the most happy there because the way of living is a lot different than here. It's real competitive in [this] area and there's soooo many people here. I feel kind of out of place. I feel kind of uncomfortable. It's gotten better, but in Maine I went to school there and that's where I got my nursing degree from and it's just home for me. I'm real comfortable there and it's a really comfortable place to live. People are really friendly. . . . My father just loves my son, he just really loves him and my father would love to have him back there, so that's really hard for me too,

knowing that he's missing out spending time with my son. But [my son's] father is more important to him. So in a way I'm sacrificing to stay out here because [this] area is nice, but I really would prefer to live in Maine. But I'm staying here so my son can have a relationship with his father and then of course the new baby, too. Who knows where I'll be five years from now. But maybe when he's old enough, [my son] could like fly out here and stay summers here with his dad or something.

We have no way of knowing whether Jackie is really making a sacrifice for the sake of her child's relationship with his father or whether she has reasons for continuing to hope that things will work out, but in any case her actions lead her away from the life that she envisioned for herself and her children. If we view Jackie's life as a tapestry she is weaving, the work/family pattern in this tapestry is coming apart. Where will Jackie be in five years? Will her life resemble those of the single mothers I interviewed, who lived with or near their parents and raised their children with their help and support? Will she have divorced and remarried someone who holds up his share of responsibility for family life? Will her husband begin to support the family and care for his children? Or will she be in the same situation as she is in now?

I don't know what has happened to Jackie Patton in the years since I interviewed her, but five months after my interview with her, one of the clerical workers I interviewed mentioned Jackie to me:

> Like this one lady I know—I guess her and her husband are in the process of getting a divorce, and she'll be at work and he'll call and she'll have to tell [the nursing supervisor] that she has to leave. And she's gotten reprimanded for it.[3] And I felt really sorry for her. She has a daughter about three months old and son who is four, and he [her husband] makes it really difficult for her. . . . It really hurts my feelings to see . . . 'cause she's really really trying and she's a twelve-hour nurse and it's really hard to find someone to watch your kids for twelve hours a shift.

As staff nurses made clear to me, there is no flexibility once a nurse is on her shift at the hospital, which is why so many of them stressed the need for reliable, stable child care and for a responsible family member to handle emergencies that might arise while they were at work.

Jackie Patton's situation was not typical of the women I interviewed. I include her story because it illustrates one way that intended patterns can be undermined or destroyed. Husbands and fathers play a pivotal role in shaping work/family life. Reports of fathers, like Rachel's husband, who took on equal or greater responsibility for the day-to-day care of their children were rare, but fathers' contributions could make or break family arrangements. Sharon Baker, for example, faced the second shift with little help from her husband, but his income helps to cover the one-thousand-dollar-a-month child-care costs for her three children. And when her husband does pitch in, Sharon's quality of life improves.

> My husband, every time I say he's doing something wonderful, something happens. And I shouldn't say it but I just hope he keeps it up, but over the last week he's been picking the boys up . . . And last week I was going by the school and the babysitter to pick my sons up. They're gone! They are? Who picked them up? And now I'm just like, "Ohhh, he's gonna pick them up." And so this week you asked me at a good time. If you had asked me three weeks ago, I would have said "My husband's no good." [Laughs.] I do it all myself! Then he does pick up the boys the last two weeks.

For the most part, when fathers were present, their contributions helped rather than hindered, even though it is also true that in most cases fathers' contributions to the care of their children were far smaller than mothers' contributions. Child care by fathers enabled some mothers to work the night shift, and economic contributions by fathers enabled some mothers to work part time. However, in some cases, like Jackie Patton's, fathers actively sabotaged their wives' work/family arrangements.

I also included Jackie's story because it was a pattern in transition. It had to be, because it was clear that things could not continue as they were for long. But most patterns are in transition, on their way to becoming something else, changing as children grow and family needs change, as the economy becomes better or worse, as the unforeseen occurs, and as opportunities arise. Looking at one point in time can never tell us about types of people, because people are not fixed in time. It can, however, reveal the patterns that have been woven and the processes by which patterns change. In the next chapter, I focus on patterns over time.

7 Sequencing: Patterns over the Life Course

A SEQUENCE is "a following of one thing after another" or "a related or continuous series."[1] Thus the term "sequence" captures both images of time (duration, lifetimes, longitudinal perspective, life-course studies) and images of weaving (where patterns are formed from a series or sequence of threads). In music a sequence is a pattern, "a melodic or harmonic pattern successively repeated in different pitches."[2] The term "sequence" also captures the concepts of continuity and relationship—what comes before is related to what follows; results are con*sequences.* I use the term "sequencing" to refer to changing patterns over the life course.

In previous chapters, I presented a cross-sectional view of employed women with children, focusing on these women at the particular point in their lives when I interviewed them. In this chapter, I step back and take the longer view, focusing on how some of the women I interviewed changed work and family patterns over time and how others plan to change those patterns in the future. Flexibility and variation are central characteristics of the lives of employed women with children (Yeandle 1982). These patterns, however changing, are nonetheless part of a single tapestry.

There were different sequencing patterns in the life stories of the women I interviewed. Although I use examples from the women I interviewed to illustrate particular sequences, it should be understood that, over time, most women use several of these patterns, and they sometimes overlap.

CHANGING PATTERNS

In all of our lives, we have "before and after," "then and now," "more and less." Very few people weave the same pattern throughout their lives. The women I interviewed were all employed, and I interviewed them at only one point in their lives, so my view of their sequencing patterns is limited and must rely on retrospective accounts and statements about future plans. There were five basic types of pattern changes practiced by the women I interviewed:[3]

1. a change from being employed to being a nonemployed mother
2. a decrease in hours of employment after the birth of children
3. a change from being a nonemployed mother to being employed
4. an increase in hours of employment
5. a qualitative change in one's relationship to work, family, or the combination of the two; for example, a change in professional status, the birth of a first child, retirement, and so forth.

These five types of pattern changes can be combined in a variety of ways. A combination of pattern changes 1 and 3 is practiced by women who left the labor force after the birth of children and reentered it again at some point when their children were older. Pattern changes 2 and 4 are practiced by women who decreased or increased their hours of employment in relation to life-course developments. Pattern change 5 is often combined with other pattern changes, but is marked by a qualitative change in relation to employment or family. Women rarely practice or plan for only one of these changes. For example, a woman may practice the third type of change by entering the labor force after her children are in school and subsequently practice the fifth pattern change by returning to college. Or a woman may practice the second type of pattern change by reducing her hours of employment after the birth of a child and plan for the fourth and fifth types of changes, an increase in hours of employment and a change in professional status.

In this chapter, I describe how women use sequencing to support particular constructions of themselves as mothers and workers over the life course. My descriptions and analyses of women hospital workers are intended to serve as examples of the patterns that women can weave over time and of the threads or elements that go into those patterns.

Joyce Anderson

Joyce Anderson, a fifty-three-year-old, Euro-American registered nurse, grew up in the Midwest in a family and a community where, she told me, women's and men's roles were narrowly and strictly defined. Women did not go to college, they did not have careers, and they did not work in paid employment after their children were born. Joyce said that she "came from an area where women were barefoot and pregnant and walked three steps behind their husbands." Joyce was married when she was eighteen years old, her first baby was born two years later, and at two-, three-, and six-year intervals, she had three more children. When she was thirty-six years old, her husband's job necessitated a move to California, where she found "it was alright to be a woman and to have ideas." When her youngest child entered first grade, Joyce started college to earn her B.S.N. degree; she was thirty-eight years old and had spent twenty years as a nonemployed wife and mother. It took Joyce five years to earn her degree, and she began her first job as a nurse at the age of forty-three; at that time, she had two children in college, one in high school, and the youngest in sixth grade. She worked nights for over two years, sleeping during the day while her husband and children were away and spending the evenings with her family. At the age of forty-five, Joyce changed her work schedule to the evening shift and returned to school during the day to earn her master's degree in nursing. Two years later, at the age of forty-seven and with her master's in hand, she changed her work schedule to the day shift. When I interviewed her, Joyce was celebrating ten years as a nurse.

The broad outlines of Joyce's story fit a typical model of sequencing. Marrying in the mid-1950s, bearing and raising four children from the late 1950s through the 1970s, and returning to school or employment when the youngest child enters public school is a familiar pattern for women of Joyce's generation.[4] But Joyce's pattern is not simply the result of applying a well-used template. Historical moment, geographical location, and level of resources come together in specific ways to shape Joyce's life.

While growing up, Joyce had never received any encouragement or support for future plans other than marriage; her father often commented that college was a waste of time for women. Nevertheless, after high school, Joyce entered a hospital diploma program for nurses,[5] but her family's attitudes toward women's education were shared by the community.

> I was always interested in nursing. I was in a [nursing] diploma pro-
> gram before I was married, and at that time you could not be married
> and be in a diploma program, so I chose marriage.

Although Joyce talked in terms of choosing marriage, she clearly did not *choose* to leave the nursing program. Her choice to marry, occurring as it did in the Midwest in the 1950s, necessitated an involuntary change from nurse-in-training to full-time house-wife. Dropping out of college or training programs, abandoning careers or jobs, and deferring plans or dreams for long periods were common experiences for women of Joyce's generation (Dinnerstein 1992:63–64). Joyce stayed at home for twenty years.

In telling her life story, Joyce repeatedly emphasized the dif-ferences between the Midwest and California in terms of oppor-tunities for women, and she claimed that not much had changed in the small, rural, Midwest community she came from. Geo-graphical location and historical moment are particularly con-founded in Joyce's history, since her move to California—which undoubtedly held greater opportunities than the community from which she moved—occurred in the 1970s, a period of much greater opportunities for women in general.[6] Her return to college and the attainment of her B.S.N. degree were the result of both opportunity-taking and planning. Joyce recounted with feeling a pivotal episode that had occurred fifteen years earlier, after she had moved to California.

> A neighbor and I were talking about going back to school and she had
> a catalog—and it was a neighbor I rarely ever saw. I took her over to
> pick up a car that was being fixed. It was like a two mile drive, so it
> was a very short conversation. But in this ride, she's telling me about
> this friend of hers who was very young, had four little kids, and her
> husband dropped dead. And she said, "You know, this friend of mine
> can't *do* anything. She's not employable, she's got four little kids, and
> she's got the rest of her life ahead of her." She said, "You know, I'm
> not in any better shape." I said, "You know, I'm not either." And we
> got the catalog out and she said would I go with her if we took college
> for mature women. . . . I think that shook both of us—the fact that you
> can't just sit there.

A chance conversation with a neighbor led Joyce to think about resuming her education in terms of "hedging her bets." Changing social norms, which were manifested in such programs as the "college for mature women," provided the support for Joyce to formulate a plan. And residence in a state that had an accessible college system provided the opportunity to put her plan into action.[7]

> Moving to California, you cannot afford to avoid college, . . . junior colleges were free at that time. I remember paying a total sum of $68 a quarter at [a four-year state college], a wonderful sum of money to take all these gorgeous classes.

Joyce and her neighbor supported each other in their first tentative steps to return to college, taking courses together in the "college for mature women" program. Once Joyce decided to go to college, Joyce's husband supported her decision, but he didn't want her to do it halfway, and she didn't.

> He said, "[classes in the college for mature women program] is a waste of your time. If you go back to college, you take math and English, and that's not a waste of your time. Don't waste your time." So I got mad and took all three and went from there.

Just as she had devoted herself for twenty years to being a wife and mother, Joyce now threw herself wholeheartedly into obtaining her nursing degree.

This transition was facilitated, however, by the weaving together of a number of threads. Joyce's youngest child was just beginning first grade, so that by scheduling her courses during public school hours, child care was not an issue. At this stage in her family's life course, she was living in a state with an accessible and inexpensive college system, enabling her to enter college easily and to afford it once there. In addition, Joyce belonged to a generation of women who at midlife were entering a world that offered wider possibilities to women than had been available in the world in which they had grown up and married (Moen, Downey, and Bolger 1990). The intersection of biography and history within social structures (Mills 1959:143) stands out clearly in Joyce's sequencing pattern.

In addition, lack of family support and the needs of family members affected the patterns Joyce could weave. When Joyce and her husband lived in the Midwest, near their families of origin, Joyce didn't have the support to return to school or take a job, even if the opportunity had presented itself.

> My mother-in-law especially is very much "you should be home with
> your kids," and she certainly never helped anybody because "she was
> home for her kids and no one *ever helped her*" and why should she help
> anybody else.

Nor did Joyce's husband provide any help at home; theirs was a
strict division of labor in which Joyce had total responsibility for
the children. As a sales representative for a large national company, he provided well for the family, but Joyce explained that his
job involved a lot of traveling and, when the children were young,
he did not do anything around the house.

> He was gone a good bit of the time, out of town probably 50 percent of
> the time. He never did any of the cooking, cleaning, or basic kid care.
> He was never there when any of them were very small.

Nonfamilial child care was not an acceptable option for Joyce.
In addition to the messages she received growing up and the atti-
tude of her extended family that mothers should be at home with
their children, Joyce's youngest child exhibited a number of be-
havioral problems, and Joyce was afraid to leave him with a nonfamily member. Joyce recalled that

> my youngest was . . . *a real handful.* That was one of my major con-
> cerns was child care *for him.* Because I had had some friends who had
> had some real hassles with child care with a kid who was real easy, and
> I couldn't see anybody managing [my son]. I could see it even getting
> to be an abusive situation. And I felt that he really needed to be older.
> He *needed* the time.

Just as Lisa Harris and Jane Bradley had decreased their hours of
employment in response to signs of "acting out" by their children, Joyce Anderson felt that her son's behavior prevented her
from leaving her child in the care of anyone else. "He needed the
time," Joyce stresses, and by this Joyce means that her son needed
his mother's time. The work/family patterns that women weave
are not simply designs worked out in advance; they are patterns
that begin with an idea (of direction and content) and emerge in
response to and in interaction with others. Family members, especially children, are both part of the work/family pattern and
help to produce it.

Joyce did not postpone her own education or career as part of a
conscious, long-range plan. During the first twenty years of her

marriage, Joyce was making choices within the limits of the options she felt were available to her—options that limited her possibilities for weaving a pattern very different from the life patterns of other women of her class, racial-ethnic group, and
generation. But then Joyce found herself in a more supportive environment with more choices just when her youngest child entered public school and child care was no longer the issue it had
been. Schooling for children becomes mandatory at age six and is
culturally acceptable in a way that child care is not. Mothers are
not seen to be *choosing* to send their children to school; they are
required to do so. Part of being a "good mother" at this stage of a
child's life is ensuring that the child attends school. Whether
Joyce's son was "a handful" or not, Joyce was fulfilling her duties
as a mother by sending him to school.

> I was home. I took classes purposely. I had to be out [of school] by the
> time [my son] got home. . . . That way I could see him off to school,
> then I could go to my classes and be home. And that worked well dur-
> ing those first years. Boy, child care would have been a real hassle.

Indeed, by arranging her own schedule around the needs of her
children, Joyce continued to function as an "at-home mom" for
the next few years.

Joyce continued to use a sequence of patterns in which work
and family interacted. When her youngest child entered high
school and her older children had graduated, Joyce began graduate school and earned her master's degree in nursing. Now her
son has graduated from high school, there are no longer any children living at home, her husband has retired, and grandchildren
have been born. Joyce tells me that she and her husband have
had "a real role reversal" as her husband, who was seldom home
when their children were small, now does child care three or
four days a week for their two-year-old granddaughter. He began
doing this when the baby was three months old and their
daughter-in-law returned to work. Joyce's husband is also now
sharing some of the household work with Joyce and filling some
roles that would traditionally have been hers. Based on research
comparing housework division by younger and older couples,
Frances Goldscheider (1992) noted that some couples become
more egalitarian after their children are grown (7–8).[8] "So,"

Joyce concluded confidently, "the roles can be changed, and it makes everybody's life so much easier."

The theme of roles permeated Joyce's narrative: the rigid sex-role division with which she had grown up, the loosening of sex roles as part of the social change of the 1970s, the opportunities that enabled Joyce to expand her own roles within both the family and the labor force, and the greater sharing of previously sex-specific roles after children had left home and her husband had retired. We are a long way from gender equality in the workplace and in the home (Reskin and Padavic 1994), but Joyce's observation that "the roles can be changed" is both a fair summation of her narrative and a statement of hope for the future.

Theresa Lang

Theresa Lang, a forty-six-year-old, Euro-American registered nurse, is the nursing director of one of the hospital wards at Sierra Hospital, but her switch from staff nurse to administrator was not part of a conscious, long-term career plan. At the age of twenty-two, Theresa graduated from a hospital nursing program with a nursing diploma and got married. She worked full time as a nurse in a doctor's office until the birth of her son three years later and then, for the next ten years, she worked part time. When her son entered school, Theresa says, she "started getting antsy" and enrolled in college to attain her B.S.N. degree and freshen her nursing skills. By the time she was thirty-seven, Theresa had gone through a divorce and earned her B.S.N. and was working part time as a staff nurse at Sierra Hospital. She loved clinical nursing, enjoyed the freedom of her part-time schedule, and, as her son grew up, became more and more interested in the administrative aspects of nursing. When her son graduated from high school, Theresa returned to college for a master's degree in nursing and soon thereafter landed the job as nursing director, one of only twelve such positions at Sierra Hospital.

Control over time is a theme that runs through Theresa's pattern of sequencing. Theresa told me that she could afford to work part time when her son was small because her husband's income provided enough for them to live on, and his job benefits meant that she did not have to receive benefits through her job. Her divorce settlement was such that this continued to be the case even after she was no longer married, and she was thus able to continue to work part time while she earned her B.S.N.

> I've always worked interesting hours. I've pushed the system so that I've always worked three or four days a week, but generally unbene-fited, so that I had a lot of control over my life. . . . What's wonderful about being an on-call nurse . . . is that it gave me control to say what days I'm available; if they needed me I was called or I could preschedule certain days. I could definitely meet my son's needs, as a single mom now . . . I could meet his needs or I could work at the school or I could do whatever I needed to do. The pay was better, you know as long as you didn't need the benefits, the pay was better.[9] And I didn't get burned out, like a lot of nurses do, because of that control. The control felt wonderful. So when I was off, I was delighted. When I was working, I was delighted to work.

Theresa's reasons for working part time match those of the voluntary part-time nurses described earlier. But Theresa, now about fifteen years older than most of the voluntary part-time nurses I interviewed, was at a later stage in her life course, and her only child was grown and in college. Having only one child also reduced the span of Theresa's child-raising years. She could, for instance, work part time all during the years her son was living at home and return to full-time work much sooner than women who had two or more children and waited until their youngest child was grown to return to full-time work. From the vantage point of Theresa's life, we can observe both life-course changes in work/family patterns and life-course changes in what constitutes control over time. Theresa described her current position as "a very administrative job. I allocate resources, keep a budget, and try and make sure that [the nurses] have everything they need to do their job. I do a lot of personnel and interpersonal conflict management." Theresa has twenty-four-hour responsibility for her ward, and she explained what this means:

> If there's a shift they cannot staff, I would have to come in. It means that if there are questions that cannot be answered, that we don't have a policy set or whatever, that at any time there's something that affects this unit, that the bottom line is it comes back to me. So I can be called at any time of the day—or night. That doesn't happen often, but it happens. It also means that in a time of disaster, no matter what

time it is, that I would be here. And it means, what it truly means, is that whatever happens on any shift, I'm responsible for. . . . I have to know what's going on there because I'm responsible.

Theresa said she could not imagine having had this kind of position when her child was young. She credited the few mothers of young children who are in hospital administration with being better able to set limits on work than she was. Theresa reported working twelve-hour days during the week and taking about six hours of work home on the weekends, totaling about sixty-five hours of work a week. Based on my interviews with other nursing directors, Theresa's weekly hours on the job are not unusual. Once, when calling to schedule an interview with another nursing director, I asked the ward clerk who answered the phone to tell me when I would be most likely to reach the nursing director. She replied, "Well, she usually comes in about 6:00 A.M. and is here until six in the evening."

Yet the move from a part-time schedule to twenty-four-hour administrative responsibility and sixty-five-hour work weeks was not interpreted by Theresa as a loss of the control over her life that the part-time schedule provided. Theresa saw her new position as providing exactly the one kind of flexibility that staff nurses reported not having: flexibility over the work day.

> I have flexibility of hours. I put in a lot of hours, but I can take care of what I need to do. I can go to the gym; I come early on two mornings so I can see the night shift [and] I go to the gym three mornings a week, and I can come in between 8:30 and 9:00 if I don't have meetings. So that flexibility is delightful.

The control that nursing directors and other administrators had over their work time and space is illustrated by the fact that all the administrators I interviewed met with me in their private offices during their workday. The staff nurses, nurses' aides, clerical workers, and housekeepers I talked to did not have the privilege of incorporating activities that were not work related into their workdays or work environments, and I met with these women in their homes, in coffee shops, or in the hospital cafeteria. Theresa made it clear that this new kind of flexibility suits her needs well.

> It's a perfect time in my life. My child is older. . . . My mother was living with us for the last year and died in January . . . but before that, that

year, she was just so easy. She had not a lot of demands, and again the flexibility allowed me to take care of her needs and take her to the doctor and things like that.

Theresa described staff nurses as "captive" when they are working their shifts, and she felt she had traded the freedom of having more time away from the job for the freedom of controlling her time on the job. Her life course position and family needs make this a positive trade-off.

In reference to the difference between her life then and now, Theresa said that she might have "sold [her] family short" if she had worked full time or gone into administration before this, and added:

> I feel very good, very good about what I did for my son. I felt as committed then. I felt I had an opportunity to be a mom, and it would . . . only be very very short. And I was gambling again that I could do just what I'm doing now, which is sort of pull myself into something else at a proper time. So that's what's worked for me.

Women who use this pattern of sequencing shared a feeling that they were taking a chance in terms of their future employment options and career development, but they also shared a degree of confidence that this gamble would pay off. Many of the women I interviewed were in an early stage of this sequence, decreasing their hours of work while their children were young, but they already had ideas about returning to college to earn a master's degree in a nursing specialty when their children were older, as Theresa had done. The resources that enabled some women to reduce their employment to part time also enabled them to "retool" at a later point in the sequence.

Nursing, a traditionally female-dominated profession, has been organized in a manner that, more readily than many other occupations, allows its members to increase and decrease their participation and to develop higher levels of skills at varying points in both their nursing careers and their own life courses. The demand for nurses has certainly been an important factor, but this type of organization is not inherent to the work of nursing—traditionally male-dominated professions, such as law and engineering, could be similarly organized. Many of the women I interviewed talked about friends who worked "in business" who had to return to their jobs soon after the birth of children and to work full time or face losing both their jobs and their positions on the career ladder. Theresa recognized that nursing had allowed her a certain freedom.

> Nursing has been great for me. It waited for me when I needed to wait
> . . . I think that it's one of the things that nursing offers, is that it
> doesn't close you off at an age gap . . . I think part of this is not "nurs-
> ing"; I think part of this is the women's movement—is that your life
> is not over at forty, and I think I'm a real example of that.

Both Joyce and Theresa credit the women's movement with giving them more options and enabling them to create a wider variety of patterns. At a time when a mythical, monolithic women's movement is being blamed for creating many of the problems women face when combining employment and mothering (see, for example, Graglia 1998; Hewlett 1986; Cardozo 1986:6–14; Popenoe 1988), it is refreshing to be reminded by these women of the degree to which women's lives have been expanded by virtue of the social changes of the last twenty years.

Grace Johnson

Sequencing refers not only to pattern changes that involve decreasing or increasing one's labor force participation, but also to qualitative changes in one's relationship to the interconnection of work and family. For many women, like Joyce Anderson and Theresa Lang, qualitative changes occur in conjunction with changes in labor-force participation. For others, like Heather Macleod, qualitative changes accompany the incorporation of a child into lives that have up until then been work-centered, child-free, and couple-oriented.

Grace Johnson, a forty-five-year-old, African-American mother of three, is an example of someone who experienced a transformative pattern change. Grace is single and has always worked full time. For twenty-four years, she worked as a ward clerk while her daughters, now twenty-five, nineteen, and sixteen years of age, were growing up. Working full time was an economic necessity, but it prevented her from being with her children as much as she would have liked when they were young. When I asked her what the good things were about combining employment and mothering, she listed the things she was able to provide for her children: private (Catholic) school, vacations, and a role model of an independent woman.

When the service employees union began to hire from its rank-and-file membership, Grace, an active union member, was offered a staff position with the union. Grace was not sure at first that she wanted to make the change.

> I think when you've been in a job for twenty-four years, it's kind of hard to start all over again. Or *should* I start all over again? I was over forty, I was like forty-one, forty-two. And I said, "Do I really want to do this?" You know, this is really scary, making that change. But I figured that I wasn't gonna advance being a ward clerk, and this was something new and challenging to me.

Grace did make the change, and her new schedule was very different from the one she had when she worked as a ward clerk.

> I mean especially [as a ward clerk] when you're talking about a 7:00 [A.M.] to 3:30 [P.M. shift] because you *know* at 7:00 I'm at work and at 3:30 I got off. . . . But here, what I like about it is that, for the union you [are] your own, let's say, *person*. You visit your facilities whether it's day or night or 6:00 in the morning, and you know, you answer your calls, so there's really no time line. . . . our weekly [hours] are sometimes like fifty, you know, and some people do sixty, but [that's] for those who don't have a family. But it's like fifty hours a week . . . if there's a crisis, it's longer.

Grace went from punching a time clock and performing clerical duties at the nurses' station to a position more like that of Theresa Lang, in which she has an office of her own and flexibility over her time within a structure of long working hours. Grace asked me to interview her in her office during working hours, just as the nursing directors had done.

Grace's transformative pattern change came about through a combination of her experience as a steward within the union, a change in union hiring practices, and abilities that were recognized. It also occurred at a point in her life when Grace felt she could take advantage of and accommodate such a development. Although Grace had always worked full time, she made it clear that her current position would not have worked as well when her children were younger. Grace emphasized to me that her change of jobs is a change that meshed with her life-course position.

> I'm kind of glad that I took this job when I did, because there's a lot of long hours . . . or traveling a lot. So I'm glad my kids are at the age when I don't have to worry about a babysitter, and that they can take care of themselves.

In answer to my question "What were the hardest things about working full time and having young children," she replied:

> One of the things was . . . not really being there with my kids and doing things. I can remember when they were like, like toddlers, and when they finally realized that their mommy is going to work, and they start crying and [that] would *pull* at my heartstrings. And sometimes I was saying, "Darn, I need to be at home with my kids," and then I say, "Now how am I gonna survive?"

Grace then recalled a time when her children were in elementary school—the memory still saddened her:

> There was another moment I never forget—I was going to work one day and I was running kind of late and I told the kids they would have to catch the bus to school and that was, you know, my youngest ones. And they said, "Okay," and they were walking down the street, and tears came to my eyes because—*they don't give me no trouble,* you know. They don't say, "Mommy, how come you don't stay at home with me," or "Mom, why do you have to go to work today, how come you can't take us to school?" They were really humble and understanding, and [the reason] it kind of broke me up is because *my* parents was always, although both of them worked, but I had that mother and father bonding and I knew that, like, one was [always] home. But you come from a single parent, and you have to work and take care of your kids, and they don't ask questions [like] "Why you don't spend enough time with me," or [they are not] really rebellious. You know, I was grateful and like, you know, like, just really saddened, you know. And they are still, still great kids at nineteen and sixteen.

The memory evoked a sense of loss, because Grace felt that she had not provided them with their complete entitlement as children: a ride to school, the room to be rebellious, a parent at home even when both parents worked. She felt this way because she had an idea of what a family should be (two parents) and what a mother should do (spend "enough" time with her children), and her own life had not fully permitted either.

These regrets were connected to expectations about what mothers should be doing for young children, such as "being there." But Grace had raised her children, and she now felt entitled to put long hours into her job. She told me that her children can now take care of themselves when she is at work:

> I mean they cook for themselves, wash—you know. So it's not like, "Mom, what are we going to have for dinner?" It's like, "What did you guys leave me for dinner?"

Transformative pattern changes represent a qualitative change in one's relationship to work and family, and can occur in response to life-course developments, new opportunities, or changes in perspective.

MODES OF SEQUENCING

There are three different modes in which sequencing came about: planned, situational, and involuntary. Modes of sequencing may overlap, and most of the women I interviewed used all of these approaches at different times and to varying degrees. Making plans, responding to opportunities, and being forced to change course are not only ways of charting action, but are also vocabularies of motive that the women I interviewed invoked in their strategies of being.

Planned Sequencing

Women who planned their sequenced changes had mapped their routes and identified the signposts—they intended to quit their jobs or decrease their hours after children were born, or to increase their hours or switch jobs after their children reached a particular age. Their plans might be quite specific or fairly vague, but they knew that in the future they would alter the pattern of their work/family lives.

Jane Bradley is an example of someone who planned her sequencing.* After working full time for a number of years, Jane cut back to part time after her second child was born. At the time I

---

*Jane Bradley was introduced in Chapter 3; she is a voluntary part-time nurse who is married and has two young children.

interviewed her, she was working at the hospital about two days a week and was in the early stages of a planned sequencing pattern:

> I *know* I'm not going to stay home always [laughs]. And I am also thinking about going on in school, so I have ideas of what I want to do, kind of after my kids are a little bit out of the nest. I also feel strongly that I don't want to work full time even when they're in high school, because I feel that's an important time to be around, too.

Jane thus indicates a plan to continue in part-time employment for at least the next sixteen years, although she intends to increase her hours of employment from their present level once her children are a little older. Later in the interview, Jane mentioned that she actually had another plan she intends to implement when her daughter enters kindergarten in two years.

> I think I'm going to go to law school, but my plan is . . . to go part time. What I've been doing is talking with a lot of my friends (ladies, particularly) that are attorneys to get an idea. . . . Women that I've talked to who are attorneys have said it's hard to work part time. But it really kind of depends. I would like to do mostly either medical malpractice consulting or child advocacy.

"I think I'm going to law school" may sound tentative, but it was actually an expression of clarity about the pattern she had in mind. She wanted to go to law school part time, and she had thoroughly investigated which law schools in the area offered part-time programs. She had identified areas of law that were both of interest to her and, theoretically, conducive to part-time employment, and she was currently investigating the likelihood of finding a part-time job as an attorney. Jane was actively gathering information, preparing, and planning for the changes ahead.

Situational Sequencing

Situational sequencing is not the product of long-range planning, and situational changes are usually motivated by opportunities that present themselves in the course of events. Those who use situational sequencing see themselves as doing what they're doing for now, but they do not give specific thought to future changes. In looking back, they may see the changes they made as opportunities that were presented and taken. Grace Johnson is a good example of someone whose pattern change was the result of situational sequencing. She did not plan to change jobs, and she had not intentionally done anything to prepare for a job as a union employee, but when the opportunity presented itself, she took advantage of what the change could offer her.

Lynda, a forty-four-year-old ward secretary who is married and has three children, expressed the most extreme version of situational sequencing. Unlike most of the women I interviewed, Lynda did not even try to represent her life in terms of plans or decisions. Telling me about how she spent her weekends, she said:

> What I like to do is, like on my day off, I'll get in the car and I'll say, "Ok, I'm going somewhere." And if you say, "Where are you going?" I'll say, "I don't know where I'm going." And I'll get on a highway and if I see an exit with a name for a little town or a street that looks interesting, I'll get off and go find out what's going on. So I find a lot of places that way.

Lynda told me that she lives her life in much the same way. She had moved frequently and changed jobs often, and she told me that she does not really have "ambitions." Her life story is full of change, contingency, funny stories, and tragedies, but when I asked her if she would have done anything differently, Lynda replied:

> I probably would go the same route. I probably wouldn't even make any changes. . . . I think that I've basically done what I wanted to do—whatever it is. . . . And I'm satisfied with it the way it is. I'm satisfied with me the way I am. I'm satisfied with my life. . . . I feel like I've been really strong in my life, because I've gone through things that I've never dreamt that I could. I've survived. . . . I've always survived whatever came up in my life and I feel like I probably wouldn't change it. I don't think I would change anything.

In the United States in the twentieth century, where the dominant discourse is primarily one of planning, aims, goals, and progress, Lynda nonetheless presented her life in terms of situational changes that she felt had worked for her. She explained it this way:

> I do what I feel like doing at the moment and I try to make the best choices, you know. . . . you can be on top of the world today and unemployed tomorrow [laughs]. I mean if you identify so much with your

job, you fall apart. If it doesn't work out, you fall apart. I think you have to be open, flexible, to anything. Even your family, you know. . . . In case anything happens. People die, people leave, people grow up. They leave home.

While any one change in her life might be involuntary, Lynda presented the overall design as situational. Her situational approach was both a strategy for survival and a protection against pain and disappointment.[10]

Most people use situational sequencing at some point in their lives, often as a way of taking advantage of opportunities that present themselves. Most of the women I interviewed, however, presented themselves as planners who sometimes make unplanned changes in response to new opportunities and who sometimes have to make changes involuntarily.

Involuntary Sequencing

Those who are forced by external changes to alter the pattern of their lives experience what I call involuntary sequencing. External changes include such events as job loss, unwanted divorce, unplanned pregnancy, illness, husband's loss of job, or financial setback. Although involuntary changes may result in positive outcomes, there is no choice about whether to change or not, as there is in situational sequencing.

Lillian Santana, a forty-two-year-old, Mexican-American registered nurse, had been forced to deal with involuntary changes in her life.* Married at the age of twenty-one, Lillian was employed in clerical jobs while she and her husband postponed children and saved to buy a house. After five years, their first child was born, Lillian quit her job, and they bought a home. Lillian said that both she and her husband planned that she would stay at home with the children. The first crack in their original plan came when, after ten years of marriage, Lillian and her husband separated. Out of the labor force for five years and with two children under the age of six, Lillian, then thirty-one, was struck by a major feature of their joint plan: it was based on the permanence of her marriage. Just as Joyce Anderson's return to school was

---

*Lillian Santana was one of the part-time nurses introduced in Chapter 3.

fueled by the recognition that her marriage might end in widow-hood, the possibility of divorce altered Lillian's perception about her own position. Lillian and her husband were reunited two months later, but Lillian began to make a new plan. Thinking back on that period of her life, she told me:

> I realized then—I had to go on food stamps—that I never wanted . . . I *never* wanted to go through that again. And so I was determined to go to school. . . . it was a challenge, but I was able to do it, and thank God I did.

She entered the local community college and started taking courses toward a degree in nursing. It took her almost six years to complete a three-year program; by the time she was thirty-six, she was working as a part-time, on-call nurse at the hospital. When she was forty-one, her husband left her again. For Lillian, it was an involuntary change.

> I didn't want the divorce; after twenty years it was just sprung on me, when [his] midlife crisis hits—something I didn't want. But now I have to make myself independent . . . and for me that means not only emo-tionally but financially. . . . It [has] been a very hard haul both ways.

The need for financial independence meant that Lillian in-creased her days of employment from one or two days a week to four days a week. When I interviewed Lillian, her final divorce decree was imminent and, with it, the loss of health-care benefits derived from her husband's job. Lillian told me that she knew she would have to move from her on-call position, in which she was required to work only one weekend a month, to a full-time posi-tion, in which she would be required to work more hours, in-cluding two weekends a month—and she resented this change.

> The part I resent most about it [voice rises] is having to [work] the every other weekend, 'cause we still give the kids every other week-end with each parent. And so [now] the [weekend] I work is when I don't have them, and then I'm free when they're here, and then I'll have one weekend that's just mine. And [when I change to full time] I'll be giving my weekends up because I'm not about to work when my kids are home. So, I resent that.

Lillian's part-time position had enabled her to hedge her bets in case she faced a future as a single mother by maintaining skills and employment, and it enabled her to be at home with her children; it gave her the flexibility that many mothers desire. Divorce changed all this. As resources diminished (husband's income and employment benefits), Lillian had to choose another pattern in which to weave her work/family design. *Being there* with and for her children was still a major priority: "I'm not about to work when my kids are home." Lillian worked a day shift, lived near the hospital, and was usually home soon after her children, now adolescents, returned from school. The norm of motherhood to which she aspired had not changed, but her ability to implement it had. For now, Lillian solves the problem by giving up the time that is reserved for neither employment or family, the time that is just for her.

Involuntary changes can often turn out to be opportunities. For Lillian, a forced change provided the opportunity to think about herself as an independent person.

> [I] went from home to marriage and I'm forty-two now. I'm just trying to develop my own life, you know, [as well as] finding out who I am. I don't even know what I *like*, honestly. And it's such a shame, you know, that it took *this* [the divorce] to bring me to *that*.

Despite the fact that the divorce has enabled Lillian to see her marriage and her role in it from a different angle, she said she would not have altered her work/family pattern if she had it to do over again. It is still her construction of motherhood, intertwined with her construction of work and structured around available resources, that motivates her work/family pattern. Lillian admitted,

> In retrospect, probably [long pause] I think I would have [long pause] worked like I'm doing, like I was doing prior to the divorce, maybe a couple days a week. I think that's a very healthy balancing thing.

But Lillian was troubled by the implications of her earlier model; it had worked well for her construction of motherhood, but it was based on a model of marriage that did not, in the end, fulfill its promise. Lillian recalled the past with a new sense of inequity.

> [My husband] skyrocketed in his job. His job just moved so fast, but a lot of it came with my staying home with the kids and his traveling and entertaining and that kind of stuff. And my job was kind of on the

back burner, and so . . . in those days, when I went to make out a [work] schedule . . . I always came home and went over my schedule with him, so that [my work] days didn't interfere with either his trips or the family. . . . We always went over it. And looking at it now, I think [makes a face]—"Phew."

But she also remembered what made this arrangement make sense at the time.

I was going to retire with this man into—we were going to be in rocking chairs—into the sunset. And the children, we were going to get them off, and I figured when the kids got off to [college], I would probably work a little more or maybe take on, I don't know, working in the library with the literacy program or something like that. . . . I never thought that I would be primary breadwinner.

Lillian told me that the arrangement she and her husband had had is similar to that of many part-time, on-call nurses and that "it makes sense, but it doesn't." Now, when she hears a nurse respond to a scheduling request by saying, "I have to go home and check with my husband," she says she hears herself and thinks,

"I remember that," but it's like not me anymore. And then I think, *It makes sense, but it doesn't.* And I don't know how to put it other than: she may be married for the rest of her life, but to me, it's like, it makes sense but it doesn't [laughs]. And I don't know how to put that.

Life doesn't hold out assurances. Just as Theresa Lang "gambled" that she "would pull [herself] into something else at a proper time," Lillian gambled that her marriage would last. She might never have questioned the sense of her plan if it had, but from her new vantage point she tried to articulate the contradiction of an arrangement that benefits the man regardless of marital status and the woman only as long as she stays married (Arendell 1986; Kurz 1995).

The timing of involuntary changes can make the difference between whether such changes are devastating or opportunity-producing. Ten years earlier, when they were first separated, Lillian's educational and occupational resources were much more limited, and the age of her children circumscribed her choices even further. At midlife, having acquired professional skills and employment status and with two children in high school, Lillian was much better prepared to shape new patterns after involuntarily giving up the old one.

The Midlife Switch

For mothers, sequencing is often timed in relation to the age of children, particularly the age of the youngest child. The points at which the youngest child enters elementary school, junior high, or high school are more influential transitions for women's midlife labor-force reentry than is the point at which all children are grown and have left home (Moen, Downey, and Bolger 1990:238). My interviews revealed that work/family pattern changes are timed in conjunction with children's age transitions not only because these transitions correspond to the greater independence of children and to the child care or supervision that being in school provides, but also because of the cultural idea that, *as mothers*, there is a point at which the task is to "let go" of children, to allow children to separate from their mothers. For Joyce Anderson, kindergarten not only provided child care for Joyce's son and child-free time for Joyce, but it also represented a cultural switch in which the work of mothering became sending her son to school rather than keeping him home.

"Being there for your children," a fundamental premise of good mothering for the women I studied, is a delicate balance, and its content changes over time. Even Jane Bradley, who had severely reduced her hours in order to "be there" when her children were young, felt that it was possible to be overinvolved in one's children:

> I think you can also be obsessed. My husband has a colleague whose wife . . . [has] become totally obsessed with her children and her children's education. He jokingly said something . . . like, "She's gonna have to get a job," and [she said,] "My job is seeing that the children do well at school" [laughs] or something like that. And it's like, she considers that her job. Well, I think parenting is a job, but I mean she's almost to the [trails off]. . . . Every project she goes to the library with them to assist, every single—it's that kind of involvement where you worry about what the child's gaining out of doing their science competition or anything they do.

Jane said her own plans are to increase her hours of work after her children "are a little bit out of the nest." The image is telling; it is the children who are moving on and entering the world, and it is *their* transition that enables Jane to change her work/family pattern in relation to their needs as well as her own.

Lisa Harris* worked full time and took a position as charge nurse before the birth of her children. Difficulties in becoming pregnant led Lisa to resign from her more administrative nursing position in the hopes that less job stress would increase her chances of conceiving. After her first child was born, she went from full time employment to a two-fifths, part-time nursing position. Lisa is a planner who would like to return to an administrative position when her children are older, and she explicitly links her future work plans not only to the age of her children, but also to their relative independence.

> I'd like to get into administration later, if . . . if I had a lot more time. Managers, I mean-whew, they work long long hours. . . . you have to really really be dedicated to it and put a lot of time into it for it to run right. So my kids will have to be really very busy doing other things, and not need me.

If her children are "busy," then Lisa would be performing both her work as a mother and her work as an administrative nurse by being more involved in her job when her children are more involved in their own extrafamilial lives.

In *Habits of the Heart*, the authors write that "in a culture that emphasizes the autonomy and self-reliance of the individual, the primary problems of childhood are what some psychoanalysts call separation and individuation—indeed, childhood is chiefly preparation for the all-important event of leaving home" (Bellah et al. 1985:56–57). If our culture has defined achieving autonomy as one of the central tasks of childhood, then the work of mothering includes fostering self-reliance by "letting go" of children at developmentally appropriate, age-appropriate, and socially appropriate times.

Lillian Santana's children were both teenagers. When I asked her if increasing her work hours after her divorce was causing any difficulties with meeting her children's needs, she told me that she would not feel guilty about calling in sick if something came up that was important to her children, but that, for the most part, it had not been a problem. She expressed a mix of

---

*Lisa Harris is one of the voluntary part-time nurses discussed in Chapter 3.

feelings, however, when she recounted a recent occasion when her sixteen-year-old daughter, a high school junior, had punctured her hand on a nail, and Lillian had not left work to take her to the doctor.

> Like my daughter went to the doctor the other day, she . . . had to get a tetanus shot and she went on her own—she's a teenager, granted, she took the bus and got there and I know the doctor—it's part of just letting go maybe.

The inflexibility of the work day once a nurse is at work makes it difficult for Lillian to leave in the middle of a shift, but if her daughter had been younger, Lillian would no doubt have called it an emergency and left. Lillian felt conflicted about letting her daughter go to the doctor on her own, and we don't know how her daughter felt about going to the doctor alone, but Lillian was able to construct the incident as one in which she is fulfilling the task of being a good mother by allowing her daughter independence at an age-appropriate time and in an appropriate way. Lillian stresses that her daughter is old enough ("she's a teenager"), that this arrangement had worked ("she took the bus and got there"), and that she was in touch with the situation ("I know the doctor"). Having emphasized that she was not abandoning the work mothers do, she talked about her daughter's solo trip to the doctor in terms that continued to describe her work as a mother—in this case, the work of letting go.

Transitions are not always discrete points with clearly defined before and after segments. Sometimes there are distinct borders between patterns, but often patterns merge into each other and there are no single boundaries. Letting go is a process, but part of children's ability to individuate rests on their ability to see their mothers as separate people (Chodorow 1978:83–84, 135–40). In a study of part-time workers, one woman reported that "her daughter sees her as 'more open, more fun to be with, and more understanding' since she took her part-time position" as a teaching assistant (Duffy and Pupo 1992:119). Part of the work of mothering can therefore be seen as both allowing children to individuate and fostering a presentation of self in which the mother is also an individual, with outside interests, responsibilities, and demands.

Taking Opportunities, Gambling, or Drifting?

Most people practice a combination of approaches to sequencing. However, whether they have a specific plan for a new pattern or are forced to alter the pattern of their work/family lives, it is op-portunity-taking that is the hallmark of sequencing in the lives of the women I interviewed. Looked at in a less positive light, it has been said that "traditional gender socialization has meant that most women . . . have been brought up to 'drift'; that is, 'to allow extraneous events and significant others to make major life deci-sions for them and not to plan their lives'" (Duffy and Pupo 1992:136). This way of describing women's actions valorizes a par-ticular concept of planning and diminishes the extent to which women are actively making major life decisions within a context of extraneous events and in relation to significant others. Al-though both women and men make major life decisions based on external events, and one might argue that this is the human con-dition, there are gender differences in terms of whose external events have precedence. A typical example is geographical reloca-tion based on the husband's job, which is often not a choice or a plan on the part of the husband any more than it is for the wife. Relocation, however, is often part of a career move, and it is con-ventionally assumed that women will quit their own jobs to move with their husbands, but not that men will do so for their wives.

The concept of a single trajectory, mapped out in advance and from which few deviations are made, is foreign to most of the women I interviewed. Nor does the "career model," in which oc-cupational status is central and all-consuming, resonate with most of them. The women I interviewed are weaving patterns in which employment and mothering are not two independent lines but are overlapping, interwoven, and entangled.

By looking at sequencing over the life course rather than ob-serving only a piece of the pattern at one point in time, we take a more holistic view of the pattern of work/family designs.[11] The patterns of the women I interviewed are not based on the de-tailed blueprints common to male-oriented career trajectories. Women gambled that occupational advancement could wait or that marriages would last, and they often hedged their bets on both possibilities by working part time or earning professional degrees or skills while their children were young. They were aware that the social changes of the last twenty years had provided a greater range of possibilities for women, and they took advantage of those opportunities. In order to shape and respond to the interconnection of their work and family lives, they wove life patterns that were flexible and varied. And, through all of this, they were implementing strategies of being by which they constructed identities as workers and as mothers.

8 Conclusion

JUST BEFORE Memorial Day, I stopped by the printing shop to pick up some copies I had ordered. The person behind the counter was an African-American woman in her mid-twenties— I'll call her Carrie. As Carrie helped me with my order, she asked what I was doing for the three-day weekend ahead, and I asked about her own plans for the holiday. She then proceeded to tell me what she had done last year, which was to join with her whole family to celebrate her grandmother's birthday. Her story continued: her grandmother had had triple bypass surgery, diabetes, and a leg amputated and was now living with Carrie's mother, who had quit her job as a nurse to care for her. Carrie said that her mother asked her, "Would you do that for me?" and then Carrie looked at me and said: "You know, I don't know—quitting your job and all. My brother, he says I would, but I don't know." We chatted some more, and Carrie told me that she has a five-year-old child and a ten-month-old baby, that her mother has started back to work part time as a visiting nurse in the evenings, that Carrie goes over to stay with her grandmother several nights a week while her mother is at work, that her mother could not have left full-time employment to care for Carrie's grandmother if it had not been for the financial support of Carrie's father, and that Carrie's mother and father have been divorced for years but remain good friends. Our conversation would have continued, but I had to leave for an appointment.

Carrie's story raises a great many issues of interest to sociologists and could be analyzed in terms of intergenerational care, obligations to kin, family responsibilities, dependence and independence, work identity, gender, class, and generation. No one of these concepts on its own would take us very far in understanding Carrie's life. They are not independent categories—they are overlapping, connected, interwoven. My conversation with Carrie was short, and it was not an interview. If I had been interviewing Carrie, I would have asked her questions that aimed to get at the meaning she gives to this web of interconnections. But even in this short narrative, it is obvious that Carrie doesn't separate her life into disconnected pieces—it would not make sense to her to do so. She presents the elements of her life as interconnected because she thinks about and experiences them that way.

I have suggested that we think of this interconnectedness through the metaphor of weaving, and I argue that the metaphor of "weaving" better represents the actions and intentions of employed women with children than the current dominant model of individual orientation that pervades discussions of work and family for women. The conceptual framework of weaving allows us to step back and view the whole, to think of the fabric of a life, the strength of the weave, and the intricacy of design. It reminds us not to get lost in the close examination of one moment or one strand, and to remember that moments and strands are parts of the weave but not the weave itself. Work, family, friendships, reflection, vocation, and recreation are parts of a person's life. They are not, separately and on their own, the life or the person.

NOT A ZERO-SUM GAME

In this book, I have argued that the orientation model of work and family that underlies much of the discussion and thinking about working mothers misrepresents the intersection of employment and motherhood in the lives of women. Motherhood and employment are not incompatible activities in a zero-sum game. And "mothers" and "paid workers" are not opposed categories. The way that we conceptualize the relationship of employment and motherhood is important because the way that we think about an issue shapes what we do about it—or what we think we should do about it. Sociologists stress the importance of understanding the individual's or the group's "definition of the situation," because those definitions—those answers to the question "What's going on here?"—have concrete implications (Thomas 1928).[1]

There are consequences to defining the situation of employment and motherhood for women in terms of opposition and orientation—and these consequences are not good for women, men, children, and families. By describing as "family oriented" women who are employed on the night shift or who are employed less than forty hours a week (or who put in less than the sixty or seventy hours a week expected in some professions), the orientation model reinforces standard myths about women's marginal relationship to employment—myths that are belied by women's work histories and their expressed feelings about the place of employment in their lives. Defining women's relationship to employment as marginal has had negative consequences for wages, benefits, job security, and national employment and child-care policies (Reskin and Padavic 1994).

By describing as "work oriented" mothers who are in male-dominated professions, mothers who are employed forty hours or more per week, mothers who travel as part of their jobs, or even mothers who admit to liking their jobs, the orientation model reproduces cultural ideas that mothers who care about their families do not work full time, or like their jobs, or want to be employed. The expectation that mothers should immerse themselves, to the exclusion of other activities, in the care and nurturance of their children has consequences. For mothers who are employed, the results are often exhaustion from trying to do everything and guilt from feeling they are never doing enough. For nonemployed mothers, the results include economic vulnerability and feelings of resentment toward "working mothers."[2] For fathers, the assumption that children are primarily the responsibility of mothers often results in assumptions that support their nonparticipation in their children's lives.[3] And for children, the result is the lack of societal responsibility for their care and the associated child-unfriendly environment (Folbre 1994; Lopata 1993:185).

Not only does the categorization of these mothers as work oriented reinforce certain cultural constructions of motherhood, it also reproduces cultural understandings of career or commitment to one's job as all-encompassing. This definition of work has consequences for men's and women's relationship to employment and for the organization of the workplace. If work commitment is understood as inherently conflicting with family responsibilities, then men, as breadwinner-fathers, will not be socially expected to share in family work as fathers, sons, and brothers. And women, as mothers, daughters, and sisters, will not be treated seriously in the workplace. Furthermore, employers can use this definition and standard of commitment to rationalize ever-increasing work loads, speed-ups, and demands on workers. If a commitment to job or career is conceptualized as being in conflict with participation in family life, then there is little reason to expect changes in the workplace that will accommodate *both* work *and* family needs.

INDIVIDUAL SOLUTIONS

> The good we secure for ourselves is precarious and uncertain . . . until it is secured for all of us, and incorporated into our common life.
> —Jane Addams

Each of the women I interviewed negotiated her own way through the structural complexities of combining employment and motherhood. Finding child care, arranging schedules, achieving job flexibility, and earning an income were connected to both resource constellations and to strategies of being. There is great diversity in the work patterns of women with children—a diversity created out of many individual solutions to a dilemma held in common. But individual solutions do not solve social problems.

Without a broader vision and a social program, individual solutions keep us rooted where we are, rather than advancing us toward any significant change. Part-time work and shift work, for example, are used by some women as ways of both participating in the labor force and having enough time or flexibility to do particular kinds of things with and for their families. As long as part-time employees are treated as marginal workers, however, women who work part time will be disadvantaged in the workplace in terms of their current and future earnings, medical benefits, Social Security, and retirement. In addition, both part-time and non-day shift workers are perceived by employers and many coworkers to be less committed to their jobs and are often treated as if invisible in terms of promotions, office politics, and workplace involvement. This brings disadvantages to men as well as women. As long as fatherhood is socially understood to be equated with breadwinning, and as long as breadwinning remains a cultural sign of masculinity, men's attempts to gain workplace flexibility in order to participate more fully in daily family life will not receive support or will be actively undermined.[4] Furthermore, to the extent that it is women rather than men who reduce their hours from the arbitrary but socially defined forty-hour week, so-called "traditional patterns" of men's and women's gendered relationships to work and family are supported and further entrenched.

Individual solutions may even rest on and perpetuate the problems of others. Many middle-class parents, for example, are able to afford private child care because child care workers are paid so little. Many middle-class parents employ poor, often immigrant women whose job options are limited (Hertz 1986; Macdonald 1998b; Rothman 1989b). While this could be viewed as a mutually beneficial arrangement, these child-care workers, in addition to earning very little, rarely get benefits such as Social Security, disability and unemployment insurance, health coverage, sick leave, or paid vacations, and they are excluded from most government policies covering workers, such as the Family and Medical Leave Act. Many, if not most, of these child-care workers have children of their own to care for and, given the income from their jobs, clearly do not earn enough to avail themselves of many of the individual solutions that are used by the middle class.

But in the absence of social solutions that address both the needs of families and the structure of work, employed women with children are left to find individual solutions.[5] For sociologists, however, analyzing individual solutions can tell us something about what kinds of social solutions are needed. Understanding the kinds of individual solutions that are implemented can tell us something about what people value and about the toll they are willing to pay to preserve what they hold dear.

In their strategies of being workers and mothers, what are employed women with children willing to sacrifice? What do they maintain in spite of difficulties? What kind of patterns are they attempting to weave?

Night-shift workers, for example, sacrifice sleep (and therefore often sacrifice health and feelings of "normalcy") in order to be at home during the day and available to their children after school. Voluntary part-time workers sacrifice advancement opportunities and future earnings for some flexibility in their schedules, gambling their own and their children's economic futures on the continuation of their marriages. Involuntary on-call workers sacrifice family routine and endure economic insecurity in the hope of being able to adequately support their children. Nursing directors sacrifice work-free time, but gain more control over the organization of their time and the use of their work space. Full-time, day-shift workers sacrifice leisure time, rest, and sometimes the feeling of "sanity" in order to do everything and be everywhere at once.

What many of these individual solutions reveal is that a large group of employed women with children are not looking for ways to mother less but *are* looking for work structures that will enable them to be employed while continuing to do much of the work of mothering. My interviews with women hospital workers indicate that employed women with children value *both* their identities as mothers *and* their identities as workers. Being a mother did not mean exclusive and total immersion in the care and nurturance of their children—fathers, other family members, and nonfamilial child care workers were involved, to varying degrees, in the day-to-day care of children.[6] Being a worker, however, did not mean that, as mothers, they simply divided up or delegated the care of children. The women I interviewed all retained for themselves some aspects of the care and nurturance that they experienced as part of being a mother, and they often went to great lengths to preserve them.

The finding that many mothers want to be able to do certain things *as mothers* does not mean that these women are not also committed *as workers*. The women I interviewed want solutions that enable them, as workers, to participate fully in the world of paid work, and, *as mothers*, to perform a self-defined portion of the culturally defined work of mothering. Most commonly, women expressed the desire to have adequate time to be with a new baby, to be with a child when he or she is ill, to have family times with their children on a regular basis, to be accessible to their children, and to attend children's school and extracurricular events. The importance of these various aspects of the work of mothering varies between mothers. One mother may feel that a three-month maternity leave from work is adequate, while another may need a one-year leave. Which childhood illnesses a mother considers to require her attendance, as opposed to that of another family member or child care provider, will vary from one mother to the next. The working definitions of stability, regularity, and routine will differ among mothers, but the differences are variations on a shared theme.

Workplace policies such as parental leave, sick leave policies that cover the illnesses of children, flex-time, part-time work with benefits, job shares, and increased vacation time would address many of these needs. But we need to think about these policies not simply as ways to deal with emergencies such as serious illness or as concessions to so-called family-oriented mothers. In order to address the stated needs of employed women with children, the work of motherhood cannot be conceptually subsumed under the category of child care. In such a conceptualization, the care of children by someone other than the mother becomes the solution and corollary to mothers' participation in the labor force. The availability of stable, quality child care is an absolute necessity, but it does not address a crucial area of concern to the mothers I interviewed: having the flexibility and the time to perform certain components of the work of mothering themselves. Public and workplace policies should be based on concepts of motherhood, fatherhood, and parenthood that include the *relationships* of mothers and fathers to their children, rather than ones that reduce motherhood or fatherhood to the delegatable tasks of caring for children.

REFOCUSING ATTENTION AT THE SOCIAL LEVEL

An article in *Working Mother* on "tips for getting the family up and out of the house" suggests that the working mother "consider the possibility that life might be easier if everyone eats in the car. A box of juice and a whole-wheat bagel are relatively mess-free in the hands of school-age children" (Marzollo 1991:48). This and the other suggestions in the article are all individual solutions that focus on how mothers and children can speed up, streamline, or eliminate morning activities in order to get everyone out of the house to meet external schedules, which are left unquestioned.

Individual solutions not only leave larger social problems unaddressed, but they may also impede progress toward solutions at the social level. The way in which a problem is formulated is sometimes part of the problem itself, and that is particularly true when social problems are formulated in terms of individual solutions. The question "What do we want for this society's children?" becomes reduced to an issue of affordable child care. The question "What employment schedules best meet the combined needs of business productivity, the social good, and the individual?" gets presented as, "How does one balance the ever-increasing demands of the workplace with the unquestioned requirements of motherhood?" The need for individual families to deal with the immediate problems facing them directs attention away from crucial collective issues relating to the kind of society we want to have, the kind of people we want to be, the kind of families we want to form, and the kind of work we want to encourage.

A Chinese proverb warns, "If we do not change our direction, we are likely to end up where we are headed." Many other countries have chosen a different direction, and those countries provide far more social support for parents and children. A United Nations study of maternity protection for employed women found that, of the 152 International Labor Organization member countries, only six (Australia, New Zealand, Lesotho, Swaziland, Papua New Guinea, *and the United States*) do not require paid maternity leave. All of the other countries either provide or require that employers provide paid maternity leave, ranging from twelve to twenty-eight weeks. In the United States, the Family and Medical Leave Act, which does not cover all places of employment, requires only twelve weeks of *unpaid* leave (Olson 1998).

One way to change direction is to challenge the structure of the workplace, particularly in terms of the hours that employers claim from or make available to their employees. With the exception of Japan, workers in other industrialized countries have fewer working hours and longer vacations than U.S. workers have (Schor 1991). In the United States, increasing workloads, speed-up on the job, and fears about the security of one's position all play a part in the phenomenon of ever-increasing hours of employment. Long workdays and six- or seven-day work weeks are becoming equated with "commitment to work" (Hochschild 1997). The increase in hours is not confined to professional or high-level corporate executive positions. In 1997, a telephone repair service worker with sole custody of his children was fired after twenty-four years of employment when he refused to work overtime because he needed to pick his children up from school (Galvin 1998). Increasingly, forced overtime has been a central issue in labor-management contract negotiations in manufacturing and service industries.

At the same time, temporary, contingent, and involuntary part-time employment has been on the rise. While some workers are working more hours than they want or need, other workers, such as the involuntary part-time workers discussed in Chapter 4, are unable to find stable, full-time employment and are working fewer hours over the week or over the year than they want or need. There is no morally or economically sound reason why all workers in the United States should not be able to make a living wage working thirty-five-hour weeks over a forty-eight-week year (McCarthy and McGaughey 1989). In addition, workplace options such as flex-time, parental leaves, and telecommuting for both men and women would address many of the problems now faced by employed women with children, as well as meeting the needs of most workers for daily lives that include familial, community, and social involvement. But these structural changes need to be accompanied by changes in the ways we think about employment, family responsibilities, and the organization of work.

Another way to change direction is to reconceptualize work and family for both women and men.[7] An American attorney who moved to France was amazed at the social support for employed women with children and the child-care options available there: "I think that the French have a better—I think that they integrate family life and work life. I think they have a better balance. I think that the bottom line is that the family is king. There is no question that the family comes first. The job would never come first" (Chayes 1998). Yet what it means to say that "family comes first" in France is very different from what it would mean in the United States. In France, quality child care for all children is provided by the society as a whole. By the age of four, 99.6 percent of French children are in some type of government-funded preschool, and fees for full-day care are on a sliding scale, depending on each family's income. Preschool teachers have degrees in child development, and the child/teacher ratio is low (Chayes 1998). But social responsibility for the care of children is only part of the reconceptualization that needs to take place in the United States, where an orientation model of work and family conceptualizes motherhood in opposition to employment and portrays working mothers as less committed to the workplace and as less than fully committed mothers. Social support for families in France is linked to a very different way of thinking about work and family. In comparing her experience as an employed mother in the United States to her experience in France, the attorney noted, "What it comes down to is that, for women, they don't have to make the choices that American women have to make. It's not a choice *between* work and family" (Chayes 1998).

What would it take for the United States to move in this direction? One answer is that is would take a cultural reconceptualization of motherhood and employment as activities that are woven together by women who are *both* mothers *and* workers. Joan Acker (1992) points out that "institutional structures would have quite different forms if reproduction were not cordoned off in a separate sphere. They would have to organize within their boundaries childbirth, sexual activities, sleeping, eating, and other daily maintenance activities. . . . The divide between reproduction and production . . . is perpetuated in institutional processes that, except for the family and certain 'total institutions,' are organized on the assumption that reproduction takes place elsewhere and that responsibility for reproduction is also located elsewhere" (567). Acker is pointing out that institutional structures embody ideologies. I suggest that structural changes in the workplace and social changes in the society would help to accomplish a reconceptualization of work and family.

There are already myriad recommendations that would address many of the issues faced by employed women with children and that would lead to better social support for families (flexibility of work schedules for women and men, work-site child-care facilities, paid parental leave, a national child-care policy and government-funded child care, a shorter work week, a national health-care policy that would cover everyone). And we have the examples of countries such as Norway and Sweden, which already have policies and structures that enable women and men to more easily and equitably weave work and family in their lives. The reference to other countries that have better support for families is not meant to indicate that these countries have found perfect or even near-perfect solutions or that their programs and policies are not without problems of their own. But a comparison of the social support available in the United States with that of other countries does indicate that the United States does far less for families that do many other countries, and it provides ideas about the directions in which the United States could move.[8]

The kinds of changes we need are changes that will enable Marcia Collins *both* to earn a living wage *and* to be home in the evening with her children, changes that will enable Sharon Baker to be fully involved in her marriage, her children's lives, her occupation, and her community without feeling like she is going "crazy half the time," and changes that will enable Jackie Patton to find high-quality, affordable child care that covers the hours she works. We need the kinds of changes that socialize responsibility for the care of children and that build employees' family responsibilities and relationships into the organization of the workplace. As a society, we should expect work life and family life to be compatible. After all, almost all workers are connected to families in some way—as children, siblings, grandchildren, grandparents, uncles, aunts, cousins, spouses, partners, fathers, and mothers.

Notes

CHAPTER ONE

1. A number of scholars have been led to examine areas where their experiential knowledge clashes with the analyses of professionals. Suzanne Carothers (1986), for example, writes that she began her research on Black mothers and daughters because of "the contradiction that emerged between my experience in the Black community of Herrington and my graduate school reading of the social science literature on Black family life and mother-daughter relationships" (316). See also Joyce Ladner (1972), Shulamit Reinharz (1984), and Dorothy Smith (1979).

2. Adolescents are often self-absorbed, but more is going on here than an adolescent's lack of interest in her parents. Children know that their fathers are employed, regardless of how focused they are on their own lives. The fact that children did not know their mothers were employed was surprising but can be understood as a result of the conflation of cultural expectations for mothers, the ways mothers presented themselves and were represented by others, and the way "work" is defined and recognized.

3. The labor-force participation rates for both Black and White women increased rapidly over the twenty years from 1975 to 1995. In 1975, of married women with children under the age of eighteen, 43.6 percent of White women and 58.4 percent of Black women were in the labor force. In 1995, the figures were 70.0 percent for White women and 79.3 percent for Black women. Although a gap remained between the labor-force participation rates of the two groups, that gap had decreased by more than a third. The gap had narrowed even more for White and Black married mothers with children ages six to thirteen. In 1975, the figures were 50.7 percent and 65.7 percent respectively; by 1995, the rates had converged to 74.9 percent and 79.1 percent respectively (U.S. Bureau of the Census 1996:400, table 627). Over the period, there has been an increase in the labor-force participation rates of married women of all racial-ethnic groups in the United States.

4. The proportions of all employed men in these occupations are also small, but my point is to call into question the popular image of the working mother as professional or managerial when compared with the actual occupations of most employed women. In 1995, 0.8 percent of employed men were physicians, 1.0 percent were lawyers, and 0.7 percent were college and university professors. While only about one-fourth of all lawyers and physicians

are women, lawyers and physicians of both sexes account for only 1.3 percent of employed people (U.S. Bureau of the Census 1996:405, table 637).

5. So too does the idea that there are boundaries between "public" and "domestic" obscure the interaction between the structures, images, and meanings assigned to each sphere (Pleck 1976; Sokoloff 1980). Although the concept of separate spheres may be useful analytically and for understanding the way in which some people have viewed the world, a rigid adherence to the idea that a boundary exists between public and private masks the fluidity of social life (Hansen 1994; Lopata 1993; Ryan 1990:10). In some cases, even innovative studies that attempt to examine the issue of boundaries don't escape the pervasiveness of this vision of the world as divided into two discrete parts. See for example Christena Nippert-Eng's (1986) investigation of how people construct and maintain the boundaries between their jobs and their personal lives. She describes a continuum along which people "integrate" or "segment" these realms to different degrees and argues that "the ways people manage their keys reflect and reinforce their mental and experiential levels of segmentation/integration between home and work. . . . we keep keys together or apart in accordance with the mental distance between the worlds and ways of being they signify" (48). She focuses, however, only on keys she has categorized as "work keys" and "home keys," never addressing where other keys fit. Where are the car keys, or the key to the bicycle lock or the gym locker? To leave for home after work, I must lock my office, my locker, or whatever my work keys apply to. To leave my house on my way to work, I must lock my front door. If I drive, I must use my car keys in both directions. By transferring the conceptual split between the workplace and the home to the physical problem of how to organize one's keys, Nippert-Eng neglects to account for the keys that are not directly connected to either the workplace or the home and to account for the keys that are connected to both. In other words, the fluidity of social life is missed.

6. There are sometimes good scholarly reasons for focusing on the extreme ends of a distribution, but this depends on the research question. Kristin Luker (1984), for example, interviewed anti-choice and pro-choice abortion activists as part of her research "to discover how people come to differ in their feelings about the rightness or wrongness of abortion" (3). Her focus is useful in understanding the social context of two opposing viewpoints. It would not, however, be an appropriate research design if one wanted to study nonactivists' beliefs and perceptions about abortion. Similarly, if we want to understand the meaning of work and family to most employed women with children, it does not make sense to focus only on those few mothers in male-dominated professions.

7. Throughout her book *Black Feminist Thought,* Patricia Hill Collins (1987) points to the limitations of either/or thinking and to the need for conceptualizations in terms of *both/and.* See particularly pages 29–31, 225–26.

8. Danielle was one of the women I interviewed during pilot interviews.

I include this excerpt from her interview because it captures so well the problems with the the term "working mothers."

9. Smith (1987) refers to this as a "line of fault" between conceptual organization and the world of lived experience (49–50). Herbert Blumer (1969) refers in similar terms to "a gap between theory and empirical observation" (173), but although Blumer and Smith describe this division in similar terms, their projects differ. For Blumer, the "separation between conceptual usage and empirical investigation establishes the major dilemma in our field" (173), the solution to which is connecting the concept with the empirical world. Concepts are applied to experience to observe the degree to which they explain that experience and the degree to which the experience is made sensible by the concepts; they are thus changed, shaped, and reordered in the process. The success of this process rests on improving the observation by using a symbolic interactionist approach (173–82). The resulting concepts are more precise, valid, and reliable. Smith also argues for the study of the world of lived experience, and while she would also like to construct concepts that more adequately reflect that experience, she is additionally concerned with what the line of fault tells us about who defines experience. The division between conceptual frames and experience is thus not simply the product of poor scholarship or a faulty approach, but is a product of certain relations of power (51–53). Smith argues that groups in power influence and shape the concepts we use.

10. In *Maternal Thinking*, Sara Ruddick (1989) argues that the practice of mothering is organized around three "universal" demands: demands for preservation, personal growth, and socialization. My discussion of the work of mothering is not based on claims of universality—I am talking explicitly about the work of mothering done by many mothers in the United States in the last quarter of the twentieth century. This work, and the way one feels about doing it, is socially constructed, not natural or universal.

11. There is a vast literature on women and employment, as book-length bibliographies of the subject attest. Space prevents listing all the excellent books and articles in this area, but the following citations refer to some of the most important books on women and employment in the United States. For general overviews of women and employment, see *Race, Gender, and Work: A Multicultural Economic History of Women in the United States* (Amott and Matthaei 1991, rev. ed. 1996), *Out to Work: A History of Wage-Earning Women in the United States* (Kessler-Harris 1982), and *Women and Men at Work* (Reskin and Padavic 1994). *Women, Work, and Family* (Tilly and Scott 1978) is fundamental reading on the topic.

For studies focusing on blue-collar women workers, see *Kellogg's Six-Hour Day* (Hunnicutt 1996), *Sunbelt Working Mothers: Reconciling Family and Factory* (Lamphere et al. 1993), *Bitter Choices: Blue Collar Women In and Out of Work* (Rosen 1987), *Wage-Earning Women: Industrial Work and Family Life in the United States, 1900–1930* (Tentler 1979), and *Women's Work and Chicano Families: Cannery Workers of the Santa Clara Valley* (Zavella 1987).

For studies focusing on women service workers, see *Pink Collar Workers: Inside the World of Women's Work* (Howe 1977), *Fast Food, Fast Talk: Service Work and the Routinization of Everyday Life* (Leidner 1993), and *Dishing It Out: Power and Resistance among Waitresses in a New Jersey Restaurant* (Paules 1991). A good collection on service-sector employment is *Working in the Service Society* (Macdonald and Sirianni 1996). For studies of office workers, see *Woman's Place Is at the Typewriter: Office Work and Office Workers, 1870–1930* (Davies 1982), *Men and Women of the Corporation* (Kanter 1977), and *Gender Trials* (Pierce 1995).

12. Classic works in the scholarship on motherhood include *The Reproduction of Mothering* (Chodorow 1978), *Of Woman Born* (Rich 1976), *Recreating Motherhood* (Rothman 1989a), and *Maternal Thinking* (Ruddick 1989). Important recent works include *Mothering Against the Odds* (Coll, Surrey, and Weingarten 1998); *Mothering: Ideology, Experience, and Agency* (Glenn, Chang, and Forcey 1994), *The Cultural Contradictions of Motherhood* (Hays 1996), and *Engendering Motherhood* (McMahon 1995).

There is a small, growing, and important literature that does take as its subject mothers, as mothers, outside the family. These works start from what they describe as the standpoint of mothers, and they focus on the connection between the work mothers do, the consciousness that arises from that practice, and mothers' actions in the world (Bouvard 1994; Collins 1987; Gilkes 1980; Jetter, Orleck, and Taylor 1997; Martin 1990; Naples 1992; Pardo 1990; Ruddick 1989). These works tend to focus on political and community action, however, and have not addressed mothers' labor force participation in the same manner.

13. Helene Lopata (1993) argues that "the concept of separate spheres has now emerged as the theory of role conflict" (181).

14. The image of weaving is different from the image of balance, which is frequently used to describe women's approach to work and family in an integrated way. While the notion of balance can convey the idea of equilibrium, the picture often used on magazine and book covers is of a balance scale, and the image is one of constant "teetering" as women attempt to equalize the weights of work and family. Presented in this way, "balance" fits into a dichotomous view of work and family in which employment and motherhood are conceived of as being at odds. In her study of families engaged in home-based, income-producing work, Betty Beach (1989) notes that the "supermom" model has been replaced by the model of "the juggler" or "the balancer," and that articles in popular magazines conceptualize balance as the management of issues such as child care, scheduling, housework, and guilt in pragmatic, organizational ways (9–10).

15. Individual hospital wards provided a bounded work setting in which hospital staff were in interaction with each other as well as with the larger institution. The hospital ward can be seen as a microcosm of the hospital, and each ward contained basically the same job categories and relation to the larger institution. While the hospital ward represents only one of the set-

tings in which these women construct the meanings that frame their actions, it is the one setting that my interviewees share. Interviews with women who share the same work setting also allowed me to contextualize my research findings by using other sources of information, such as interviews with coworkers, conversations with supervisors, knowledge of personnel policies, and knowledge of the institutional structure of the workplace. My interviews with hospital workers invariably contained references by them to others with whom they worked. By interviewing primarily workers in the same hospital ward, I found that the stories interviewees reported about their interactions with coworkers and the meanings they gave to the actions of others were transformed from the level of individual interpretation into a network of meanings and interactions.

16. Although the hospital ward provided the "whole" with which I started, I did not interview everyone on the two wards. First, I did not interview men. Hospital work does not characterize the employment of most men. The hospital is primarily a feminized work site, even though hospital administrators and physicians are predominantly male. A study of gender and occupation by Christine Williams (1991) looks at male nurses precisely because they work in a feminized occupation, but that is not the focus of this study. Second, although I interviewed an additional eight women hospital workers who did not have children, I chose to concentrate my efforts on interviewing the women who were mothers. Third, some women hospital workers declined to be interviewed. In addition, I interviewed some hospital workers who worked outside the two wards I selected. For example, because each ward has only one nursing director, I also interviewed nursing directors from other wards. And I interviewed some African-American nurses from outside the ward because there were so few in any one ward.

17. Occupational segregation within the wards, which is reflected in the demographic profile of the interviewees, confounds class (as represented by occupational status) and race. Karen Sacks (1984) provides a detailed discussion of the occupational segregation by race in the hospital she studied in her research on ward secretaries and union organizing. Of the women I interviewed, all of the administrators were White and all of the janitorial service workers were African American. None of the nursing directors in the hospital were women of color. The nursing staff was more ethnically and racially diverse, and I interviewed six White nurses, five Black nurses, five Filipina nurses, three Chicana nurses, and one Chinese-American nurse.

18. Registered nurses, for example, obtain their qualifications by completing either a two-year A.S. degree program or a four-year B.S.N. degree, and some nurses, called diploma nurses, got their nursing qualification in hospital training programs, which are being phased out. While the difference in type of degree does not affect wages for entry-level nursing positions, one's ability to gain a medical specialty or go into administration is connected to whether or not one has a bachelor's degree or is in a position to go on for a master's degree. Seven staff nurses had two-year degrees, and thirteen had

four-year degrees. One nursing director had only a B.A. degree, but the other nursing directors and hospital administrators had master's degrees. One nurses' aide had a two-year degree, and three of the clerical workers had completed some college-level work, but the other clerical workers, janitorial workers, and nurses' aide had only high school diplomas. Educational and occupational qualifications are part of the constellation of resources that helps shape the lives of employed women with children.

19. The interviews with women whose children were over eighteen focused on their work and family lives when their children were younger. The content, issues, and themes of these interviews did not differ substantively from the interviews with women whose children were younger.

20. The two Jewish women were both of Eastern-European heritage, and they identified their race/ethnicity as Jewish or Jewish/Caucasian in addition to listing their religion as Judaism. In terms of ethnic identification, their Jewish ethnicity distinguishes them (in terms of perceived cultural differences) from the more general category of Euro-American. As American Jews in relation to African Americans, Latinos, and other people of color, they benefit from White privilege (Delgado and Stefancic 1997), so I have placed them in this social category at the group level.

21. Since the 1965 Immigration Act, immigration from the Philippines has been high. Between 1966 and 1994, there were consistently more legal immigrants to the United States from the Philippines than from any other country except Mexico. Over the period, the number increased from about thirty thousand to about fifty thousand immigrants each year (U.S. Bureau of the Census 1996:11, table 8). In 1990, 52 percent of the Filipino population of the United States lived in California, primarily in the San Francisco and Los Angeles areas, and 3.6 percent of California's population was Filipino, making that the largest Asian-ancestry group in the state (U.S. Bureau of the Census 1990a, table P9).

22. In addition to the methodological reasons for not limiting my study to one racial-ethnic group, a personal experience sensitized me to additional problems with that approach. When I was a teaching assistant for a sociology course, the class read a book about women, work, and family that was based on an interview sample drawn only from White women. The author had done this intentionally and for standard sociological reasons. A number of African-American undergraduate women strongly objected to the limitation of the sample. Their objection was not that their experiences were different from those related in the book—indeed, the issues the book raised resonated for them in many ways; their objection was that Black women were not represented as part of the category "women," which the book purported to be about.

23. I conducted in-depth, open-ended interviews that focused on issues of work and family. I collected employment and family histories from the people I interviewed and asked them about their jobs, children, daily schedules, child care, and future plans. The interviews were recorded with the per-

mission of the respondents and lasted from one to three hours. My aim in the interviews was to allow people to shape their own answers to very general questions, such as "Tell me about your work" or "Describe what a typical day is like for you." Subsequent questions took their direction from interviewee's responses as I tried to understand how each person defined and acted on the meanings they gave to their actions and identities as workers and as mothers. Interviews conducted in this manner facilitate a grounded theory approach in which emergent themes from respondents' accounts guide subsequent interviews and the development of analysis and theory (Glaser and Strauss 1967; Strauss and Corbin 1990).

24. In the chapters that follow, I quote extensively from the interview transcripts. I used ellipses if I omitted any portion of the excerpt being quoted. These omissions remove repetition or unrelated comments; I did not omit anything if its absence might have changed the meaning of what was being said. I used dashes in the excerpts to indicate short pauses or to separate what, in written form, were not complete sentences. I used italics in the excerpts to indicate words or phrases on which the interviewee put verbal stress.

25. My focus is on understanding the meanings employed women with children give to their experiences. Therefore, this book does not address the issue of what is good or bad for children, which is an entirely different topic.

26. The general point that research starts from experience has been elaborated by other sociologists, for example Blumer 1969:178–82; Hughes 1971: 339; Reinharz 1984:256; Smith 1987:154.

CHAPTER TWO

1. In their views of the future and their assumptions about marriage, family, and employment, these college students resemble the young women described in Ruth Sidel's book *On Her Own: Growing Up in the Shadow of the American Dream* (1990).

2. Research on the work of nannies and au pairs (Macdonald 1998a) and on the child-care choices of mothers (Uttal 1996) reveals that mothers and child-care workers must negotiate the situation to reconcile particular definitions of motherhood with the fact that people other than the mothers are providing a large proportion of children's care.

3. Many employed women with children do talk about sharing child care with fathers, but I found that most of the college senior women in my classes looked ahead to a version of marriage in which the husband's job was sacrosanct and children were the mother's responsibility.

4. It is important to keep in mind that activities that constitute mothering or parenting are culturally and historically specific. During my fieldwork in Botswana, a Scandinavian visitor remarked that she thought the Batswana treated their children badly. I was surprised at this observation, since Tswana culture values children and integrates them very thoroughly

into daily life. Tswana babies are carried next to their mothers' or caretakers' bodies until they can walk, and young children are incorporated into large multi-age play groups of siblings and cousins. Children are cared for, watched over, and played with, although not always by their parents. The visitor explained that she thought that Tswana children were badly treated because she never saw parents playing with or reading to their children. She was completely unaware of the cultural specificity of the criterion she was using to evaluate the treatment of Tswana children by their parents. For a discussion of the association between "cultural place" and the developmental needs of children, see Weisner 1996. For discussions of the problems with importing assumptions about family life from one culture to another, see Ambert 1994, Garey and Townsend 1996.

5. "Doing gender" refers to the way that a person performs activities *as a man* or *as a woman*, and to the way that the performance of these activities is judged by others as being either inside or outside the bounds of appropriate behavior for a man performing a particular activity or appropriate behavior for a woman performing that activity. Much of the gender assessment of people's activities does not happen at a conscious level; most people, most of the time, behave within a range of gender appropriateness, and it is behavior that appears to be outside those norms that warrants notice or comment. West and Zimmerman (1987) note that "to 'do' gender is not always to live up to normative conceptions of femininity or masculinity; it is to engage in behavior *at the risk of gender assessment*" (136).

6. Lynn Davidman tells me that the theme of "being there" is also very strong in her interviews with people who were children or young adolescents when their mothers died. What is interesting is that they do not see anyone else as able to "be there" in the way that mothers are expected to be (Davidman 1999).

7. Susan Ostrander's *Women of the Upper Class* (1984) provides a number of examples of how upper-class women organize their lives to "be there" for their children.

8. A MassMutual survey found that, whether the mother in the family worked or not, 82 percent of families ate dinner together (*Providence Journal-Bulletin*, 31 December 1994:10).

9. Sensitizing concepts orient and focus attention, but they can also work to redirect attention and shape perception (Blumer 1969:164–68; Hughes 1971:339; Smith 1987:61–64).

10. For studies that address how women talk about their reasons for working, see Potuchek 1997; Wandersee 1981.

11. That many employed women with children are negotiating within an orientation model does not support the validity of the model, nor does it mean that these women are suffering from "false consciousness." The mothers I interviewed are using the tools (concepts, definitions) available to them to make sense of their realities and to explain them to others. The lack of "fit" between concept and experience is a product not of false consciousness,

but rather of inarticulateness in the face of a situation for which concepts and definitions do not yet exist or are not widely shared.

12. For a discussion of White privilege, see McIntosh 1997.

CHAPTER THREE

1. Although almost one third of employed women with children under six are employed less than thirty-five hours a week, of all women who are employed part time, only 20 percent have children under six years of age (Jacobs 1997:103). The vast majority of part-time workers are not women with preschool children.

2. Internationally, the definition of part-time work varies; Japan and the United States place the cut-off at thirty-four hours, while Canada, Finland, France, New Zealand, and the United Kingdom all define part-time work as thirty hours or less per week (Blyton 1985:106). Of all part-time workers in the United States in 1995, 30 percent worked between thirty and thirty-four hours a week (U.S. Bureau of the Census 1996, table 630) and would be classified as full-time workers in most other industrialized countries. In 1995, about one quarter (27.6 percent) of the total female labor force (mothers and non-mothers) was employed part time (Jacobs 1997:103).

3. In 1994, 62.6 percent of all full-time employees had health plan coverage provided by employers or unions, but only 19 percent of part-time employees had health plans provided by their employers or unions (U.S. Bureau of the Census 1996, table 670).

4. Some voluntary part-time employees are working part time while they are in educational or training programs; others are adding a part-time job in addition to holding a full-time or another part-time position. These uses of part-time work were exemplified by the two voluntary part-time employees I interviewed who were clerical workers. One of these women was also employed at another hospital. In 1995, 6.2 percent of employed women held more than one job, and employed women who were widowed, divorced, separated, or never married were more likely to hold multiple jobs (U.S. Bureau of the Census 1996:403, table 634). The other voluntary part-time clerical worker was working as a ward clerk while attending nursing school. Of all part-time workers in 1996, 19 percent were also in school or training (U.S. Bureau of the Census 1996:403, table 633).

5. Jane is obligated to the hospital to work her scheduled weekends, but she can trade with someone else if she wants to take a weekend off to travel with her husband.

6. If Marianna stayed out of work until her youngest child was nine years old, and assuming a two-year spacing between the four children she would like to have, she would be out of the work force for fifteen years, not nine years.

7. In 1986, the nationwide vacancy rate for registered nurses doubled— from 6.5 percent to 13.6 percent. In response, hospitals increased average maximum salaries for registered nurses by 40 percent between 1986 and 1990

(Greiner 1991:15). In California, there was a 15 percent Registered Nurse vacancy rate between 1988 and 1990, but by 1993 the R.N. vacancy rate in the state had fallen to 8 percent. In an effort to address the nursing shortage problem, the author of a study that found a negative relationship between having children under six years of age in the home and the number of hours worked by nurses suggested that hospitals offer "subsidized child care facilities and flexibility in scheduling" to "increase the number of hours a nurse is willing and able to engage in market activities" (Bahrami 1988:332).

8. For an ethnographic account of the way supervisors of low-status service employees are unsympathetic to the family constraints of their women employees and a discussion of why union officials often do not challenge organizations on these issues, see Kahn and Blum 1996.

9. By family strategy, I am referring to a conscious plan that aims to achieve certain goals for the family as a unit by placing the interests of that family unit above individual interests or the interests of other configurations (for example, the couple). The family unit may be the larger kinship group, in which case the interests of individuals, couples, and nuclear family groups may be secondary, or the unit may be defined as the nuclear family unit, in which case the interests of individuals, couples, and the larger kinship group are secondary. In general, a family strategy is associated with a collective view of familial obligations. One problem with family strategies is that they may, in practice, reflect the interests of one member of the unit while sacrificing the interests of the less powerful members of the family unit.

10. Other studies have also noted the facilitating nature of parents' employment schedules on fathers' involvement in the care of their children (Beach 1989:21; Coltrane 1996:71; Hertz 1998; Hood and Golden 1984; Townsend 1992).

11. For studies of mothers' definitions of self in relation to their negotiations of child care and with child-care providers, see Macdonald 1998b; Uttal 1996.

12. My own interviews revealed the prevalence of these assumptions in the day-to-day interactions of part-time employees. A part-time social worker who had a job-share position told me that she had been told repeatedly that she would not be considered for a promotion unless she increased her hours to full time. A clerical worker told me that when she asked her supervisor why she had not been informed of a staff meeting, she was told that the supervisor assumed that she would not be interested since she had reduced her hours to part time.

CHAPTER FOUR

1. Bureau of Labor Statistics data show that the proportion of involuntary part-time workers began declining after 1993, but changes in the BLS questionnaire for 1994 and after "made it more difficult for workers to be classified as involuntary part time" (Clark 1997:940).

2. This does not mean that casual on-call employees have to get through only ninety days of exploitative schedules. The hospital administration has an interest in distributing available hours among casual employees so that an individual employee does not get enough hours to be reclassified or is reclassified for only the minimum number of hours. The unit supervisor thus exerts great control over which employees will be retained. And reclassified on-call employees have a continuing interest in working as much as possible in order to be reclassified again at a higher number of guaranteed hours.

3. See Harriet Presser and Amy Cox (1997) for a discussion of the relationship between low education (high school or less) and working nonstandard hours and days or nonfixed schedules. The authors find that "low-educated mothers are disproportionately represented in occupations with high rates of nonstandard schedules [and] that many of these women who work nonstandard hours do so primarily for labor market rather than personal reasons" and conclude that "low-educated mothers appear drawn into working nonstandard hours by a lack of options" (33). In their study of nonstandard working hours among low-status service workers, Peggy Kahn and Linda Blum (1996) argue that the assignment of nonstandard working hours has "a gendered substructure based on the male norm of the unencumbered, family-free worker" (1).

4. For studies of kin assistance comparing race and family structure, see Hofferth 1984; Hogan, Hao, and Parish 1990. For an account of the importance of kin assistance in buying a first home, see Townsend 1998b. Nazli Kibria (1993) discusses the ideology of family collectivism in the Vietnamese-American community and refers to the sharing of resources among family members and between families as "patchworking."

5. Marcia's description of being able to sense when one of her children has a problem is what Sara Ruddick (1989), in her philosophical investigation of the work of mothering, refers to as "the scrutinizing gaze, the watchful eye of preservative love" (72).

Chapter Five

1. In the early part of the twentieth century, census enumerators were explicitly instructed not to count the work involved "in taking in boarders as employment unless it provided the majority of [a woman's] economic support" (Bose 1987:98). Furthermore, many women employed outside the home in the 1900, 1920, and 1930 censuses were listed as "housewife" because the census question asked for one's "usual occupation." Women were encouraged to list "housewife," and men, regardless of whether they were gainfully employed or not, listed some occupational category.

2. There are, of course, exceptions, but for the people I interviewed, the difference between the educations, occupations, and incomes of the husbands of the part-time nurses and the husbands of the full-time, night-shift nurses was striking.

3. Sierra Hospital has been phasing out its practical nurse positions in favor of having only registered nurses and nurses' aides on the ward. Although practical nurses have more training than those who qualify to be nurses' aides, Shirley's current job title is "nurses' aide."

4. The Filipina nurses I interviewed did not mention personally facing racism or discrimination in California hospitals, although two of them talked about dealing with institutional and personal racism when they had worked as nurses in other states, such as Texas.

5. A *New York Times* article notes that "the peak hours for juvenile crime are 3 P.M. to 8 P.M., with the biggest, most dangerous burst coming in the first hour after school" (Herbert 1997).

CHAPTER SIX

1. Thirteen of the eighteen women I interviewed who worked full time on the day shift had children under eighteen years of age. Four of these women had children between the ages of fourteen and seventeen. Of the nine women with children younger than fourteen, three were clerical workers, five were registered nurses, and one was the manager of a nonmedical unit. Of the five registered nurses, two worked twelve-hour shifts three days a week, two were nursing directors, and one worked for the hospital as a community nurse. Many of the full-time, day-shift nurses on the ward did not have children, and most of the day-shift nurses who were mothers worked part time.

2. Some people react critically to Heather's style of being a mother, partly because they feel that women like Heather have the resources to make different choices. Those who expect women with children to abide by the dominant cultural norms for mothers interpret Heather's commitment to her career as interfering with her mothering. But in making this judgement, they are applying unexamined standards of what children need and what mothers should do. For a discussion of the cultural construction of intensive mothering, see Hays 1996.

3. Nurses receive "reprimands" from their nursing supervisor when they have not performed as required, such as by doing sloppy charting, not carrying out doctor's orders, being late, and so on. Leaving the hospital during one's shift would be considered a serious offense. Reprimands in one's file can affect salary increases and can lead to being dismissed.

CHAPTER SEVEN

1. *American Heritage Dictionary,* Second College Edition (Boston: Houghton Mifflin, 1985).

2. Ibid.

3. This list of changes is meant to be not exhaustive, but simply de-

scriptive of the patterns I found. There are more varieties of pattern changes than just these five, but these were the primary types that emerged from my interviews.

4. Joyce's generation was the focus of a study by Myra Dinnerstein (1992) of white, married women at midlife who entered the professions after years as full-time housewives and mothers. The women in her study, all born between 1936 and 1944, grew up in what she labels a "traditional" world in which marriage and motherhood were expected and primary; desires or plans for a career were either never developed or abandoned in the wake of husbands' careers and the advent of children. The interview excerpts in Dinnerstein's book remind me very much of my interview with Joyce.

5. Diploma programs are hospital-run, apprenticeship-type programs that train registered nurses. These programs were much more common when Joyce was a young woman but are now being phased out in the United States in favor of either two- or four-year, college-affiliated nursing programs. Registered nurses from hospital diploma programs are often referred to as "diploma nurses." Many of those who got their nursing qualification from a hospital program later went to college for associate or bachelor's degrees.

6. Between 1970 and 1974, "there was a 102 percent increase in female college students (ages 25 to 34) . . . compared to 46 percent for men" (Dinnerstein 1992:194 n. 16).

7. A study of labor-force reentry among midlife women during the 1970s found that women in their early forties in 1970 were "three times less likely to reenter employment than those in their early 40s only five years later. . . . [However], 40-year-old homemakers in 1970 were more likely to become employed as 45-year-olds in 1975 than they had been in 1970, suggesting that it was not their upbringing or their own goals and values that accounted for the period differences we found. A more compelling explanation directs attention to the social changes that occurred in the United States during the 1970s" (Moen, Downey, and Bolger 1990:238–39).

8. For men, life-course changes such as retirement or the advent of grandchildren can result in second careers or avocations and in increased involvement with young children (Townsend 1998a). In four of my interviews, I was told of men who, upon retirement, took care of their grandchildren while their daughters or daughters-in-law were at work.

9. Part-time nurses without benefits received a pay differential; they were paid more per hour than nurses in positions with benefits. A number of hospital workers pointed out to me that if you didn't need benefits, the extra money was great, but that it wasn't enough to make up for the lack of health benefits if you needed them.

10. In her interviews with young women, ages twelve to twenty-five, Ruth Sidel (1990) classified one group as "Outsiders" and says of them that "they are either so burdened by day-to-day living or feel so hopeless about

their lives that they can barely envision a future for themselves" (63). Such hopelessness can derive from poverty, discrimination, ostracism, drug and alcohol dependence, or emotional trauma. It is not necessary to experience situations such as these to feel like an outsider (nor does everyone who experiences trauma become an outsider), but, for whatever reasons, outsiders feel too hopeless or too "outside the culture" to plan their futures. Lynda presented herself as "adventurous" rather than "hopeless," and she validated her life by telling me she wouldn't change a thing, so that, in essence, there would not have been any point in planning.

11. Although now somewhat dated, a study by Phyllis Moen (1985) found that "women follow no modal pattern of labor force participation; combinations of full-time and part-time work, as well as periods of absence from the labor force, are more the rule that the exception" (150). Current employment statistics for mothers indicate that this is still true, although increasingly women remain in the labor force and work full time for much of their adult lives.

Chapter Eight

1. W. I. Thomas's (1928) often-quoted statement that "if men define situations as real, they are real in their consequences" best summarizes this point. I have found, to my surprise, that Thomas's statement is often misunderstood to mean that people can create particular circumstances simply by thinking them to be true. Thomas's point, and the point of other sociologists who take meaning into account, is that there are concrete consequences of people's actions, and that people's actions are based on their subjective understandings of objective circumstances.

2. Articles discussing the problems of guilt and feelings of inadequacy on the part of mothers are a staple of women's magazines, and new survey results are released periodically on how American women feel about their performance as mothers. See Satran (1998) for one of the better popular overviews of the topic. The popular media also likes to focus on animosity between mothers who are employed and those who are not. One of the consequences of dichotomously categorizing mothers as either family oriented or work oriented is that it undermines the possibility of mothers uniting together over shared issues. Class issues, however, complicate the divisions between mothers (Luker 1984; Pollitt 1997).

3. The timing of school events or Parent-Teacher Association meetings is one example of the way that fathers' noninvolvement is institutionally assumed. Arendell's (1995) discussion of divorced fathers includes the frustration some of them expressed about being excluded from participation in certain areas of their children's lives by the assumptions and practices of their children's schools and medical institutions (185–87). This is not to say that fathers are prevented from taking on the responsibility for the day-to-day

care of their children, but only to point out that institutional arrangements often support their noninvolvement.

4. Benjamin Kline Hunnicutt (1996) has written a fascinating account of the rise and fall of the Kellogg Company's six-hour day, which lasted from 1930 to 1985. When Kellogg decided to phase out the six-hour shifts, they led a concerted campaign to link eight-hour shifts with the masculinity of work. Hunnicutt notes that many of the male workers he interviewed talked with great pride about the times they had worked sixteen-hour days and the times they had worked every day for months without a break, but that he "frequently detected embarrassment or something like a guilty unwillingness to talk about shorter hours among the men" and that he "often had the distinct feeling that male workers became uncomfortable, even hostile, as soon as six-hours came up in conversation" (136–37).

5. For example, there has been little, if any, movement toward a social solution that addresses the continuing need for affordable, high-quality child care in the United States. In 1980, the author of a *Newsweek* article reported that "even day-care stalwarts admit glumly that a national system may be a decade away" and quoted Eleanor Holmes Norton, then head of the Equal Employment Opportunity Commission, as saying, "there is going to be a crisis if nothing is done about day care in this decade" (Langway 1980:79). Not only was nothing done in the 1980s, but we have not moved any closer to dealing with this issue as the 1990s and the twentieth century come to an end.

6. Greater involvement of fathers in day-to-day parenting would, in general, be good for mothers, fathers, and children. If fathers share in the parenting of their children in a substantial way and on a large scale, the "work of mothering" will no doubt be altered. Involving fathers, however, still leaves us with individual "solutions." In addition, proposing fathers' involvement as a panacea ignores the situation of large numbers of families in which, for a variety of reasons, there are no fathers.

7. Although work and family need to be reconceptualized for both women and men, my focus in this book has been solely on the meaning and experience of motherhood and employment for women. Other studies have focused on fatherhood and employment (Coltrane 1996; Gerson 1993; Hood 1993; Townsend 1992) and on dual-earner couples (Barnett and Rivers 1996; Ehrensaft 1990; Hertz 1986; Hochschild and Machung 1989).

8. Sheila Kamerman has written extensively about child-care and family-support policies in various nations (Kamerman 1995; Kamerman and Kahn 1997).

References

Abelson, Reed. 1997. "When Waaa Turns to Why: Mom and Dad Both Work? Sure, But What to Tell the Children?" *New York Times*, 11 November, Business/Financial Section.

Acker, Joan. 1992. "Gendered Institutions: From Sex Roles to Gendered Institutions." *Contemporary Sociology* 21(5):565–69.

Ambert, Anne Marie. 1994. "An International Perspective on Parenting: Social Change and Social Constructs." *Journal of Marriage and the Family* 56:529–43.

Amott, Teresa, and Julie Matthaei. 1991. *Race, Gender, and Work: A Multicultural Economic History of Women in the United States*. Boston: South End Press.

———. 1996. *Race, Gender, and Work: A Multi-Cultural Economic History of Women in the United States*. Revised edition. Boston: South End Press.

Arendell, Terry. 1986. *Mothers and Divorce: Legal, Economic, and Social Dilemmas*. Berkeley: University of California Press.

———. 1995. *Fathers and Divorce*. Thousand Oaks, Calif.: Sage.

Aymer, Paula. 1997. *Uprooted Women: Migrant Domestics in the Caribbean*. Westport, Conn.: Praeger.

Baca Zinn, Maxine. 1991. "Family, Feminism, and Race in America." Pp. 119–33 in *The Social Construction of Gender*, edited by Judith Lorber and Susan Farrell. Newbury Park, Calif.: Sage.

Bahrami, Bahman. 1988. "Hours of Work Offered by Nurses." *Social Science Journal* 25(3):325–35.

Barker, Kathleen. 1993. "Changing Assumptions and Contingent Solutions: The Costs and Benefits of Women Working Full- and Part-Time." *Sex Roles* 28(1–2):47–71.

Barnett, Rosalind C., and Caryl Rivers. 1996. *She Works/He Works: How Two-Income Families Are Happier, Healthier and Better-Off*. San Francisco: Harper.

Bateson, Mary Catherine. 1989. *Composing a Life*. New York: Plume (Penguin).

Beach, Betty. 1989. *Integrating Work and Family Life: The Home-Working Family*. Albany: State University of New York Press.

Bellah, Robert N., et al. 1985. *Habits of the Heart: Individualism and Commitment in American Life*. New York: Harper and Row.

Belous, Richard. 1989. *The Contingent Economy: The Growth of the*

Temporary, Part-Time, and Subcontracted Workforce. Washington, D.C.: National Planning Association.

Benenson, Harold. 1984. "Women's Occupational and Family Achievement in the U.S. Class System: A Critique of the Dual-Career Family Analysis." *British Journal of Sociology* 35(1):19–41.

Bennett, Sheila Kishler, and Leslie B. Alexander. 1987. "The Mythology of Part-Time Work: Empirical Evidence from a Study of Working Mothers." Pp. 225–41 in *Women, Households, and the Economy,* edited by Lourdes Beneria and Catherine R. Stimpson. New Brunswick, N.J.: Rutgers University Press.

Bergmann, Barbara R. 1986. *The Economic Emergence of Women.* New York: Basic Books.

Bernard, Jessie. 1975. *Women, Wives, Mothers: Values and Options.* Chicago: Aldine.

———. 1981. "The Good-Provider Role: Its Rise and Fall." *American Psychologist* 36(1):1–12.

Blum-Kulka, Shoshana. 1997. *Dinner Talk: Cultural Patterns of Sociability and Socialization in Family Discourse.* Mahwah, N.J.: Lawrence Erlbaum Associates.

Blumer, Herbert. 1969. *Symbolic Interactionism: Perspective and Method.* Englewood Cliffs, N.J.: Prentice-Hall.

Blyton, Paul. 1985. *Changes in Working Time: An International Review.* New York: St. Martin's Press.

Bose, Christine E. 1987. "Devaluing Women's Work: The Undercount of Women's Employment in 1900 and 1980." Pp. 95–115 in *Hidden Aspects of Women's Work,* edited by Roslyn Feldberg, Christine Bose, and Natalie Sokoloff. New York: Praeger.

Bouvard, Marguerite Guzman. 1994. *Revolutionizing Motherhood: The Mothers of the Plaza de Mayo.* Wilmington, Del.: Scholarly Resources.

Cardozo, Arlene Rossen. 1986. *Sequencing.* New York: Collier Books.

Carothers, Suzanne C. 1998. "Catching Sense: Learning from Our Mothers to Be Black and Female." Pp. 315–27 in *Families in the U.S.: Kinship and Domestic Politics,* edited by Karen V. Hansen and Anita Ilta Garey. Philadelphia: Temple University Press.

Chayes, Sarah, reporter. 1998. "French Child Care." *Morning Edition.* National Public Radio. 28 February. 4:37.

Chodorow, Nancy. 1978. *The Reproduction of Mothering: Psychoanalysis and the Sociology of Gender.* Berkeley: University of California Press.

Clark, Charles S. 1997. "Contingent Work Force." *CQ Researcher* 7(40): 937–60.

Cole, Johnetta B. 1986. "Commonalities and Differences." Pp. 1–30 in *All American Women: Lines That Divide, Ties That Bind,* edited by Johnetta B. Cole. New York: Free Press.

Collins, Patricia Hill. 1987. "The Meaning of Motherhood in Black Culture and Black Mother/Daughter Relationships." *Sage* 4(2):3–10.

———. 1990. *Black Feminist Thought: Knowledge, Consciousness, and the Politics of Empowerment*. Boston: Unwin Hyman.

Coltrane, Scott. 1989. "Household Labor and the Routine Production of Gender." *Social Problems* 36:473–90.

———. 1996. *Family Man: Fatherhood, Housework, and Gender Equity*. New York: Oxford University Press.

Contratto, Susan. 1987. "Father Presence in Women's Psychological Development." Pp. 138–57 in *Advances in Psychoanalytic Sociology*, edited by Jerome Rabow, Gerald M. Platt, and Marion S. Goldman. Malabar, Fla.: Robert E. Krieger.

Coontz, Stephanie. 1992. *The Way We Never Were: American Families and the Nostalgia Trap*. New York: Basic Books.

Daniels, Arlene Kaplan. 1987. "Invisible Work." *Social Problems* 34:403–15.

Davidman, Lynn. 1999. *Motherloss*. Berkeley: University of California Press.

Davies, Margery W. 1982. *Woman's Place Is at the Typewriter: Office Work and Office Workers, 1870–1930*. Philadelphia: Temple University Press.

Delgado, Richard, and Jean Stefancic, eds. 1997. *Critical White Studies: Looking Behind the Mirror*. Philadelphia: Temple University Press.

DeVault, Marjorie L. 1991. *Feeding the Family: The Social Organization of Caring as Gendered Work*. Chicago: University of Chicago Press.

di Leonardo, Micaela. 1987. "The Female World of Cards and Holidays: Women, Families, and the Work of Kinship." *Signs* 12(3):440–53.

Dill, Bonnie Thornton. 1980. "'The Means to Put My Children Through': Child-Rearing Goals and Strategies among Black Female Domestic Servants." Pp. 107–23 in *The Black Woman*, edited by La Frances Rodgers-Rose. Beverly Hills, Calif.: Sage.

Dinnerstein, Myra. 1992. *Women Between Two Worlds: Midlife Reflections on Work and Family*. Philadelphia: Temple University Press.

Dixon, Ruth B. 1982. "Women in Agriculture: Counting the Labor Force in Developing Countries." *Population and Development Review* 8(3):539–66.

Duffy, Ann, and Norene Pupo. 1992. *Part-Time Paradox: Connecting Gender, Work, and Family*. Toronto: McClelland and Stewart.

DuRivage, Virginia. 1986. *Working at the Margins: Part-Time and Temporary Workers in the United States*. Report. Cleveland: 9 to 5, National Association of Working Women.

Ehrensaft, Diane. 1990. *Parenting Together: Men and Women Sharing the Care of Their Children*. Urbana: University of Illinois Press.

Etaugh, Claire, and Gina Gilomen Study. 1989. "Perceptions of Mothers: Effects of Employment Status, Marital Status, and Age of Child." *Sex Roles* 20(1–2):59–70.

Fausto-Sterling, Anne. 1992. *Myths of Gender: Biological Theories about Women and Men*. Second edition. New York: Basic Books.

Ferree, Myra Marx. 1976. "Working-Class Jobs: Housework and Paid Work as Sources of Satisfaction." *Social Problems* 23(4):431–41.

———. 1987. "Family and Job for Working-Class Women: Gender and Class

Systems Seen from Below." Pp. 289–301 in *Families and Work*, edited by Naomi Gerstel and Harriet Engel Gross. Philadelphia: Temple University Press.

Fishman, Pamela M. 1983. "Interaction: The Work Women Do." Pp. 89–101 in *Language, Gender, and Society*, edited by Barrie Thorne, C. Kramer, and Nancy Henley. Rowley, Mass.: Newbury House.

Folbre, Nancy. 1991. "The Unproductive Housewife: Her Evolution in Nineteenth-Century Economic Thought." *Signs* 16(3):463–84.

———. 1994. *Who Pays for the Kids? Gender and the Structures of Constraint*. New York: Routledge.

Galvin, Kevin. 1998. "Some Workers Protest Increase in Forced Overtime." Associated Press Wire Service, 11 November.

Garcia Coll, Cynthia, Janet L. Surrey, and Kathy Weingarten, eds. 1998. *Mothering Against the Odds: Diverse Voices of Contemporary Mothers*. New York: Guilford Press.

Garey, Anita Ilta, and Karen V. Hansen. 1998. "Introduction: Analyzing Families with a Feminist Sociological Imagination." Pp. xv–xxi in *Families in the U.S.: Kinship and Domestic Politics*, edited by Karen V. Hansen and Anita Ilta Garey. Philadelphia: Temple University Press.

Garey, Anita Ilta, and Nicholas W. Townsend. 1996. "Kinship, Courtship, and Child Maintenance Law in Botswana." *Journal of Family Issues* 17(2):189–202.

Garson, Barbara. 1994. *All the Livelong Day: The Meaning and Demeaning of Routine Work*. Revised edition. New York: Penguin.

Gerson, Kathleen. 1985. *Hard Choices: How Women Decide about Work, Career, and Motherhood*. Berkeley: University of California Press.

———. 1993. *No Man's Land: Men's Changing Commitments to Family and Work*. New York: Basic Books.

Gerzer, Annemarie. 1986. "The Beck Department Store: A Case Study." Pp. 118–63 in *Women, Work and Family in Britain and Germany*, edited by Kate Crehan, T. Scarlett Epstein, and Annemarie Gerzer. New York: St. Martin's Press.

Gilkes, Cheryl Townsend. 1980. "Holding Back the Ocean with a Broom: Black Women and Community Work." Pp. 217–31 in *The Black Woman*, edited by LaFrances Rodgers-Rose. Beverly Hills, Calif.: Sage.

Glaser, Barney, and Anselm L. Strauss. 1967. *The Discovery of Grounded Theory: Strategies for Qualitative Research*. Chicago: Aldine.

Glenn, Evelyn Nakano. 1980. "The Dialectics of Wage Work: Japanese-American Women and Domestic Service, 1905–1940." *Feminist Studies* 6(3):432–70.

Glenn, Evelyn Nakano, Grace Chang, and Linda Rennie Forcey, eds. 1994. *Mothering: Ideology, Experience, and Agency*. New York: Routledge.

Goffman, Erving. 1959. *The Presentation of Self in Everyday Life*. Garden City, N.Y.: Doubleday.

Goldscheider, Frances K. 1992. "Family Relationships and Life Course Strategies in Aging Populations." Paper presented at the annual meeting of the Population Association of America, Denver, April 30–May 2.

Graglia, F. Carolyn. 1998. *Domestic Tranquility: A Brief Against Feminism.* Dallas: Spence.

Gramsci, Antonio. 1971. *Selections from the Prison Notebooks.* London: New Left Books.

Granrose, Cherlyn S., and Eileen E. Kaplan. 1996. *Work-Family Role Choices for Women in Their 20s and 30s: From College Plans to Life Experiences.* Westport, Conn.: Praeger Publishers.

Greiner, Ann Claire. 1991. "Desperately Seeking Nurses: Hospital Restructuring Makes R.N. Jobs Less Attractive." *Anthropology of Work Review* 12(1):13–16.

Hansen, Karen V. 1994. *A Very Social Time: Gender, Class, and Community in Antebellum New England.* Berkeley: University of California Press.

Harley, Sharon. 1990. "For the Good of Family and Race: Gender, Work, and Domestic Roles in the Black Community, 1880–1930." *Signs* 15(2):336–49.

Hays, Sharon. 1996. *The Cultural Contradictions of Motherhood.* New Haven: Yale University Press.

Herbert, Bob. 1997. "In America; 3:00, Nowhere to Go." *New York Times,* 26 October, editorial desk.

Hertz, Rosanna. 1986. *More Equal Than Others: Women and Men in Dual-Career Marriages.* Berkeley: University of California Press.

———. 1998. "The Parenting Approach to the Work-Family Dilemma." Pp. 767–75 in *Families in the U.S.: Kinship and Domestic Politics,* edited by Karen V. Hansen and Anita Ilta Garey. Philadelphia: Temple.

Hertz, Rosanna, and Joy Charlton. 1989. "Making Family Under a Shiftwork Schedule: Air Force Security Guards and Their Wives." *Social Problems* 36:491–507.

Hertz, Rosanna, and Faith I. T. Ferguson. 1996. "Childcare Choices and Constraints in the United States: Social Class, Race and the Influence of Family Views." *Journal of Comparative Family Studies* 27(2):249–80.

Hewitt, John P. 1997. *Self and Society: A Symbolic Interactionist Social Psychology.* Boston: Allyn and Bacon.

Hewlett, Sylvia Ann. 1986. *A Lesser Life: The Myth of Women's Liberation in America.* New York: Warner Books.

Hochschild, Arlie Russell. 1979. "Emotion Work, Feeling Rules, and Social Structure." *American Journal of Sociology* 85(3):551–75.

———. 1983. *The Managed Heart: Commercialization of Human Feeling.* Berkeley: University of California Press.

———. 1988. "Gender Strategies in Women's Advice Books: A Look at Surface and Deep Acting." Paper presented at the annual meeting of the American Sociological Association, Atlanta, August.

———. 1997. *The Time Bind: When Work Becomes Home and Home Becomes Work.* New York: Henry Holt.

Hochschild, Arlie Russell, and Anne Machung. 1989. *The Second Shift: Working Parents and the Revolution at Home.* New York: Viking.

Hofferth, Sandra L. 1984. "Kin Networks, Race, and Family Structure." *Journal of Marriage and the Family* 46:791–806.

Hogan, Dennis P., Ling-Xin Hao, and William L. Parish. 1990. "Race, Kin Networks, and Assistance to Mother-Headed Families." *Social Forces* 68(3):797–812.

Holden, Karen. 1990. "Comment on 'Are Part-Time Jobs Bad Jobs?' by Rebecca Blank." Pp. 156–64 in *A Future of Lousy Jobs? The Changing Structure of U.S. Wages*, edited by Gary Burtless. Washington, D.C.: Brookings Institution.

Hood, Jane C., ed. 1993. *Men, Work, and Family.* Newbury Park, California: Sage.

Hood, Jane, and Susan Golden. 1984. "Beating Time/Making Time: The Impact of Work Scheduling on Men's Family Roles." Pp. 133–43 in *Work and Family: Changing Roles of Men and Women*, edited by Patricia Voydanoff. Palo Alto, Calif.: Mayfield Publishing.

Howe, Louise Kapp. 1977. *Pink Collar Workers: Inside the World of Women's Work.* New York: G. P. Putnam's Sons.

Hughes, Diane, and Ellen Galinsky. 1994. "Work Experiences and Marital Interactions: Elaborating the Complexity of Work." *Journal of Organizational Behavior* 15:423–38.

Hughes, Everett C. 1971. *The Sociological Eye: Selected Papers.* Chicago: Aldine-Atherton.

Hunnicutt, Benjamin Kline. 1996. *Kellogg's Six-Hour Day.* Philadelphia: Temple University Press.

Hunt, Janet G., and Larry L. Hunt. 1982. "The Dualities of Careers and Families: New Integrations or New Polarizations?" *Social Problems* 29(5):499–510.

Ibsen, Henrik. 1958 [1879]. "A Doll's House." Pp. 1–68 in *Four Great Plays by Ibsen.* New York: Bantam.

Jacobs, Eva E., ed. 1997. *Handbook of U.S. Labor Statistics: Employment, Earnings, Prices, Productivity, and Other Labor Data.* Lanham, Md.: Bernan Press.

Jetter, Alexis, Annelise Orleck, and Diana Taylor, eds. 1997. *The Politics of Motherhood: Activist Voices from Left to Right.* Hanover, N.H.: University Press of New England.

Jones, Jacqueline. 1987. "Black Women, Work, and the Family Under Slavery." Pp. 84–110 in *Families and Work*, edited by Naomi Gerstel and Harriet Engel Gross. Philadelphia: Temple University Press.

Kahn, Peggy, and Linda M. Blum. 1996. "'We Didn't Hire You for Your Children': Gendered Practices and Non-Standard Working Hours in the Service Sector." Paper presented at the annual meeting of the American Sociological Association. New York, August.

Kahne, Hilda. 1994. "Part-Time Work: A Reassessment for a Changing Economy." *Social Service Review* 68(3):417–36.

Kamerman, Sheila B. 1995. "Innovations in Toddler Day Care and Family Support Services: An International Overview." *Child Welfare* 74(6):1281–301.

Kamerman, Sheila B., and Alfred J. Kahn, eds. 1997. *Family Change and Family Policies in Great Britain, Canada, New Zealand, and the United States.* New York: Oxford University Press.

Kanter, Rosabeth Moss. 1977. *Men and Women of the Corporation.* New York: Basic Books.

Kessler-Harris, Alice. 1981. *Women Have Always Worked: A Historical Overview.* Old Westbury, N.Y.: Feminist Press.

———. 1982. *Out to Work: A History of Wage-Earning Women in the United States.* Oxford: Oxford University Press.

Kibria, Nazli. 1993. *Family Tightrope: The Changing Lives of Vietnamese Americans.* Princeton: Princeton University Press.

Komarovsky, Mirra. 1967 [1962]. *Blue-Collar Marriage.* New York: Vintage Books.

Kurz, Demi. 1995. *For Richer, for Poorer: Mothers Confront Divorce.* New York: Routledge.

Ladner, Joyce. 1972. *Tomorrow's Tomorrow: The Black Woman.* Garden City, N.Y.: Doubleday.

Lamphere, Louise, Patricia Zavella, Felipe Gonzales, with Peter B. Evans. 1993. *Sunbelt Working Mothers: Reconciling Family and Factory.* Ithaca: Cornell University Press.

Langway, Lynn. 1980. "The Superwoman Squeeze." *Newsweek,* 19 May, 72–79.

Leidner, Robin. 1993. *Fast Food, Fast Talk: Service Work and the Routinization of Everyday Life.* Berkeley: University of California Press.

Lopata, Helena Znaniecka. 1993. "The Interweave of Public and Private: Women's Challenge to American Society." *Journal of Marriage and the Family* 55(1):176–90.

Luker, Kristin. 1984. *Abortion and the Politics of Motherhood.* Berkeley: University of California Press.

Macdonald, Cameron. 1998a. "Manufacturing Motherhood: The Shadow Work of Nannies and Au Pairs." *Qualitative Sociology* 21(1):25–53.

———. 1998b. "Working Mothers and Mother-Workers: Nannies, Au Pairs, and the Social Construction of Motherhood." Ph.D. diss., Brandeis University.

Macdonald, Cameron Lynne, and Carmen Sirianni, eds. 1996. *Working in the Service Society.* Philadelphia: Temple University Press.

Machung, Anne. 1989. "Talking Career, Thinking Job: Gender Differences in Career and Family Expectations of Berkeley Seniors." *Feminist Studies* 15(1):35–58.

Malone, Beverly L., and Geri Marullo. 1997. "Workforce Trends among U.S. Registered Nurses." A report for the International Council of Nurses ICN Workforce Forum. Stockholm, Sweden, September 21-October 1, 1997. ANA Policy Series. Washington, D.C.: American Nurses Association (www.ana.org/readroom/usworker.htm).

Martin, Joann. 1990. "Motherhood and Power: The Production of a Women's Culture of Politics in a Mexican Community." *American Ethnologist* 17(3):470–90.

Marx, Karl. 1963 [1869]. *The Eighteenth Brumaire of Louis Bonaparte.* New York: International.

Marzollo, Jean. 1991. "Managing Morning Madness." *Working Mother,* March, 47–49.

Mason, Mary Ann. 1988. *The Equality Trap.* New York: Simon and Schuster.

Matthaei, Julie A. 1982. *An Economic History of Women in America: Women's Work, the Sexual Division of Labor, and the Development of Capitalism.* New York: Schocken Books.

McCarthy, Eugene, and William McGaughey. 1989. *Nonfinancial Economics: The Case for Shorter Hours of Work.* New York: Praeger.

McIntosh, Peggy. 1997. "White Privilege and Male Privilege: A Personal Account of Coming to See Correspondences through Work in Women's Studies." Pp. 291–99 in *Critical White Studies: Looking Behind the Mirror,* edited by Richard Delgado and Jean Stefancic. Philadelphia: Temple University Press.

McMahon, Martha. 1995. *Engendering Motherhood: Identity and Self-Transformation in Women's Lives.* New York: Guilford Press.

Mead, George H. 1962 [1934]. *Mind, Self, and Society: From the Standpoint of a Social Behaviorist.* Edited by Charles W. Morris. Chicago: University of Chicago.

Mills, C. Wright. 1940. "Situated Actions and Vocabularies of Motive." *American Sociological Review* 5:904–13.

———. 1959. *The Sociological Imagination.* London and New York: Oxford University Press.

Mirchandani, Kiran. 1998. "Protecting the Boundary: Teleworker Insights on the Expansive Concept of 'Work.'" *Gender and Society* 12(2): 168–87.

Moen, Phyllis. 1985. "Continuities and Discontinuities in Women's Labor Force Activity." Pp. 113–55 in *Life Course Dynamics: Trajectories and Transitions, 1968–1980,* edited by Glen H. Elder, Jr. Ithaca: Cornell University Press.

———. 1989. *Working Parents: Transformations in Gender Roles and Public Policies in Sweden.* Madison: University of Wisconsin Press.

Moen, Phyllis, Geraldine Downey, and Niall Bolger. 1990. "Labor-Force Reentry Among U.S. Homemakers in Midlife: A Life Course Analysis." *Gender and Society* 4(2):230–43.

Montagu, Ashley. 1963 [1945]. "'Ethnic Group' and 'Race.'" Pp. 61–71 in *Race, Science, and Humanity.* Princeton: D. Van Nostrand.

———, ed. 1964. *The Concept of Race.* London: Collier.

Morgan, D. H. J. 1975. *Social Theory and the Family.* London: Routledge and Kegan Paul.

Naples, Nancy A. 1992. "Activist Mothering: Cross-Generational Continuity in the Community Work of Women from Low-Income Urban Neighborhoods." *Gender and Society* 6(3):441–63.

National Center for Education Statistics. 1996. *The Condition of Education 1996*. Washington, D.C.: U.S. Department of Education, Office of Educational Research and Improvement, National Center for Education Statistics.

Nippert-Eng, Christena E. 1996. *Home and Work: Negotiating Boundaries Through Everyday Life*. Chicago: University of Chicago Press.

Olson, Elizabeth. 1998. "U.N. Surveys Paid Leave for Mothers." *New York Times*, 16 February, A5.

Ortner, Sherry B. 1990. "Gender Hegemonies." *Cultural Critique* 14:35–80.

Ostrander, Susan A. 1984. *Women of the Upper Class*. Philadelphia: Temple University Press.

Pardo, Mary. 1990. "Mexican American Women Grassroots Community Activists: 'Mothers of East Los Angeles.'" *Frontiers* 11(1):1–7.

Parsons, Talcott, and Robert F. Bales. 1955. *Family, Socialization and Interaction Process*. New York: Free Press.

Paules, Greta Foff. 1991. *Dishing It Out: Power and Resistance among Waitresses in a New Jersey Restaurant*. Philadelphia: Temple University Press.

Pierce, Jennifer L. 1995. *Gender Trials: Emotional Lives in Contemporary Law Firms*. Berkeley: University of California Press.

Pleck, Elizabeth H. 1976. "Two Worlds in One: Work and Family." *Journal of Social History* 10(2):178–95.

Pollitt, Katha. 1997. "Killer Moms, Working Nannies." *The Nation*, 24 November.

Popenoe, David. 1988. *Disturbing the Nest: Family Change and Decline in Modern Societies*. New York: Aldine de Gruyter.

Potuchek, Jean L. 1997. *Who Supports the Family? Gender and Breadwinning in Dual-Earner Marriages*. Palo Alto: Stanford University Press.

Presser, Harriet B. 1987. "Work Shifts of Full-Time Dual-Earner Couples: Patterns and Contrasts by Sex of Spouse." *Demography* 24(1):99–112.

———. 1988. "Shift Work and Child Care among Dual-Earner American Parents." *Journal of Marriage and the Family* 50(1):133–48.

———. 1989. "Can We Make Time for Children? The Economy, Work Schedules, and Child Care." *Demography* 26:523–43.

Presser, Harriet B., and Amy G. Cox. 1997. "The Work Schedules of Low-Educated American Women and Welfare Reform." *Monthly Labor Review*, April, 25–43.

Ratcliff, Kathryn Strother, and Janet Bogdan. 1988. "Unemployed Women: When 'Social Support' Is Not Supportive." *Social Problems* 35(1):54–63.

Reinharz, Shulamit. 1984. *On Becoming a Social Scientist: From Survey Research and Participant Observation to Experiential Analysis*. Second edition. New Brunswick, N.J.: Transaction.

Reskin, Barbara, and Irene Padavic. 1994. *Women and Men at Work*. Thousand Oaks, Calif.: Pine Forge Press.

Rich, Adrienne. 1976. *Of Woman Born: Motherhood as Experience and Institution.* New York: W. W. Norton.

Rollins, Judith. 1985. *Between Women: Domestics and Their Employers.* Philadelphia: Temple University Press.

Rosen, Ellen Israel. 1987. *Bitter Choices: Blue-Collar Women In and Out of Work.* Chicago: University of Chicago.

Rosenfeld, Rachel A., and Gunn Elisabeth Birkelund. 1995. "Women's Part-Time Work: A Cross-National Comparison." *European Sociological Review* 11(2):111–34.

Rothman, Barbara Katz. 1989a. *Recreating Motherhood: Ideology and Technology in a Patriarchal Society.* New York: W. W. Norton.

———. 1989b. "Women as Fathers: Motherhood and Child Care under a Modified Patriarchy." *Gender and Society* 3(1):89–104.

Rothman, Sheila. 1978. *Woman's Proper Place: A History of Changing Ideals and Practices, 1870 to the Present.* New York: Basic Books.

Ruddick, Sara. 1989. *Maternal Thinking: Toward a Politics of Peace.* New York: Ballantine Books.

Ryan, Mary P. 1990. *Women in Public: Between Banners and Ballots, 1825–1880.* Baltimore: Johns Hopkins University Press.

Sacks, Karen Brodkin. 1984. "Computers, Ward Secretaries, and a Walkout in a Southern Hospital." Pp. 173–90 in *My Troubles Are Going to Have Trouble with Me: Everyday Trials and Triumphs of Women Workers,* edited by Karen Brodkin Sacks and Dorothy Remy. New Brunswick, N.J.: Rutgers University Press.

Satran, Pamela Redmond. 1998. "Are You a Good Mother?" *Parenting,* May 1998, 88–95.

Schor, Juliet B. 1991. *The Overworked American: The Unexpected Decline of Leisure.* New York: Basic Books.

Segura, Denise. 1994. "Working at Motherhood: Chicana and Mexican Immigrant Mothers and Employment." Pp. 211–33 in *Mothering: Ideology, Experience, and Agency,* edited by Evelyn Nakano Glenn, Grace Chang, and Linda Rennie Forcey. New York: Routledge.

Sidel, Ruth. 1990. *On Her Own: Growing Up in the Shadow of the American Dream.* New York: Viking.

Skolnick, Arlene. 1991. *Embattled Paradise: The American Family in an Age of Uncertainty.* New York: Basic Books.

Slater, Philip. 1964. "Parental Role Differentiation." Pp. 350–70 in *The Family: Its Structure and Functions,* edited by Rose Laub Coser. New York: St. Martin's Press.

———. 1976 [1970]. *The Pursuit of Loneliness: American Culture at the Breaking Point.* Revised edition. Boston: Beacon Press.

Smith, Dorothy E. 1987. *The Everyday World as Problematic: A Feminist Sociology.* Boston: Northeastern University Press.

———. 1979. "A Sociology for Women." Pp. 135–87 in *The Prism of Sex:*

Essays in the Sociology of Knowledge, edited by Evelyn Torton Beck and Julia A. Sherman. Madison: University of Wisconsin Press.

Smith, Vicki. 1983. "The Circular Trap: Women and Part-Time Work." *Berkeley Journal of Sociology* 28:1–17.

———. 1997. "New Forms of Work Organization." *Annual Review of Sociology* 23:315–39.

Sokoloff, Natalie J. 1980. *Between Money and Love: The Dialectics of Women's Home and Market Work*. New York: Praeger.

Stacey, Judith. 1990. *Brave New Families*. New York: Basic Books.

Stack, Carol B. 1974. *All Our Kin: Strategies for Survival in a Black Community*. New York: Harper and Row.

Strauss, Anselm L., and Juliet Corbin. 1990. *Basics of Qualitative Research: Grounded Theory Procedures and Techniques*. Newbury Park, Calif.: Sage.

Tentler, Leslie Woodcock. 1979. *Wage-Earning Women: Industrial Work and Family Life in the United States, 1900–1930*. New York: Oxford University Press.

Thomas, W. I. 1928. *The Child in America: Behavior Problems and Programs*. New York: Knopf.

Thorne, Barrie. 1993. *Gender Play: Girls and Boys in School*. New Brunswick, N.J.: Rutgers University Press.

Tilly, Louise A., and Joan W. Scott. 1978. *Women, Work, and Family*. New York: Holt, Rinehart and Winston.

Townsend, Nicholas W. 1992. "Paternity Attitudes of a Cohort of Men in the United States: Cultural Values and Demographic Implications." Ph.D. diss., University of California, Berkeley.

———. 1998a. "Fathers and Sons: Men's Experience and the Reproduction of Fatherhood." Pp. 363–76 in *Families in the U.S.: Kinship and Domestic Politics*, edited by Karen V. Hansen and Anita Ilta Garey. Philadelphia: Temple University Press.

———. 1998b. "Assistance from Kin with the Purchase of a First Home: The Importance of Definitions of Help." Unpublished manuscript. Department of Anthropology, Brown University, Providence, R.I.

U.S. Bureau of the Census. 1975. *Historical Statistics of the United States, Colonial Times to 1970, Bicentennial Edition, Part 1*. Washington, D.C.: U.S.G.P.O.

———. 1990a. *Census of Population and Housing 1990, Summary Tape File 3C—Part 1*. Washington, D.C.: Bureau of the Census.

———. 1990b. *Statistical Abstract of the United States: 1990*. Washington, D.C.: U.S.G.P.O.

———. 1990c. *Work and Family Patterns of American Women*. Current Population Reports, Series P-23, No. 165. Washington, D.C.: U.S.G.P.O.

———. 1996. *Statistical Abstract of the United States: 1996*. Washington, D.C.: U.S.G.P.O.

———. 1997. *Statistical Abstract of the United States: 1997*. Washington, D.C.: U.S.G.P.O.

Uttal, Lynet. 1996. "Custodial Care, Surrogate Care, Coordinated Care: The Meaning of Child Care to Employed Mothers." *Gender and Society* 10(3):291–311.

Walker, Karen. 1990. "Class, Work, and Family in Women's Lives." *Qualitative Sociology* 13:297–320.

Wandersee, Winifred D. 1981. *Women's Work and Family Values, 1920–1940*. Cambridge: Harvard University Press.

Waters, Mary C. 1990. *Ethnic Options: Choosing Identities in America*. Berkeley: University of California Press.

Weisner, Thomas S. 1996. "Why Ethnography Should Be the Most Important Method in the Study of Human Development." Pp. 305–24 in *Ethnography and Human Development: Context and Meaning in Social Inquiry*, edited by Richard Jessor, Anne Colby, and Richard A. Shweder. Chicago: University of Chicago Press.

Welter, Barbara. 1973. "The Cult of True Womanhood: 1820–1860." In *The American Family in Social-Historical Perspective*, edited by Michael Gordon. New York: St. Martin's Press.

West, Candace, and Don H. Zimmerman. 1987. "Doing Gender." *Gender and Society* 1(2):125–51.

White, Lynn, and Bruce Keith. 1990. "The Effect of Shift Work on the Quality and Stability of Marital Relations." *Journal of Marriage and the Family* 52(2):453–62.

Williams, Christine. 1991. *Gender Differences at Work: Women and Men in Nontraditional Occupations*. Berkeley: University of California Press.

Yeandle, Susan. 1982. "Variation and Flexibility: Key Characteristics of Female Labour." *Sociology* 16(3):422–30.

Zavella, Patricia. 1987. *Women's Work and Chicano Families: Cannery Workers of the Santa Clara Valley*. Ithaca: Cornell University Press.

Index

abortion debate, orientation model of, 204 n. 6

Acker, Joan, 200

African-American women: kin support among, 100–102, 213 n. 4; labor force participation rates, 203 n. 3; nursing as profession among, 120, 214 n. 4; provider concept of motherhood among, 51–52; research issues concerning, 203 n. 1, 208 n. 22; and working mothers, 6 n, 51–52

Arendell, Terry, 93

"at-home mothers," 7, 121–23; definition of, 110; shift workers' ability to appear as, 138–39

au pairs, research on, 209 n. 2. *See also* child care

Baca Zinn, Maxine, 17 n

balance metaphor, motherhood and labor force participation and, 14–15, 206 n. 14

Bateson, Mary Catherine, 14–15

Beach, Betty, 206 n. 14

behaviorist theory, orientation model of work and family and, 7–8

"being there" strategy: and emotional presence, 33; for involuntary part-time working mothers, 102–5; involuntary sequencing and, 184–85; midlife switch and changes in, 186–88; rejection of career concept and, 46–49; shift work by mothers as, 128–29; for voluntary part-time working mothers, 70–72; for working mothers, 32–33, 210 n. 6

Belous, Richard, 56

benefits, employment, 56–59, 89. *See also* medical benefits

Bernard, Jessie, 12–13

Black Feminist Thought, 204 n. 7

blue-collar working mothers: as invisible workers, 4–5; research on, 205 n. 11

Blum, Linda, 213 n. 3

Blumer, Herbert, 205 n. 9

Bose, Christine, 108–9

breadwinner ideology, 7, 109

breastfeeding, for working mothers, 150–51

career concept, working mothers' distancing from, 45–49, 71, 74

Carothers, Suzanne, 203 n. 1

Chicanas, 17, 51

child care: college students' views of work/family strategies and, 22–23, 209 n. 2; familial child care, preferences for, 97–100; French–U.S. comparisons, 199–200; for full-time day-shift workers, 145–57; for involuntary part-time workers, 90–107; kin assistance and, 100–102; lack of national consensus on, 195, 217 n. 5; midlife switch and changes in, 186–88; nonfamilial, 70–71; for part-time workers, 66, 68; for shift workers, 112–13; supervisory role of mothers, working mothers' perceptions of, 127–29; during twelve-hour shifts, 158–64; voluntary part-time work as solution to, 61–63, 66–72, 78–79. *See also* fathers, as child-care providers

children: focus on, 209 n. 25; of interviewees, 214 n. 1; invisibility of mothers' employment among, 2–3, 108–9, 203 n. 2; letting go of, 186–88; protests from, 83–84, 97, 102, 170; socialization of, 36, 41. *See also* schools

White women, 17. *See also* racial-
ethnic privilege
Women of the Upper Class, 210 n. 7
women's movement, 175–76
work: cultural norms regarding, 108–9,
193–94; definition and meaning of, 1,
41–44, 78, 105–6, 213 n. 1
work/family patterns: of college students, 20–23; gender-neutral conceptualization of, 199–200; individual-
ization of solutions and, 194–97;
involuntary sequencing and, 184–85;
midlife switch in, 186–88; voluntary
part-time work as, 60–63
Working Mother magazine, 4, 197
working mothers: blue collar, 4–5, 205
n. 11; career concept, rejection of,
45–49; college students' plans for being, 20–23; as conceptual category,
10–12; conflicting vocabularies of
motive for, 45–52; cultural norms
and, 5–9, 24–25, 209 n. 4; employment patterns in 1950s and, 1–2; images of, 4–5, 9–12, 25, 203 n. 4, 216
n. 2; as invisible workers, 2–3, 108–9;
noneconomic rewards for, 43–44; orientation model of work and family
and, 5–9; perceptions of, 6–7; in professional positions, 151–57; research
methodology on, 12–19; resource
constellations for, 52–55; sequencing
of patterns of, 165–90; shift work
and, 108–39; strategies of being for,
23–25, 129, 138–39; terminology regarding, 2 n, 10–12; U.S. labor force
participation patterns, 2–5; as voluntary part-time workers, 56–87; working-class, 43–44. *See also* labor force
participation; maternal visibility;
motherhood
workplace environment, work/family
patterns and, 198–201

Zavella, Patricia, 109
zero-sum game metaphor, work/family
patterns and, 192–94